Strategic Management for Hospitality and Tourism

Fevzi Okumus
Levent Altinay
Prakash Chathoth

ELSEVIER

AMSTERDAM • BOSTON • HEIDELBERG • LONDON • NEW YORK • OXFORD • PARIS
SAN DIEGO • SAN FRANCISCO • SINGAPORE • SYDNEY • TOKYO
Butterworth-Heinemann is an imprint of Elsevier

Butterworth-Heinemann is an imprint of Elsevier
The Boulevard, Langford Lane, Kidlington, Oxford OX5 1GB UK
30 Corporate Drive, Suite 400, Burlington, MA 01803, USA

First edition 2010

British Library Cataloguing in Publication Data
A catalogue record for this book is available from the British Library

Library of Congress Cataloging-in-Publication Data
A catalog record for this book is available from the Library of Congress

ISBN: 978-0-7506-6522-3

For information on all Butterworth-Heinemann
visit our website at elsevierdirect.com

Printed and bound in Great Britain
10 11 12 13   10 9 8 7 6 5 4 3 2 1

Working together to grow
libraries in developing countries

www.elsevier.com | www.bookaid.org | www.sabre.org

ELSEVIER   BOOK AID
            International   Sabre Foundation

Dedication

My work on this book is dedicated to my family, my wife Bendegul, and our daughters, Ezgi and Eda for their patience and support necessary to complete this task. Without their endless and unconditional love, support, care and understanding, completing this project would not have been possible.

Fevzi Okumus

I would like to thank my family for their support and encouragement in this endeavor.

Levent Altinay

I would like to dedicate my work on this book to my family.

Prakash Chathoth

Contents

Part IV The Strategy Process

Preface

This textbook equips students—the future leaders and managers of the hospitality and tourism industry—with an advanced and contemporary knowledge of strategic management. Specifically, it helps students to develop the analytical and practical managerial skills they will need to do their jobs professionally and efficiently. In this book, we take a holistic approach to strategic management, emphasising the importance of establishing synergies between the external and internal environments. The book is structured in a staged approach, to both help students understand the basics of strategic management and develop their own independent approaches to the complexities and uncertainities of the business environment.

One of the distinctive characteristics of this book is its straightforward style in establishing the key dimensions of the external and internal contexts in which the strategy content and the strategy process are embedded in the hospitality and tourism industry. It also emphasises an appreciation of the major cultural differences and the various ways of doing business in different countries.

The book has an innovative structure that consists of four main sections: the introduction, strategy content, strategy context, and strategy process. Each of the chapters in these sections has a thorough pedagogic structure consisting of an introduction, examples and vignettes, discussions points, exercises, case studies, and further reading and websites.

Chapters 1 and 2 describe the characteristics of strategic decisions and strategic management and define the context and characteristics of hospitality and tourism organizations. They also establish the key dimensions of the external and internal contexts in which both the strategy content and the strategy process are shaped. Chapter 3 defines and explains the different layers of the hospitality and tourism organization's external environment and examines their likely impacts on the organization's operations. Chapter 4 identifies different elements of the hospitality and tourism organization's internal environment and evaluates their influence on strategy formulation and implementation.

Chapters 5 and 6 address business- and corporate-level strategies and show how an organization may attempt to respond to the external environment and gain competitive advantage. Chapter 7 identifies and evaluates different methods of collaboration for H&T firms in order to develop new products and to penetrate new markets. Chapters 8 and 9 define strategy formulation and implementation, respectively, and discuss the real-life complexities of both formulation and implementation. Finally, Chapter 10 brings the main threads of the book together and encourages readers to be "learning individuals" while remaining being learning oriented in their approach toward managing organizations.

The book introduces "user-friendly" analytical techniques and applies them to international case studies. The case studies are specific and contemporary and carefully related to different aspects of strategic management. The global dimension of the hospitality and tourism business is a core focus, with a particular emphasis on the impacts of internationalisation and cross-cultural issues on development of strategic decisions and their implementation. The first author is based in the US, the second author is based in the UK and the third author is Hong Kong, China. The authors have extensive experience in teaching strategic management to students from various countries and cultures.

This text also provides online support material for tutors and students in the form of guidelines for instructors on how to best use the book, Power-Point presentations, and case studies, plus additional exercises and Web links for students.

We take this opportunity to thank all of our students who have greatly helped us to develop and refine this book. Our special thanks go to Stephen Taylor for his contribution to the first proposal of this book. We fully acknowledge his input in developing this book during the initial phase. Finally, we thank all of the scholars and researchers who contributed to the strategy literature in the hospitality and tourism field. Two of them deserve special acknowledgement: Professor Michael Olsen and Dr. Angela Roper. Dr. Roper was the main advisor of the first two authors' Ph.D. work, and Professor Olsen was the main advisor of Dr. Chathoth's Ph.D. work.

We look forward to receiving your constructive comments to further enhance this book for future editions.

Dr. Fevzi Okumus	Dr. Levent Altinay	Dr. Prakash Chathoth
August 30, 2009	August 30, 2009	August 30, 2009
Orlando, Florida, United States	Oxford, United Kingdom	Hong Kong, SAR China

PART 1

Introduction to Strategy

Chapter 1 introduces the subject of this book and strategic management, and Chapter 2 introduces the subject's application in the context of the international hospitality and tourism industry. The primary objectives of these two introductory chapters are to establish the importance and relevance of strategic management as an area of academic study and as a key executive practice for aspiring hospitality and tourism professionals.

CHAPTER 1

Introduction to Strategic Management

Learning Objectives

After reading this chapter, you should be able to:

1. Discuss the historical origins of strategic management.
2. Identify the schools of thought on strategic management.
3. Describe the strategic management framework and its objectives.
4. Define key terms pertaining to strategic management.
5. Assess various perspectives of strategic management and their significance.

CONTENTS

3

Opening Case

The Great Eastern hotel, a privately owned, independent, five-star deluxe hotel located in Hong Kong's commercial district, is faced with a turbulent external environment owing to the current financial crisis. Since its inception six years ago, the hotel has grown in prominence during the bustling economy from 2003 to 2007, and it has been one of the top performers in the upscale and luxury market segments over the four years preceding the economic crises. The hotel's main target market segment is the business traveler (75 percent of room bookings) who has no problem with paying USD 350 per night for a room.

During the past six months, however, the hotel has been a victim of the severe economic upheaval, which has led to a significant reduction in room bookings from the business travel segment. This has reduced profits significantly to the extent that the hotel is no longer able to cover fixed costs. The owner, Jerry Kong, has called an executive committee meeting to discuss the future direction the company should take in the immediate term and in the long term to sustain its competitive advantage.

1. What issues should Jerry and the executive committee address? Why? (Hint: Make assumptions where necessary, including mission and vision statements, as well as goals, strategies, and objectives.)

2. Given the preceding information, what are Jerry's options? How should they be evaluated? Make assumptions where necessary.

3. What should the hotel do in the short term and in the long term? Make assumptions where necessary to arrive at your decisions.

4. Why is it difficult to answer the preceding questions? Do we have clear answers for issues and challenges in real life?

5. Do managers and executives in hospitality and tourism organizations always have sufficient and reliable information to make decisions?

INTRODUCTION

This chapter introduces strategic management and provides an overview of the book's structure and contents. In doing so, strategy is presented from a historical perspective from various lenses—including schools of thought—through which strategy has been conceptualized, researched, and developed over the past several decades. This chapter then discusses key definitions of the terms used in the strategic management literature, and various schools of thought in the field are described.

HISTORICAL ORIGINS OF STRATEGY AND STRATEGIC MANAGEMENT

Before we proceed any further, it is essential to define *strategic management.* Strategic management is a field of study that involves the process through which firms define their missions, visions, goals, and objectives, as well as craft and execute strategies at various levels of the firms' hierarchies to create and sustain a competitive advantage. It helps organizations to prioritize what is important for them and provides a holistic view of an organization. It entails two distinct phases that deal with formation and implementation of strategy within an organizational setting. Figure 1.1 shows the strategic management framework/process, which is described in more detail later in this chapter and in Chapter 5.

Historic origins of strategic management have been linked to the military. The word *strategy* comes from the Greek *strategos*, which means "general." In literal terms, it means "leader of the army." Military strategy deals with planning and execution in a war setting, while taking into consideration the strategy and tactics required to implement the plan. Outmaneuvering the enemy in a "chesslike" situation requires a well-thought-out plan with emphasis on the plan's execution.

FIGURE 1.1   *The Strategic Management Framework.*

The basis of strategic management can be linked to the works of Sun Tzu that date back to 400 B.C. and to Carl von Clausewitz in the eighteenth century. Sun Tzu's reference to space, quantities, and other factors related is similar to the characteristics of the positioning school (Mintzberg, Ahlstrand, and Lampel, 1998). According to Sun Tzu, calculations underlie victorious situations in wars.

Carl von Clausewitz's considered strategy "a variation of themes" in war situations (Mintzberg et al., 1998). According to von Clausewitz, strategy was "open-ended and creative" in a situation of chaos and disorganization (Mintzberg et al., 1998). This makes a more systematic and organized approach essential, which is why planning became a part of the process. Strategy formation takes into consideration the various maneuvers and the scenarios and calculations pertaining to them. Being flexible while being proactive and deliberative, however, is essential. Literature during the twentieth century used these works to describe strategy in the corporate arena.

Strategic management as a domain of study has evolved over the past 50 years. In the 1950s and 1960s, strategic management was viewed from a general management perspective, with emphasis on the role of the leader. As a result, the focus was on leadership, interpersonal relationships, and the systems, processes, and structures in an organization. Firms used the top-down approach, with the top management at the core of the decision-making process. The strategic management process was not formalized and explicit during this phase; instead, it was more implicit and informal. During the late 1960s, the 1970s, and the early 1980s, firms adopted the strategic planning approach with an emphasis on analysis and formalized planning, with special teams assigned to develop plans. The typologies and concepts related to business and corporate strategies, with strategy formulation at the core of such conceptualizations, led to the evolution of the domain during this period.

In the 1980s, scholars emphasised more on strategy implementation as a process. There was a shift in emphasis from the leader to the development of organizational culture and its role in defining and implementing strategies. Also, as globalization began to capture the imagination of firms' executives, researchers provided more insight into the underlying concepts of globalization, including systems, processes, and structure that enabled firms to grow into a multidivisional corporation. Some scholars focused on firms' competencies to explain strategy, which led to the emergence of the resource-based view of the firm. In the hospitality and tourism domains, strategic management emerged as a field of study in the mid- to late 1980s that aimed at applying the works of scholars in the strategic management domain to hospitality organizations. Most of these efforts aimed at confirming theories related to the contingency, strategic planning, and competitive strategies.

In the 1990s, globalization led to the emergence of network strategies, and strategic alliances became the focal point around which researchers developed the literature. More efforts from a resource-based perspective led to the conceptualization of characteristics related to the firm's internal competencies that enabled them to sustain competitive advantage. The shift toward internal competencies also saw a shift in perspective toward the knowledge-based view and learning at the core of strategic competitive advantage in the late 1990s. Progress continues using the knowledge perspective from the 2000s, with increased emphasis on corporate social responsibility.

In the hospitality and tourism domains, Olsen, West, and Tse (2006) conceptually developed the coalignment concept, which has been used as a theoretical framework in other studies in the field. Efforts by Harrington (2001), Okumus (2004), and Jogaratnam and Law (2006) in the 2000s focused on environmental scanning in the hospitality industry context, whereas Harrington and Kendall (2006), Okumus and Roper (1999), and Okumus (2002), as well as others, have made attempts to develop the strategy implementation framework for hospitality and tourism firms during this period. More recent efforts in the field have moved toward a knowledge-based view and corporate social responsibility. Chapter 2 discusses in more detail the state of strategic management literature in the hospitality field.

SCHOOLS OF THOUGHT ON STRATEGIC MANAGEMENT

From a historical perspective, many schools of thought have emerged in the strategic management domain. Mintzberg and colleagues (1998) described the domain as consisting of ten schools/perspectives (Table 1.1) that pertain to design, planning, positioning, entrepreneurial, cognitive, learning, power, cultural, environmental, and configuration. As Mintzberg and his colleagues explain, the first three schools are more prescriptive, with an emphasis on strategy formulation that developed from the 1960s to the 1980s. The next six schools are less prescriptive, while emphasizing how strategies are developed. The tenth school conceptually combines and captures the other nine schools into an integrative whole. Each school is described briefly in this section.

The design school purports a fit between an organization's internal capabilities and external opportunities. This school emphasises the importance of a firm's position within the context in which it operates. The environment is used as a reference while gauging the firm's strategies, and

Table 1.1 Schools of Thought on Strategy

	Design School	Planning School	Positioning School	Entrepreneurial School	Cognitive School	Learning School	Power School	Cultural School	Environment School	Configuration School
Key Concept	Fit between organizational capabilities and external opportunities	Structured step-by-step, top-down approach	Strategy as a formal and controlled process	Leader or entrepreneur as the focal point of organizational strategy making	Decision maker's cognition and mind drive strategy making	Learning as the foundation for strategy formation	Power and politics drive this school of thought	Strategy formation as comprising social interaction	The decision maker's role is one of a boundary spanner	Strategy as transformational
Focus on	Firm's position in the market context	Mission, vision, goals, and strategies	Strategy types and positioning strategies	The leader's "intuition, judgment, wisdom, and experience" with the overall aim of creating a market niche	Managerial capabilities in strategy formation and implementation	Organizational capabilities are at the core of competitive advantage	Firms vying for position; engage in power plays, ploys, and tactics to maneuver in various contexts	Resources and capabilities are the sources of competitive advantage	Environment characteristics impact strategy formation	Transformational leadership, which forms the essence of strategy
Approach	The environment as a reference; strategy formulation is more deliberate	Planning hierarchies along with evaluation, operationalization, execution, and control	Strategy formation is deliberate and definitive	Deliberate in strategy making, yet adaptive to environment changes	Cognitive skills of managers influence perceptions of environment	Learning influences deliberate strategy, giving rise to a more emergent process	Strategy formation is more emergent	Strategy is deliberate	Strategy formation as reactive	Bottom-up change and top-bottom transformation are part of the process

Source: Developed from Mintzberg et al., 1998.

the emphasis is on how it develops its structure in order to support the strategy. Strategy creation and implementation were considered two distinct stages in the strategic management process.

The second school, planning, which developed in the 1970s, conceptualized strategy to include a structured, step-by-step approach. Mission and vision statements were set, and goals were clearly spelled out while detailing the objectives that would lead to the accomplishments of those goals. Note that goals and strategies were clearly differentiated under this approach. An environment assessment included forecasts and scenario analysis. The strengths, weaknesses, opportunities, and threats (SWOT) analysis was part of this process, and it gave the firm an overview of the various factors it had to deal with in a given context. The firm's internal and external environment-related factors are important to consider in order to assess the firm's position within a given market. The strategy process includes planning hierarchies along with evaluation, operationalization, execution, and control. The planning hierarchies per Mintzberg and his colleagues include budget hierarchies, objectives hierarchies, strategies hierarchies, and program hierarchies. These hierarchies are detailed within the corporate, business, functional, and operational levels. This school highlights planning as a formal process driven by the top management team of firms led by the CEO, and strategies appear as a result of this process.

The third school is positioning, which developed in the 1980s. Although it is not very different from the planning and design schools, it views strategy formation as consisting of a few strategy types. This school emerged from the work of Porter (1980), with an emphasis on strategy typologies. Strategy was still conceptualized as a formal and controlled process, but the focus here was on competitive strategies and industry structure. As the term suggests, *generic* strategies were applicable to firms within and across industries. Mintzberg and his colleagues describe the emergence of the positioning school as part of "three waves": "the military writings, the consulting imperatives of the 1970s, and the recent work on empirical propositions, especially of the 1980s." Notably, the works of Sun Tzu and von Clausewitz have influenced the emergence of this school, along with the BCG matrix for portfolio analysis developed in the 1960s, followed by the writings of Porter (1979, 1980, 1985) pertaining to competitive analysis (five forces model); generic strategies (cost leadership, differentiation, and focus); and value chain.

The fourth school is the entrepreneurial school, which pertains to decision making and the process of strategy formation. Here, the central role of strategy formation lies with the leader, whose "intuition, judgement, wisdom, experience and insight" are at the heart of decision making. Source: Mintzberg, H., Ahlstrand, B., Lampel, J. (1998; p. 124) The leader's vision and his or her leadership style influence the organization's strategic posture.

Strategy is conceptualized by the leader based on his or her intuition and wisdom rather than based on a calculated plan.

Mintzberg and his colleagues describe this school as both "deliberate" and "emergent," thereby emphasizing the leader's experience, while at the same time being adaptive to the changing environment of the business. Joseph Schumpeter was one of the early proponents of entrepreneurial orientation, and he described the entrepreneur as being at the crux of business innovation and idea formation. The entrepreneur provides the capital and impetus to start and grow the business into prominence. The entrepreneur's ability to search for new opportunities while providing his or her personal insights into how to best move the business forward through intuitive thinking is at the heart of the firm's ability to progress.

The philosophy and approach in organizations that live and die by the entrepreneurial spirit are top-down, with the leader having the power to decide the course the organization takes while implementation the strategy. It should be noted that organizations that have an entrepreneurial orientation tend to occupy a niche position.

The cognitive school is the fifth school, and it emphasizes strategy formation from the perspective that the decision maker's cognition and mind drive strategy making. The cognitive skills of managers influence their perspectives of how they perceive the environment. These perspectives in turn influence the strategy formation process. According to Mintzberg and his colleagues, they include "concepts, maps, schemas, and frames." This school is still emerging in terms of philosophy and contributions to the field.

The sixth school is learning, which supports the notion that strategy making is based on a foundation of learning. The strategy maker is constantly learning about the process of strategy formation and its various elements in a complex environment. In fact, the firm is learning constantly as a whole, which is incremental and continuous in a complex business environment. The knowledge perspective is part of the learning school, and the focus here is on the system as a whole rather than only a few managers at the helm of decision making.

Organizational capabilities and competencies become the core of sustainable competitive advantage. Given this perspective, it is not easy to distinguish between strategy formulation and implementation. It should be noted that learning is constantly taking place, and it influences the deliberative strategy formulation process, giving rise to a more emergent formulation process. While describing the learning school, Mintzberg and his colleagues state that "strategy appears first as patterns out of the past, only later, perhaps, as plans for the future, and ultimately, as perspectives to guide overall behavior."

The seventh school views strategy formation from a power perspective, with negotiation at the crux of the process. Power and politics drive this school of thought, with organizations vying for position in markets and transactions. Macro and micro power perspectives draw attention to transactional-level power and market-level power, respectively. Strategy formation is more emergent as firms engage in power plays, ploys, and tactics to maneuver in various contexts.

The eighth school is the cultural school, where, again, the emphasis is on the organization as a collective whole and strategy formation as comprising social interaction. Strategy is deliberate in that the members are engaged in the process that involves collective action. Resources and capabilities are the sources of competitive advantage, as firms are able to create a culture that brings forth unique decision making with a resistance toward organizational change.

The ninth school pertains to the environment while describing strategy formation as reactive. The firm's external environment influences the strategy formulation and implementation processes, and firms are viewed as being part of an environment that is simple or complex, stable or dynamic. The decision maker's role is one of a boundary spanner in being able to scan the environment while identifying the macro and micro level forces that impact the firm's position within a given business domain. The population ecology perspective describes firms as belonging to a given cluster in terms of their characteristics (resources and capabilities) and how they are able to adapt within a given environmental context.

The tenth school is the configuration school, which views strategy as transformational. *Configuration* refers to the structure that a firm adopts in a given environmental context, and *transformation* refers to a change in configuration based on a change in context. The life cycle of organization is essentially a pattern that emerges from the various configurations and transformations that occur over the various periods of change that organizations go through. The essence of strategy formation is to ensure that firms are able to recognize the need to change its configuration while transforming from one state to the other during its productive life.

Structure follows strategy and strategy follows structure are two views of the strategy formation process that are related to this school. In fact, this school is actually a compendium of all other schools put together. Transformational leadership forms the essence of strategy, and bottom-up change and top-bottom transformation are part of the process. Mintzberg and his colleagues state that "resulting strategies take the form of plan or patterns, positions or perspectives, or else ploys, but again, each for its own time and matched to its own situation."

OVERALL AIMS OF STRATEGIC MANAGEMENT: CREATING A COMPETITIVE ADVANTAGE

A firm is in business to create value for its stakeholders. Since value is created if firms have a competitive edge over their market rivals, it is imperative that a definitive and formalized approach that falls within the realm of strategic management is at the core of the process. Relying on luck and intuition may not be the best way to sustain an advantage in the firm's market domain. Creating a competitive advantage, and subsequently sustaining it over a period of time, requires a formal approach in terms of strategy formation and implementation. The firm should engage in constant evaluation of its market position, including benchmarking, that enables it to develop a strategic perspective to the value creation process. Since factors in the firm's external and internal environments are constantly changing, the complexity and variability associated with creating and sustaining competitive advantage are high.

This is why firms such as IBM, Microsoft, Hilton Hotels Corp and McDonald's have all been through ups and downs during the course of their organizational histories in terms of sustaining competitive advantage in their respective market domains. If companies plan to constantly scan the environment to detect any changes in their external environment and be able to formulate strategies at the corporate, business, and functional levels, they must engage in the strategic management process. Moreover, emphasis must be given to implementing strategies (which is even more complex), including creating strategic control systems that help to evaluate the gap between formulated and implemented strategies.

1. *At the corporate level*, strategy is about asking questions about what business the firm is in or would like to be in, the firm's potential to create value by being in the business or expanding into a new line of business, and the resources and capabilities the firm already has or needs to get to sustain/create competitive advantage in its business or businesses.

2. *At the business level*, firms need to ask themselves the following questions: How can we create competitive advantage in our product-market domains in each strategic business unit (SBU)? How can we continue to be an overall cost leader or a broad differentiator, or, for that matter, have a cost focus or be a focused differentiator in our market domain? Note that SBU is defined as a unit within a given corporate identity that is distinctly different from other units within the

corporation in terms of products and services, as well as the markets it serves with a distinct profit-making capability of its own.

3. *At the functional level*, the firm's objective is to sustain its advantage by focusing on efficiencies related to production, operations, administration, marketing, and other support functions. It also engages in constant innovation to ensure new product/service development rollout, while ensuring that the service and product qualities, as well as the customer satisfaction related to them, are at the highest level.

Note that the linkage among the three levels of strategy leads to the creation of sustainable competitive advantage. The various concepts introduced in this chapter and many other related ones are presented and discussed in detail throughout this book.

DEFINING KEY TERMS

Strategy entails futuristic thinking and developing a course of action to meet goals and objectives (more on this in Chapter 5). The strategic management framework (see Figure 1.1) captures the process sequentially and definitively. It should be noted that although we present different elements of the strategic management framework separately or in a linear step-by-step process, in fact they overlap and go hand in hand. The framework includes mission and vision statements, goals, and objectives that are linked to the mission and vision, as well as strategies and tactics to achieve the goals and objectives. Strategic analysis provides the firm with a clear picture of its situation, which includes internal and external analysis. Internal analysis pertains to strengths and weaknesses analysis, whereas external analysis pertains to opportunities and threats analysis, which is also referred to as SWOT analysis. The analysis enables a firm to engage in strategic decision making. Strategic decisions pertain to choosing an alternative among a set of alternatives that leads to strategy-related success. These decisions have an effect on the firm's long-term orientation and direction.

Strategic management includes two distinct phases: the strategy formation phase and the strategy implementation phase. Strategic formation is the process of defining the direction of the firm's futuristic course of action, which would enable the firm to allocate resources in order to achieve the set goals and objectives. An internal and external environment analysis is part of the assessment before strategy is formulated at the corporate, business, and functional levels. On the other hand, strategy implementation is the process of putting strategy into action, which includes designing the organizational structure and related systems. This process leads to effective resource allocation processes, including programs and activities such as setting budgets, developing support systems, recruiting, hiring, and training, as well as designing performance evaluation and rewards systems that lead to the attainment of set goals and objectives.

The organization must first define its mission, goals, and objectives. The mission is a brief description of the very purpose of creating the organization. The mission statement includes a clear purpose and states why the organization is in existence. For example, the following is the corporate mission statement for Four Seasons Hotels and Resorts (fourseasons.com):

> *Four Seasons is dedicated to perfecting the travel experience through continual innovation and the highest standards of hospitality. From elegant surroundings of the finest quality, to caring, highly personalised 24-hour service, Four Seasons embodies a true home away from home for those who know and appreciate the best. The deeply instilled Four Seasons culture is personified by its employees – people who share a single focus and are inspired to offer great service.*

The vision, however, describes where the organization wants to go from where it is at present. For instance, Hilton Hotels Corporation defines its vision as "Our vision is to be the first choice of the world's travelers."

Goals are more specific in terms of what the organization aims to achieve in a definite period of time so it would be able to accomplish its mission and vision. Goals are planned over the short and long terms. Short-term goals are set for a period not exceeding one year, whereas long-term goals are set for a period of time exceeding three to five years. This very much depends on the characteristics of the business. Goals need to be linked to objectives. Note that goals are more abstract than objectives. Objectives need to be definite and quantifiable, strategies clearly identify how the objectives will be met in terms of the plan, and tactics are the actions that operationalize the strategy—those that lead to the attainment of goals and objectives. For instance, in a game of chess, a tactic may be employed to corner the opponent's rook by making a series of moves. Another set of tactics could be geared toward weakening the queen. These tactics in combination may be part of the strategy to gain an advantage, which ultimately would lead to winning the game. Note that tactical decisions, which can be immediate or very short term in terms of scope, impact the implementation process at the functional/operating level.

To differentiate missions, goals, objectives, strategies, and tactics, let's consider this case: The King Hotel is in business with a mission to create value for its stockholders. To accomplish the mission, the firm has set goals for the current year of increasing the business segment productivity. The objectives that are linked to the goals include increasing the business segment revenues by 10 percent and increasing repeat clientele for this segment by 15 percent. The strategies include marketing and operations-related plans and tactics, including increasing sales calls in the business district of the city, increasing promotional campaigns for the international and domestic business markets, and creating an amenities package for business travelers that includes free airport transfers, a free welcome drink on arrival, free Internet access in the room, and free use of business centre secretarial services for three hours a day. Note that the goals are linked to the mission, the objectives are linked to the goals, the strategies are linked to the objectives, and the tactics are linked to the strategies.

> ## EXERCISE
>
> Choose an H&T organization and research this company's vision, mission, goals, and objectives. Critically evaluate and compare them with those of other H&T companies. What are the similarities and differences? Which aspects do you like in these statements and why?

THE BOOK'S APPROACH AND STRUCTURE

This book consists of four parts. The first part consists of Chapter 1, which introduces the topic of this book and strategic management, and Chapter 2, which discusses the application of strategic management in the context of the international hospitality and tourism industry. In particular, Chapter 1 opens the scene by providing a brief discussion on the historical origins of strategy, the writings of classic authors, the industrial organization model, and the resource-based view. It further discusses assumptions of dominant strategic management approaches. Based on these discussions, key terms such as *strategy* and *strategic management* are introduced.

Chapter 2 is devoted to examining and applying strategic management in the hospitality and tourism contexts. It provides a brief review of the current level of strategy literature in the hospitality and tourism field and illustrate its limitations. This chapter also discusses why tourism and hospitality organizations need strategy and strategic management and whether and how generic strategy models and theories can be applied in tourism and hospitality organizations. The primary objectives of the two introductory chapters are to establish the importance and relevance of strategic management as an area of academic study and as a key executive practice for aspiring hospitality and tourism professionals.

The second part of the book establishes the key dimensions of the external and internal contexts in which both the strategy content and the?strategy process are embedded. The specific dynamics and nature of the hospitality and tourism industry and organizations are emphasised throughout. In particular, Chapter 3 concentrates on exploring approaches to the analysis of the external environment that is confronting hospitality and tourism organizations. The relevant theories, models, and frameworks pertaining to the process?of external analysis are introduced and explored in the specific context of hospitality and tourism. Chapter 4 discusses the importance of the organization's internal environment as an influence on strategy formation and implementation. The importance of organization structure, culture, and leadership as key considerations is highlighted and discussed in the context of the international hospitality and tourism industry.

The third part of the book is devoted to exploring the varying levels of strategy content—the so-called "what" of strategy. Three levels of strategy content are explored that, although ultimately linked, can be viewed as separate areas of strategic management decision making. The importance of context as an influence on strategy content is highlighted throughout the three chapters in this section. Chapter 5 is concerned with exploring the issue of competitive strategy at the level of the strategic business unit (SBU). Particular emphasis is given to exploring the concept of generic strategies as the basis for creating superior value and ultimately a sustainable competitive advantage. Chapter 6 explores the potential roles of the corporate centre and its relationship with SBUs. The core tension between coordination and responsiveness is highlighted and discussed. Chapter 7 is concerned with the issue of the interbusiness or network level of strategy content. The central question explored here is the extent to which organizations should seek to develop cooperative arrangements when developing strategies.

The fourth part provides discussions about the strategy process and contains two chapters that cover entitled strategy formation and strategy implementation. Chapters 8 and 9 do not constitute entirely separate subjects. In other words, they are not phases or stages that can be looked at and understood in isolation. They are strongly linked and greatly overlapping. They have been selected because debates on these issues have been raging for years. Chapter 8 discusses how strategy development and implementation is viewed in different schools of thought. It critically evaluates each view's assumptions and suggestions and provides some recommendations for tourism and hospitality organizations as they engage in their strategy formation process. Chapter 9 is devoted to explaining how strategies (or strategic decisions) can be implemented and how changes can be managed. A number of implementation factors are identified, and the role and importance of each are discussed. Chapter 9 also evaluates the magnitude and pace of strategic change. Discussions are also provided on potential barriers and resistance to strategy implementation and how they can be overcome.

Part 5 contains only one chapter. This final chapter seeks to integrate the key themes explored in earlier chapters in an effort to provide readers with the holistic perspective that is inherent in effective strategic management practice. The final part of the text consists of case studies. Two cases deal with the strategy content, and two cases deal specifically with the strategy process. The fifth case study is integrative in nature and is relevant to the book as a whole. Strategy context issues are reflected in all five cases.

SUMMARY

This chapter introduces strategic management, while providing an overview of how the field has evolved from a historical perspective. Given the complexity associated with managing firms, schools of thought on strategic management have comprehensively covered the various approaches to managing the firm from a strategic perspective while highlighting their relevance and significance. Definitions of key terms used in the field, such as *mission, vision, strategy, goals and objectives*, were discussed to explain how the strategic management framework can be used effectively. The chapter also provides a description of how this book could be used to develop a good understanding and appreciation of strategic management in hospitality and tourism.

STUDY QUESTIONS

1. Explain the origins of strategy and strategic management.

2. List the main schools of thought, and explain their premises on strategic management.

3. Why are there different schools of thought on strategic management? Do you think it is confusing to have several different views on strategic management?

4. Define *strategic management, vision, mission, goals, objectives*, and *tactics*.

5. Do you think it is important for H&T companies to have such statements? If yes, why? If no, why not?

REFERENCES AND FURTHER READINGS

Harrington, R. (2001). Environmental uncertainty within the hospitality industry: Exploring the measure of dynamism and complexity between restaurant segments. *Journal of Hospitality and Tourism Research*, 25(4), 386–398.

Harrington, R. and Kendall, K. (2006). Strategy implementation success: The moderating effects of size and environmental complexity and the mediating effects of involvement. *Journal of Hospitality and Tourism Research*, 30(2), 207–230.

Jogaratnam, G. and Law, R. (2006). Environmental scanning and information source utilization: Exploring the behaviour of Hong Kong hotel and tourism executives. *Journal of Hospitality and Tourism Research*, 30(2), 170–190.

Mintzberg, Henry, Ahlstrand, B. W., and Lampel, J. (1998). *Strategy safari: A guided tour through the wilds of strategic management*, New York: The Free Press.

Okumus, F. (2002). Can hospitality researchers contribute to the strategic management literature? *International Journal of Hospitality Management*, 21, 105–110.

Okumus, F. (2004). Potential challenges of employing a formal environmental scanning approach in hospitality organizations. *International Journal of Hospitality Management*, 23, 123–143.

Okumus, F. and Roper, A. (1999). A review of disparate approaches to strategy implementation in hospitality firms. *Journal of Hospitality and Tourism Research*, 23(1), 21–39.

Olsen, M.D. (2004). Literature in strategic management in the hospitality industry. *International Journal of Hospitality Management*, 23, 411–424.

Olsen, M.D., West, J., and Tse, E (2006). Strategic Management in the Hospitality Industry, 3rd edition. Prentice Hall, New York.

Porter, M.E. (1979). How competitive forces shape strategy. *Harvard Business Review*, March/April 1979.

Porter, M.E. (1980). *Competitive Strategy*. New York: The Free Press.

Porter, M.E. (1985). *Competitive Advantage: Creating and Sustaining Superior Performance*. New York: The Free Press.

Roper, A. and Olsen, M.D. (1999). Research in strategic management in the hospitality industry. *International Journal of Hospitality Management*, 17, 111–124.

CHAPTER 2

Strategic Management in Hospitality and Tourism

Learning objectives

After reading this chapter, you should be able to:

1. Define the hospitality and tourism (H&T) context.

2. Evaluate characteristics and types of H&T organizations.

3. Discuss how characteristics of H&T organizations may influence the application of strategic management practices in H&T organizations.

4. Evaluate the current level of strategy research in the H&T field.

CONTENTS

Opening Case

Mark Bright has been working as an assistant manager in an ice cream factory. During his last annual review, he was told that he would be promoted to the general manager position at another factory within two years. Although he has been happy with his salary, benefits, and the working environment, recently he has started to think about a career change. He finds his current job very routine and not stimulating enough. He does not like routine paperwork and long meetings. He considers himself a people person, since he likes to help people and he enjoys interacting with others.

Thanks to a close friend's recommendation, a restaurant chain has offered Mark a managerial position in Orlando, Florida. He will make 30 percent more and receive a better benefits package. Before starting this position, Mark must work as an assistant manager in the Miami branch of the restaurant for six months. During this time, he will also attend some training workshops at a college in Miami. The regional human resources management director will also work with him closely to better prepare him for the position. After he starts his new job in Orlando, the company will subsidize his tuition for a master's degree at a very prestigious hospitality college in Orlando.

1. Do you think Mark should accept this offer? Explain why or why not.
2. If he accepts this position, what type of skills will Mark need in managing a restaurant compared to being a manager in an ice cream factory?
3. In your view, what are the differences in managing a restaurant compared to managing an ice cream factory?

INTRODUCTION

In Chapter 1, we introduced the topic of strategic management, with discussions on the historical origins of strategy and the writings of classic authors. We also discussed the dominant strategic management schools of thought. We believe that the first chapter is particularly important for the reader in terms of providing a foundation for discussions and debates in the following chapters.

In this chapter, we define the H&T context and evaluate characteristics and types of H&T organizations. We then question how these characteristics may impact on strategic management practices in H&T organizations. Next, we discuss how generic strategic management models and theories can best be applied in the H&T context. Finally, we provide a brief review of the current status of strategic management literature in the H&T field.

DEFINING THE HOSPITALITY AND TOURISM CONTEXT

Services are becoming increasingly an important part of the global economy. It is estimated that on average 70 percent of the gross domestic product

(GDP) of the Organization for Economic Co-Operation and Development (OECD) (2007) countries come from service industries. Moreover, it is predicted that the importance of services will continue to increase worldwide not only in the developed parts of the world but also in developing countries. Certainly H&T is an important sector in services particularly in the developed countries. Under the services sector, the H&T industry is often named as the number one industry worldwide in terms of generation of income and employment. Over the last three decades, the H&T industry has grown rapidly, and now it has become one of the most prominent sectors of the service industry. It produces over 11 percent of the world's gross domestic product and employs over 10 percent of the global workforce (UNWTO, 2003).

In 2006, international tourism arrivals worldwide achieved an all-time record of 842 million tourists. In the same year, tourism receipts, including international passenger transport, were estimated about $883 billion, which means that international tourism generated over $2.4 billion a day in 2006 (UNWTO, 2007). As an export category, the tourism industry ranks fourth after fuels, chemicals, and automotive products (UNWTO, 2007). Despite the presence of terrorism, natural disasters, health scares, fluctuations in exchange rates, and uncertainties in economic and political arenas, the H&T industry has experienced positive growth for the last two decades. This growth has not only been observed in developed parts of the world but also in developing parts of the world such as Africa, Asia, and the Middle East. It is predicted that the H&T industry will continue growing rapidly worldwide. Following economic, sociocultural trends and developments, more people will be participating both in domestic and international tourism. In meeting this growing demand, many new H&T businesses will be opened, new tourism destinations will emerge, and new tourism services and products will be introduced.

Although it is one of the largest industries worldwide, providing a concise definition for the H&T industry has been a major challenge for professionals and academics. As often acknowledged, there continues to be a lack of agreement as to exactly what hospitality and tourism encompasses and the relationship between them. According to Nykiel (2005), definitions of the H&T industry are often limited by the unique viewpoints of sectors within the industry. For example, a hotel operator may see the industry as accommodations with food and beverages. A food and beverage operator may view the industry as a dining experience with the focus on menu offerings and food service. A travel agency manager might believe that providing travel-related services to people for business and leisure defines the industry best. An executive of a theme park may see hospitality as providing a unique entertainment and educational experience. In order to overcome this confusion, Nykiel (2005) placed all of these viewpoints under a wider perspective called "hospitality" and further stated that the hospitality industry encompasses travel, accommodations, food service, clubs, gaming, attractions, entertainment, and recreation.

Kandampully (2007) notes that hospitality organizations operate within a network of service organizations. To a large extent, they are interrelated and interdependent, and include the following:

- Tour operators, travel agents, and tourism organizations

- Travel and transport operators

- Leisure, recreation, and entertainment venue

- Restaurants, bars, clubs, and cafes

- Hotels, resorts, motels, camping grounds, bed & breakfast (B&B) establishments, and hostels

Butler and Jones (2001) use *tourism* as an all-encompassing term that covers all aspects of people being away from their home and *hospitality* as a specific part of providing accommodations and meals for tourists. They note that the one difficulty in their definitions is that the hospitality industry also serves many people who are not tourists, such as local residents. They state that tourism is often interpreted as the flow of visitors from one country to another for more than 24 hours of time and less than one year.

In this book, to get a broader view and include all of the different types and sizes of organizations in the field, we use the terms *hospitality* and *tourism* interchangeably. Thus, these terms encompass travel, accommodations, food services, clubs, gaming, theme parks, attractions, entertainment, recreation, conventions, and nonprofit tourism organizations such as national tourism offices, destination management, and marketing offices. It is clear that the H&T industry is a composite of a number of distinct industries that are closely interrelated and interdependent. These industries operate within a global network. The following section will provide more explanation and discussions about different types of H&T organizations.

TYPES OF HOSPITALITY AND TOURISM ORGANIZATIONS

Organizations that operate in the H&T industry can be grouped under different categories depending on their primary activities, size, profit motives, and geographical coverage. In terms of their primary services, organizations can be categorized as follows:

1. Travel and transport

2. Accommodations (lodging)

3. Food and beverages

4. Entertainment and recreation

5. Tourism offices or destination management organizations

6. Nongovernmental tourism organizations

Each of these is often identified as a subsector under the H&T industry. In addition, each can be further broken into several subgroupings. For example, under accommodations, there are hotels, motels, guest houses, hostels, villas, and time-shares. Some of these organizations can be further grouped depending on their service level, such as luxury hotels, boutique hotels, midmarket hotels, and budget hotels, or according to their star ratings, such as five-star (diamond), four-star, and three-star hotels.

A further grouping of the H&T organizations can be made based on their size such as small, medium, and large. Independent and flexible small and medium-sized enterprises (SMEs) dominate the tourism market worldwide. An SME is defined in employment terms as a company with a workforce of fewer than 250 employees (European Commission, 2002; Wanhill, 2000). For example, it is reported that around more than 90 percent of tourism and hospitality organizations in Europe are SMEs (Bastakis, Buhalis, and Butler, 2004; European Commission, 2002, Wanhill, 2000) which are usually owner-managed, being run either by an individual or by small groups of people.

Managing SMEs is different from managing larger enterprises. For example, Quinn, Larmour, and McQuillan (1992) state that smaller hotels are not simply smaller versions of large hotel groups. They have distinct organizational structures and cultures that are often influenced by their owners. The business objectives of smaller hotels may have a different emphases compared to large hotel groups. According to Quinn and colleagues (1992), profitability, market share, and productivity are less important to small businesses. In addition, they may have less desire to expand and achieve high profitability and productivity ratios. Their views on the external environment, long-term strategies, generic positions, competitive advantages, and allocations of financial and human resources may not be similar to those of large organizations. We know that many SMEs face financial and managerial challenges (Hwang and Lockwood, 2006), and their ratio of business failures is higher compared to larger organizations (Wanhill, 2000).

Another classification of H&T organizations can be made according to profit motive. A high majority of H&T organizations aim to make a profit and achieve some financial objectives in order to satisfy their owners and shareholders. On the other hand, nongovernmental tourism organizations, associations, tourism destination management, and marketing organizations can be placed under nonprofit tourism organizations. Their primary aim is often not to make profit but to achieve other nonfinancial objectives, such as serving society, protecting the environment, and achieving sustainable tourism development in their regions over the long term. The United Nations World Tourism Organization (WTO) and Visitor and Convention Bureaus (CVBs) are examples of nonprofit tourism organizations.

Finally, H&T organizations can be further grouped based on their geographical coverage. These include local, regional, and global firms. Local organizations operate in only one city or country, whereas regional organizations operate in only a geographical region such as Europe, the Middle East, or North America. For example, the Hong Kong–based Shangri La Hotel chain is a good example of a regional hospitality firm that is found only in the Pacific-Asia rim. Finally, global hospitality and tourism firms such as Intercontinental Hotels, Marriott Hotels, Hilton, McDonald's, and KFC are examples of those that operate in many countries and almost all continents worldwide. Compared to national organizations, regional and global H&T organizations face more complex, dynamic, and challenging external and internal environments. Consequently, they must accommodate the impact of an international context when tackling strategic analysis, strategic choice, implementation, strategic control, and global competitive advantage.

The preceding categories of H&T organizations show the diverse nature of the industry. Certainly, some of the firms can be placed under multiple groupings. What is important, however, is that, depending on their functional area, size, profit, and nonprofit motives and geographical coverage, the internal and operational environments, level of competition, barriers to entry and exit, and substitutes and resource requirements may vary. This will be discussed in more depth in Chapter 3.

In addition, depending on the functional area, size, profit, and nonprofit motives and geographical coverage, organizational culture, structure, cost structure, competitive strategies, resource levels, and entry and exit barriers can be different for each company. Certainly, these differences require their managers to better understand the unique features of these organizations.

Chapter 4 will examine in more depth the internal characteristics of various H&T organizations.

As just stated, there can be major differences among hospitality and tourism organizations in terms of their primary activities, size, profit motives, and geographical coverage. These differences can have important implications on the application of strategic management theories and models that are in practice. In addition, one may further claim that because of these differences, we should be cautious about making generalizations about hospitality and tourism organizations. On the other hand, it is often claimed that although different services are offered in H&T organizations, each organization has its own unique characteristics that demand closer inspection when managing H&T organizations. The following section explains and evaluates the unique characteristics of each segment in the H&T industry.

DISCUSSION QUESTION

Based on what we have discussed so far, can we make generalizations about the hospitality and tourism industry?

CHARACTERISTICS OF HOSPITALITY AND TOURISM ORGANIZATIONS

Essentially, service sector organizations, including the H&T organizations, possess certain unique features. Ignoring the differences between service organizations and manufacturing organizations can lead to unexpected outcomes. The following are some closely related, unique characteristics of H&T organizations (Fitzsimmons and Fitzsimmons, 2004; Gronoos, 2007; Kandampully, 2007):

1. Inseparability—customer participation in the service process

2. Simultaneity

3. Perishability

4. Intangibility (the tangible–intangible continuum)

5. Heterogeneity

6. Cost structure

7. Labor intensive

Inseparability

In H&T organizations, customers need to be present and participate in the service delivery process. This is certainly not common in manufacturing industries. This means that the separation of the production and marketing functions, which are important characteristics of the traditional manufacturing industry, is not possible in the service delivery process that is found in H&T organizations. Therefore, H&T organizations must communicate with and motivate their customers to actively participate in the service delivery process.

Attracting and bringing customers to H&T organizations require careful attention to their location, brand image, and ongoing marketing and promotional activities. In addition, the presence of customers and the requirement for them to play an active role in the service delivery process necessitate ongoing careful attention to behavior, the physical appearance of employees, the interior design and decoration of facilities, furnishings, layout, and noise. This means that like Fitzsimmons and Fitzsimmons's (2004) comments on managing service organizations, operations, marketing and HRM functions in H&T, organizations need to be very closely integrated. Compared to manufacturing firms, this certainly requires that a different managerial approach, organizational structure, and culture must be developed and maintained in H&T organizations.

Simultaneity

A typical manufactured good, such as a refrigerator or a television, can be inspected before it is delivered to retail outlets, where they are then sold to customers. However, services in H&T organizations are created and consumed simultaneously, which can prevent employing active quality control mechanisms. In addition, as just noted, customers and employees need to participate and coordinate in the service delivery process. It is almost impossible to have one manager for every employee to monitor the service delivery process and make sure that frontline employees are doing their jobs well, in addition to guiding the customers' participation in the process.

Therefore, in order to make sure that services are produced and offered to customers at an expected quality that meets consistent standards, H&T organizations should rely on other measures such as investing in human resources, use of technology, building desired physical facilities, and decoration to ensure the quality of services delivered. This has implications on decision-making practices, resource allocations, operations, marketing, and human resource management practices.

Perishability

As production and consumption in H&T organizations are simultaneous, services become perishable if they are not sold. Subsequently, their value is lost forever. For example, an airline seat or a hotel room will perish if a customer does not purchase it at the time of production. Therefore, the full utilization of service capacity is a strategic task for many H&T organizations. It is particularly important to emphasize that demand for an H&T organization's services often fluctuates considerably, depending on the external developments and changes, such as seasonality and crises. For instance, terrorist attacks (such as September 11, 2001 in New York), disease outbreaks (such as SARS in the Far East), and natural weather phenomena (such as tornadoes or hurricanes) all had a negative impact on the demand for services offered by the H&T industry worldwide. Because H&T organizations cannot sell their services when such circumstances arise, they lose a considerable amount of nonrecoverable income. When the demand is low or there are sudden fluctuations in demand, it is neither easy nor recommended for H&T organizations to lower their rates greatly, since it may influence their image, change their customer segment, and upset their regular customers.

A further issue in terms of perishability is that consumer demand for H&T services exhibits very cyclic behavior over a short period of time. For example, restaurants are busy during lunchtime, evenings, and weekends, but they may not be very busy at other times. Demand for many H&T organizations, such as restaurants and theme parks, increases during public holidays such as Christmas, New Year's Day, and spring break. Depending on the location, many hotels and restaurants experience great variances in summers and winters. This puts much responsibility on the management of these firms in planning for the future and allocating their resources timely and adequately to the right purposes. In short, expected and unexpected fluctuations in demand have implications on cost structure, pricing, staffing, and resource allocation decisions.

Tangibility

Hospitality and tourism organizations offer a combination of tangible and intangible products (Kandampully, 2007). For example, a hotel room or a meal in a restaurant has both tangible and intangible qualities. Again, there may be major differences between a budget hotel and a luxury hotel or between a fast-food restaurant and an upscale restaurant in terms of tangible and intangible qualities offered. However, services are often ideas, concepts, interactions, relationships, and experiences that are not often patentable.

It is essential to note that the intangible aspects of services offered by H&T organizations are critical in customer satisfaction. This is because the main difficulty related to the intangibility of services is that customers cannot often see, feel, and test these services when they order or buy them (Gronroos, 2007; Kandampully, 2007). Prior to their purchase, they may try to evaluate services as much as they can by looking at the interior of a hotel or a restaurant and the appearance and behavior of the employees. In most cases, customers tend to rely on the image or the goodwill of H&T organizations. In order to overcome potential problems and dissatisfaction in these areas, some H&T companies publicize their service promises and offer a 100 percent satisfaction guarantee.

Legal requirements have also been proposed for H&T organizations to provide acceptable service performance for customers. However, these legal requirements vary among different countries. The expectations of customers may also vary, depending on the country or geographical location of the H&T enterprise. We know that customers' demands and expectations are constantly increasing, which puts more pressure on H&T organizations to improve their services and management practices.

Heterogeneity

Services provided by H&T organizations may also vary considerably. One hotel unit in a chain hotel, one unit in a restaurant chain, or one holiday experience of a traveler to the same destination is unlikely to be identical to another. Many factors, particularly the human element, result in variations of the service delivery process. In other words, services will be heterogeneous, and variations in service delivery from customer to customer and from time to time will always occur. It is often difficult to standardize every employee–customer interaction in the H&T business. In addition, in many H&T organizations, customers interact not only with employees but with other customers. This customer-to-customer interaction in certain service organizations, such as pubs, discos, nightclubs, and cruises, can be an important aspect of the total service delivery process. H&T organizations are also highly susceptible to external changes. One example of an external factor is the weather. Visiting an outdoor theme park can be very pleasant and entertaining on a nice day, but it can be a miserable experience if it is raining and cold.

In recent years, through the intensive use of information technology and active training of employees and design of physical facilities, attempts to improve and standardize the service delivery process have greatly increased. On the other hand, some customers expect a high level of service delivery, but this does not mean that they prefer standardized services. Therefore, H&T organizations need to achieve some degree of balance between standardization and differentiation in meeting the demands and expectations of their customers.

Cost Structure

The cost structure of H&T firms influences their managerial and resource allocation decisions. For example, luxury H&T organizations are capital, labor, and energy intensive. Typically, they have high property costs and also employ large numbers of full-time employees. It can be difficult for them to reduce such cost items even if the demand is low. In addition, they may need to renovate their facilities every five to ten years to stay competitive in their field. Another issue is that given the vast amount of investment made in these organizations, investors and owners often look at very carefully at their return on investment. Therefore, these companies need to maintain a steady flow of customers to maintain the profitability of their businesses. This often leads to creative marketing and product development strategies as well as pricing strategies.

Labor Intensive

Installing machines and computers on a car factory's assembly line or in an ice cream factory can reduce the number of employees. However, compared to many organizations in other industries, H&T organizations require a great many employees. To put it simply, H&T organizations are labor intensive. This is because personal interactions and experiences are important parts of services, and employees play a key role in this process. Despite using many machines, computers, and technological developments, H&T organizations still rely primarily on their employees to deliver a memorable and positive experience. Being served and treated nicely by employees is a major factor in getting repeat customers.

The Impact of these Unique Characteristics on Managing H&T Organizations

Previously, we examined several unique characteristics of H&T organizations. It should be noted that given the differences among organizations in this industry in terms of their size, service type, profit motive, and customer segment, the level and importance of these unique characteristics may be different. For example, the tangible aspect of service in a fast-food restaurant may be more apparent compared to eating in an expensive restaurant. The cost structure of a small-budget hotel is certainly different from the cost structure of a five-star luxury hotel.

Table 2.1	Areas Where the Industry Characteristics Impact on Managing H&T Firms

1. Analyzing the internal and external environment as an ongoing process
2. Making decisions in the areas of service delivery, pricing, and marketing
3. Strategic planning practices
4. Developing a sustainable competitive advantage
5. Achieving and evaluating intended outcomes
6. Managing capacity to maximize revenue
7. Managing the cost structure of the company
8. Allocating available financial and human resources for future strategies
9. Evaluating and improving the service delivery process
10. Interacting and satisfying customers
11. Training, developing, and motivating employees and managers (our internal guests)
12. Designing and decorating facilities

The time a customer spends in a fast-food restaurant is much shorter than when he or she enjoys a four-course meal in an upscale restaurant. Interactions between customers and employees and among customers on a cruise ship, in a five-star hotel, or in a nightclub will be very different from the interactions in a budget hotel or McDonald's. What is important here is that managers and owners of H&T organizations should be aware of the unique characteristics of their business. They also must go beyond the simple adaptation of the management techniques developed by the manufacturing industries. Table 2.1 provides some key areas where the preceding unique characteristics can have implications on the management of H&T organizations.

THE CASE FOR STRATEGIC MANAGEMENT IN H&T ORGANIZATIONS

Despite its size and growing importance, the H&T industry faces major challenges and problems worldwide. Businesses in the H&T industry operate in a dynamic and complex environment. Macro trends such as changes in legislations, regional and global economic and political crises, sociocultural trends, sophistication of customers, stiff competition, terrorism, security, global warming, multiculturalism, globalization, mergers and acquisitions, labor shortage, and advanced technological developments all pose important challenges to the management strategies of H&T organizations. According to Nykiel (2005), product design, market segmentation, franchising, real estate investment trusts, and new product concepts are some of the strategic driving forces that cause the industry to be very dynamic. All of these trends and developments require the organizations in the H&T industry to keep redefining their strategic management practices through a continuous process.

It is worth emphasizing that strategic management is not only important to H&T organizations but also to all organizations, regardless of their size and type. However, we should stress that H&T organizations operate in a unique external and internal context, which makes it especially important to understand and follow contemporary strategic management practices and theories. For example, the H&T industry has been experiencing dramatic changes in customer expectations and needs. They not only need to develop new products and service concepts as an ongoing basis, but they also need to control their costs and manage their human resources wisely.

According to Pine and Gilmore (1998), services in the H&T industry are undergoing a shift from service to experience. Today, most H&T organizations such as Disney World, Hilton, Marriott, and Starbucks refer to their respective services as "an experience." This requires changing the mindset of many managers and employees in their strategic thinking and daily actions. In order to achieve this shift, there is an essential need to know both the H&T context and how this strategic change can be achieved in that context. To better prepare and respond to these trends and keep redefining strategic management practices, H&T organizations need to have a clear knowledge about strategic management theories and apply them in the relevant context. This is because strategic management deals with the major and fundamental managerial issues that directly affect the future of H&T organizations.

Regardless of their size, type, and customer segment, all H&T organizations engage in key decisions in terms of their future intentions and resource allocations. When an H&T organization successfully prepares for its future and responds to changes and developments in its external and internal environment proactively, it can secure its survival and develop sustainable competitive advantages. It is also essential to emphasize that even successful organizations face problems and may end up making irrational investments. When they make such investments or managerial errors, they may face some dramatic consequences and perhaps even risk their own survival. For example, Delta Airlines and the once famous and successful Six Flags theme parks have both been facing serious problems in recent years due to bad investments and managerial decisions. It is known that the ratio of business failure among small and medium-sized H&T organizations is high. Applying strategic management principles and theories can certainly be helpful not only in overcoming failures in decision making and resource allocations but also in turning the organization around and making it successful. Table 2.2

Table 2.2	Areas Where Strategic Management Can Help H&T Organizations

- Providing a holistic view for the entire H&T organization
- Providing a sharper focus on what is strategically important
- Providing a link between the external environment and the internal environment
- Analyzing a complex and rapidly changing external environment
- Analyzing an organization's strategic resources
- Giving a clear sense of strategic vision and direction
- Defining organizational purposes
- Developing measurable goals and objectives
- Identifying key resources and investing in core competencies
- Formulating decisions and making them happen
- Managing change
- Coordinating organizational activities and allocating resources
- Understanding the complexities of decision making and the structuring of an organization
- Understanding the role and importance of the organizational structure and culture on the strategy process
- Reducing and managing uncertainty inside the organization
- Measuring intended and unintended outcomes of the strategy process

provides a number of important areas in which strategic management can help H&T organizations.

APPLYING STRATEGIC MANAGEMENT IN THE H&T CONTEXT

One emerging question is how we can use and apply generic strategic management theories and models in specific H&T industry context. In this section, we will examine how such theories and models can be applied in the particular context of hospitality and tourism. Most of the strategic management tools, models, techniques, and theories have traditionally been developed mainly for the manufacturing sector in the United States and have subsequently been applied to other industrial sectors (Okumus and Wong, 2005). However, H&T organizations that are concerned with a service-based output reflect the typical characteristics found across the service sector. These include customer participation in the service delivery process, simultaneity, perishability, intangibility, heterogeneity, and high fixed costs of the services provided. As explained previously, there are different types of firms with unique features in the H&T industry.

McGahan and Porter (1997) and Porter (1980) claimed that the industry context does matter because it can have a direct or an indirect impact on the strategy-making process and on the productivity and profitability of organizations. This reflects the so-called "outside-in" view that we saw in Chapter 1. Conversely, Baden-Fuller and Stopford (1994) argued that it is the internal characteristics of firm—the "inside-out" view—that matters most, not the industry. According to Baden-Fuller and Stopford (1994), successful organizations can skillfully ride the waves of industry crises, and less successful ones disappear due to industry misfortunes besetting the industry. For example, Southwest Airlines has been profitable and successful since the early 1970s, while many other major airlines have faced serious challenges, with some declaring bankruptcy. Here, the industry structure and characteristics are considered to be of secondary importance.

Given these conflicting views as to whether the industry context or that of the individual firm is more important when devising a strategic plan, we propose a different but more holistic view on this controversial issue. In support of McGahan and Porter (1997), we believe that the industry structure and the unique characteristics of the H&T sector do matter and that they can have a clear impact on the strategy-making process and on the productivity and profitability of H&T organizations. Therefore, we need to have a better and deeper understanding of how the external environment affects the H&T industry. We further acknowledge that the industry context is one of the dimensions impacting the management practices in H&T organizations and their performance.

In short, the context at both the industry and the organizational levels is crucial if one is to effectively use and apply the strategic management theories and models in H&T organizations. The importance of context to strategy making means that the preceding argument holds across all industrial sectors and not just hospitality and tourism. All issues related to the strategy process and the strategy content must always be framed in that specific context. In other words, we cannot meaningfully separate strategy from its industry context or from its internal organizational context. We will analyze and evaluate the context at the industry level in Chapter 3 and in the organizational level in Chapter 4.

STRATEGY RESEARCH IN THE HOSPITALITY AND TOURISM FIELD

When we look at the strategy literature in the H&T field, we see that strategy research dates back to the early 1980s, and the focus of these studies was mainly conceptual in nature and concerned with strategic planning rather than strategic management (e.g., Olsen and DeNoble, 1981; Reichel, 1982).

Toward the end of the 1980s, empirical work was more evident, with the focus being mainly on environmental scanning and strategy and structure alignments (e.g., Schaffer, 1987; Tse and Olsen, 1998).

The international context has attracted a considerable volume of attention, although most research in this area has largely been descriptive in nature, with a more limited amount of activity directed toward theoretical development. A notable early study concerning the international dimension is the research of Dunning and McQueen (1981). With regards to methodology, it is difficult to generalize, but strategy researchers in the United States have tended toward survey-based research, while European researchers have made greater use of case study–oriented approaches (see Taylor and Edgar, 1996; 1999).

In recent years, several attempts have been made to review the current level of strategy research in the H&T field. Athiyaman (1995) in the tourism field and Olsen and Roper (1998) and Tse and Olsen (1998) in the hospitality field reviewed the current strategy literature. However, these studies did not explicitly attempt to group the previous strategy research in the H&T field under different stages or schools of thought. Instead, the focus was essentially cataloguing relevant publications. For example, Athiyaman (1995) acknowledged that the strategy research in the tourism field is almost nonexistent. On the other hand, Olsen and Roper (1998) and Tse and Olsen (1998) indicated that most of the previous studies in the hospitality field fall into the strategic analysis aspect and that there has been limited research on strategy implementation and evaluation.

Referring back to the classifications provided by Hoskisson and colleagues, (1999), most of the current strategy work in the H&T field can perhaps be placed in early development or under the industrial economics area. Again, from the perspective of different strategic management schools of thought (Mintzberg et al., 1998), apart from some exceptions such as Edgar and Nisbet (1996), Okumus (2004), and Okumus and Roper (1999), most of the previous work on strategy in the H&T field can be put under the traditional planning school. For example, after comparing the strategy literature in the generic field and the strategy literature in the H&T field, Okumus (2002) claimed that H&T researchers tended to follow key strategy research issues and trends almost two decades later than their counterparts in the strategic management field.

In summary, the strategic management research in the H&T context contains a commendable emphasis on industry application, but no notable theoretical contributions have been made to the mainstream strategic management field. One reason for this is that strategic management did not appear on most H&T syllabi until the 1980s, and this in itself would account for the gap in mainstream interests. Another reason is that most of the research during this period was performed by researchers at Virginia

Polytechnic under the direction of Professor Michael Olsen, who has a strong commitment to the "co-alignment principle" that is deeply rooted in the planning school. Those who undertake strategy research in H&T typically encounter a view of strategy that is very much rooted in the classical planning perspective, and consequently they tend to overlook the considerable developments that have taken place in the last 30 years.

Another reason may be that many of the researchers and academics involved in teaching and researching strategy in the hospitality and tourism field have not had a formal training in strategic management but a more generalist hospitality management or business administration background. Thus, a lack of exposure to the mainstream and the limited number of strategy specialists are both likely to be contributing factors. However, the potential still exists for high-quality strategy research of relevance to both the academic community and the industry practitioners.

Finally, limitations of previous research are not unique to the strategic management on H&T organizations. Olsen (2001) and Weiler (2001) both discuss how literature and scholarly activities in the H&T field are somewhat limited and mainly conceptual. Therefore, similar comments can perhaps be made for the literature in other areas such as marketing, human resources, operations management, and financial management in the H&T field.

SUMMARY

This chapter provided a brief review of the current level of strategy literature in the H&T field and illustrated its limitations. A number of conclusions and summary points can be provided:

- Recognition of the unique characteristics can provide us with the necessary insights and understanding of the challenges in applying strategic management in the specific context of H&T.

- The characteristics and types of H&T organizations can impact on strategic management practices, particularly in strategic analysis, decision making, resource allocation, and creating and maintaining a competitive advantage.

- Strategic management theories, models, and frameworks developed in the generic field can be used and applied within the H&T context.

- To do all of the preceding, we must have a good understanding of the industry characteristics and the internal features and managerial practices of H&T organizations.

STUDY QUESTIONS

1. How can we define the H&T industry?

2. What are the main characteristics of H&T organizations?

3. Can we make generalizations about H&T organizations?

4. How are managing H&T organizations different from managing manufacturing organizations?

5. How much do the unique characteristics of H&T organizations impact the strategic management practices in H&T organizations?

6. How can we better apply strategic management theories in H&T organizations?

7. In what areas do the industry characteristics influence the management practices in H&T organizations?

8. In what situations can strategic management help H&T organizations?

9. Why has the current level of strategy research in the H&T field been limited?

SMALL CASE STUDY

A hotel group recruits a successful senior executive from a manufacturing company to turnaround the hotel group.

1. Discuss what type of challenges this new executive may face in this position.

2. Discuss the types of skills that this executive may need in this new position.

REFERENCES AND FURTHER READINGS

Athiyaman, A. (1995). The Interface of Tourism and Strategy Research: An Analysis, *Tourism Management*, 16 (6), 447–453.

Baden-Fuller, C. and Stopford, J.M. (1994). *Rejuvenating the Mature Business*. Boston: Harvard Business School.

Bastakis, C., Buhalis, D., and Butler, R. (2004). "The perception of small and medium sized tourism accommodation providers on the impacts of the tour operators' power in Eastern Mediterranean', *Tourism Management*, 25 (2), 151–170.

Bowman, E.H., Sing, H., and Thomas, H. (2002). The Domain of Strategic Management History and Evolution. In A. Pettigrew, H. Thomas, H., and Whittington, R. (Eds.), *Handbook of Strategy and Management.* London: Sage.

Butler, R. and Jones, P. (2001). Conclusions—Problems, Challenges and Solutions. In A. Lockwood and S. Medlik (Eds.), *Tourism and Hospitality in the 21st Century.* Oxford: Butterworth and Heinemann.

Dunning, J.H. and McQueen, M. (1981). The eclectic theory of international production: A case study of the international hotel industry, *Managerial and Decision Economics,* 2 (4), 197–210.

Edgar, D. and Nisbet, L. (1996). A Matter of Chaos – Some Issues for Hospitality Businesses, *International Journal of Contemporary Hospitality Management,* 8 (2), 6–9.

European Commission (2002). SMEs in Europe, Including a first glance at EU Candidate Countries. Observatory of European SMEs. Number 2.

Fitzsimmons, J. and Fitzsimmons, M. (2004). *Service Management, Operations, Strategy and Information Technology.* New York: McGraw-Hill/Irwin.

Gronroos, C. (2007). *Service Management and Marketing: Customer Management in Service Competition,* New Jersey: John Wiley.

Harrison, J. (2003). *Strategic Management of Resources and Relationships: Concepts and Cases.* New York: John Wiley.

Hoskisson, R., Hitt, M., Wan, W., and Yiu, D. (1999). Theory and Research in Strategic Management: Swings of a Pendulum, *Journal of Management,* 25 (3), 417–456.

Hwang, L. and Lockwood, A. (2006). Understanding the Challenges of Implementing Best Practices in Hospitality and Tourism SMEs, *Benchmarking: An Internatinal Journal,* 13 (3), 337–354.

Kandampully, J. (2007). *Services Management: The New Paradigm in Hospitality,* New Jersey Pearson.

Leibold, M., Probst, G., and Gibbert, M. (2002). *Strategic Management in the Knowledge Economy: New Approaches and Business Applications.* Erlangen: Publicist.

Lowendahl, B.R. (2000). *Strategic Management of Professional Service Firms.* Copenhagen: Copenhagen Business School Press.

McGahan, A. and Porter, M. (1997). How Much Does Industry Matter?, *Strategic Management Journal,* 18 (Special Issue 1), 15–30.

Mintzberg, H., Ahlstrand, B., and Lampel, J. (1998). *Strategy Safari.* London: Prentice-Hall.

Nykiel, R. (2005). *Hospitality Management Strategies.* New Jersey: Pearson Education.

Organization for Economic Co-Operation and Development (OECD). (2007). OECD in Figures 2006-2007, OECD publications. *http://www.oecdobserver.org/news/fullstory.php/aid/1988/OECD_in_Figures_2006-2007.html* (accessed October 1, 2007).

Okumus, F. (2002). Can Hospitality Researchers Contribute to the Strategic Management Literature, *International Journal of Hospitality Management,* 21 (2), 105–110.

Okumus, F. (2003). A Framework to Implement Strategies in Organizations, *Management Decision,* 41 (9), 871–883.

Okumus, F. (2004). Potential Challenges of Employing a Formal Environmental Scanning Approach in Hospitality Organizations,' *International Journal of Hospitality Management,* 23 (2), 123–143.

Okumus, F. and Roper, A. (1999). A Review of Disparate Approaches to Strategy Implementation in Hospitality Firms, *Journal of Hospitality and Tourism Research*, 23 (1), 20–38.

Okumus, F. and Wong, K. (2005). In Pursuit of Contemporary Content for Courses on Strategic Management in Tourism and Hospitality Schools, *International Journal of Hospitality Management*, 24, in press.

Olsen, M. (2001). Hospitality Research and Theories: A Review. In A. Lockwood and S. Medlik (Eds.), *Tourism and Hospitality in the 21st Century*. Oxford: Butterworth and Heinemann.

Olsen, M.D. and DeNoble, A. (1981). Strategic Planning in Dynamic Times, *Cornell Hotel and Restaurant Administration Quarterly*, 21(4), 75–80.

Olsen, M. and Roper, A. (1998). Research in Strategic Management in the Hospitality Industry, *International Journal of Hospitality Management*, 17, Special Issue, 111-124.

Pine, J. and Gilmore, J. (1998). Welcome to the Experience Economy, *Harvard Business Review*, July-August, 97–105.

Porter, M. (1980), *Competitive Strategy*. New York: The Free Press.

Quinn, U., Larmour, R., and McQuillan, N. (1992). The Small Firm in the Hospitality Industry, *International Journal of Contemporary Hospitality Management*, (4) 1, 11–14.

Reichel, A. (1982). Corporate strategic planning for the hospitality industry: a contingency approach. In R.C. Lewis, T.J. Beggs, M. Shaw, and S.A. Croffoot (Eds.), *The Practice of Hospitality Management II*. Westport, CT: AVI Publishing.

Sarathy, R. (1994). Global Strategy in Service Industries, *Long Range Planning*, (27) 6, 115–124.

Schaffer, J.D. (1987). Competitive Strategies in the Lodging Industry, *International Journal of Hospitality Management*, 6 (1), 33–42.

Taylor, S and Edgar, D. (1996). Hospitality Research: The Emperor's New Clothes?, *International Journal of Hospitality Management*, 15 (3), 211–227.

Taylor, S. and Edgar, D. (1999). Lacuna or Lost Cause? Some Reflections on Hospitality Research, in B. Brotherton (Ed.), *The Handbook of Contemporary Hospitality Management Research*, 19–38, Chichester: John Wiley & Sons Ltd.

Tse, E. and Olsen, M. (1998). *Strategic Management*. In B. Brotherton (Ed.), *The Handbook of Contemporary Hospitality Management Research*. Chichester: John Wiley & Sons Ltd., 351–374.

Wanhill, S. (2000). Small and Medium Tourism Enterprises, *Annals of Tourism Research*, 27 (1) 132–147.

Weiler, B. (2001). Tourism Research and Theories: A Review. In A. Lockwood and S. Medlik (Eds.), *Tourism and Hospitality in the 21st Century*. Oxford: Butterworth and Heinemann.

UNWTO. (2003). *Tourism and the World Economy*. Madrid: World Tourism Organization.

UNWTO (2007). *UNWTO World Tourism Barometer*, June 2007, at *http://www.world-tourism.org/facts/eng/pdf/barometer/unwto_barom07_2_en_excerpt.pdf* (accessed October 1, 2007).

Strategy Context

Part 2 establishes the key dimensions of the external and internal contexts in which both the strategy content and the strategy process are embedded. The specific dynamics and nature of the hospitality and tourism industry and organizations are emphasised throughout.

CHAPTER 3

The Hospitality and Tourism Industry Context

Learning objectives

After reading this chapter, you should be able to:

1. Define and explain the role of the external environment in the context of the hospitality and tourism businesses.
2. Explain strategy formulation from a contingency perspective.
3. Classify the environment into specific categories.
4. Define and analyze the firm's task environment.
5. Assess industry-related competitive factors and structures.
6. Discuss challenges in analyzing the general macro and the task environments.

CONTENTS

Opening Case

More information has been released on the case related to the Great Eastern Hotel we saw in Chapter 1. The turbulence in the economic environment has resulted in policy changes such that banks, financial services firms, and automobile firms—which all form an integral part of the hotel's target markets—have cut travel-related expenses for executives. No longer can executives of these firms travel first class on their business visits; they must now use only economy class travel. Moreover, they are now required to cut hotel stay–related expenses, so they have to stay in three- and four-star hotels and not pay more than USD 200 per night. These restrictions have had a major impact on hotels like Great Eastern, which Debbie and her executives must resolve.

The U.S. government is bailing out banks and financial institutions, and since Great Eastern has a major influx of business travelers from U.S. firms, it is important that Debbie and her team consider the impact of government policies on these firms as they seek a solution.

1. Assess the impact of the environment on the Great Eastern Hotel. Make assumptions where necessary.

2. How do customer-related factors affect the hotel as well as its competitors? Make assumptions where necessary.

3. How does the environment affect the hotel's formulation of strategies?

INTRODUCTION

In the previous chapters, we provided an overview of the strategic management and its application to the hospitality and tourism industry. This chapter provides an in-depth perspective of the role of the environment and its impact on hospitality and tourism firms. The internal and external environments are defined and a description of the role of the external environment and its impact on the business is elaborated on from a strategy formulation perspective.

We characterise the environment through a classification scheme and define its categories and their impact on the firm from macro and micro perspectives. Specifically, both the general and task environments and their subcategories are described to differentiate their effects on the firm. Porter (1979; 1980) discussed the forces that emanate in the firm's task environment using the five forces model, which provides a comprehensive view of how these forces impact the firm. This chapter examines the five forces model and its implications from a hospitality and tourism industry perspective. The chapter also provides a description of strategic groups and their relevance to the hospitality sector, which is followed by an overview of the external environment from an international perspective.

CHARACTERISING THE EXTERNAL ENVIRONMENT

Every day, firms deal with both external and internal environments. The external environment lies outside the firm and includes individuals, firms, systems, and institutions that have an impact on it. Influences from the external environment come in the form of changes that occur due to the forces that emanate from it. These forces arise from the trends in the macro and micro environments and could present opportunities or pose threats, depending on how they impact the firm. Organizations that scan the environment, track changes, and assess the impact of changes in terms of cause and effect have a more formalized approach to environment scanning.

Duncan (1972) defines the internal environment as the context (e.g., firm) within which social and physical factors are taken into consideration by individuals for decision making. The interpersonal interactions among the members in the internal environment of the firm are what distinguish it from the external environment. According to Duncan, the internal environment contains three components: human resource, organizational functional, and organizational level. The functional component refers to operations, sales and marketing, human resources, materials management, and administration, while the organizational level refers to products and services, goals and objectives, and the process that integrates personnel with the organization.

Scanning the environment itself is not sufficient; organizations must be able to cope with the forces by ensuring that the internal resources and capabilities are aligned with the opportunities so they can tap them as they appear in the firm's external environment. Likewise, organizations must be able to counter the threats posed by the changes in the environment. This entire process of identifying strengths, weaknesses, opportunities, and threats is referred to as the SWOT analysis.

Strengths and weaknesses lie within the internal environment of the firm. Opportunities and threats are external to the firm and emanate from the macro and micro environments in which it is located. SWOT provides a situation analysis of the firm in terms of its current position in a given market.

Strategic Fit and Strategic Intent

The SWOT analysis provides the firm with an overview of how it is positioned in a given market to tap opportunities and counter threats. This analysis was initially developed by Albert Humphrey from Stanford University from the perspective of providing firms with a framework to assess their resources and capabilities so opportunities could be tapped. The alignment between the firm's internal resources and capabilities and external opportunities is called the "strategic fit." The "fit" ensures that firms can align themselves with emerging opportunities.

This approach was developed from the 1960s through the late 1980s in the strategic management domain. However, there were many who contended that it is of paramount importance that a firm "times" their "fit" properly. In this regard, Hamel and Prahalad (1989; 1994) were the pioneers who brought about the paradigm shift in how strategy formulation and implementation were conceptualized. They purported that it is essential for firms to view such positioning from a strategic perspective so they can sustain competitive advantage in the long term.

The timing is crucial for firms to be able to ensure that as opportunities emerge, they not only have the resources and capabilities but are able to tap them at the right time. Critics of the "fit" approach have suggested that the complexity associated with acquiring the resources and capabilities should also be considered, as it would take time to acquire them. The firm would need to use these "strategic resources and capabilities" to develop products and services to tap the opportunities. Therefore, opportunities that may emerge cannot be tapped immediately unless existing resources and capabilities are sufficient to tap them. In such cases, the competitive advantage that firms are able to create may not be sustainable owing to the less "strategic" nature of the resources and capabilities employed to create the competitive advantage.

"Strategic intent" was put forth by Hamel and Prahalad (1989) based on the premise that firms would not be able to create a sustainable competitive advantage unless strategic resources and capabilities are used to tap opportunities. This approach captured a firm's posture toward its environment in terms of identifying the opportunities and threats and positioning it to address them by acquiring resources and capabilities ahead of time. Therefore, resources should be acquired and capabilities should be developed to tap tomorrow's opportunities and threats. The sustainable competitive advantage created by such an approach drives the firm to look into the future to identify potential opportunities and threats. Here, we use Porter's (1980) definition of *sustainable competitive advantage*, which is "the advantage that firms are able to create in the marketplace by being ahead of competition during the time horizon over which existing resources and capabilities are used to the fullest extent."

The opportunities and threats that emanate in the environment, as described earlier, are a result of the forces that emerge from the macro and micro external environments. The literature identifies the environmental categories as distinct, using a classification scheme. The scheme was developed so it becomes easier to conceptualize and understand a complex subject such as the external environment. The importance of understanding the environment and its impact was emphasized by scholars in the 1950s when the contingency school emerged. The characteristics of the environment are described in more detail in the next section.

Environment Characteristics

Terms used to describe the environment include *environmental uncertainty, environmental volatility*, and *environmental munificence* (Table 3.1). Environmental uncertainty relates to the difficulty of the firm's managers to accurately predict the occurrence of an event. The higher the uncertainty, the more difficulty managers have in assigning probabilistic estimates of the occurrence or nonoccurrence of the event. The literature categorizes environmental uncertainty as contingency views and perceptual views (Gerloff, Muir, and Bodensteiner, 1991).

The contingency view relates to understanding the environment and fitting the firm as per the characteristics of the environment. On the other hand, perceptual views of the environment relate to how the firm's managers are able to "notice, interpret, or learn about" the environment and its characteristics. The firm's external environment is characterized as being stable or volatile, certain or uncertain, liberal or illiberal. Volatility and uncertainty relate to the rate of change of key variables in a given environmental context. An environment in which firms have plenty of opportunities

Table 3.1 Environmental Characteristics

Environmental Characteristics	Description
Environmental Uncertainty	Difficulty in accurately predicting the occurrence of an event
Environmental Volatility	Rate of change related to factors in the external environment
Environmental Munificence	The availability of slack resources and the opportunities for firms to grow
Illiberality	The opposite of munificence; an environment in which the scope for growth is limited
Environmental Dynamism	Degree of change in key factors in the environment categories, especially the general and task environments
Environmental Hostility	The unfavorable conditions in the firm's general environment that have a negative impact on the firm
Market Hostility	Pertains to the unfavorable conditions in the firm's task environment
Environmental Turbulence	Amount of change in the firm's external environments, as well as the complexity (number of factors) in those environmental categories

to grow, including the availability of slack resources, is said to be liberal or munificent. On the contrary, illiberality is associated with an environment where maturity has taken hold, strategic resources are difficult to acquire or obtain, and firms find it difficult to grow.

The firm's environment is also described as hostile, turbulent, and dynamic. Environmental hostility refers to unfavourable conditions in the general or macro environment. For instance, the current economic environment presents a hostile environment for hospitality and tourism firms. On the other hand, market hostility refers to unfavourable conditions at the task and industry environment levels. In the hospitality industry, demand and supply conditions and competitive factors could create a hostile market environment. Environment turbulence refers to the amount of change in the firm's external environment categories, including the level of complexity in those environmental categories. Note that "complexity" refers to the number of factors in the environment. Finally, environmental dynamism is the degree of change in the key factors within the firm's external environmental categories. For instance, the change in mortgage and interest rates in the U.S. context due the economic downturn that began in mid-2008 reflects environmental dynamism. Similarly, within the hospitality and tourism industry environment, the level of dynamism is reflect in the shift in demand during a 365-day period due to a shift from high-peak to low seasons during the course of the year.

Environment Dimensions

Two environmental dimensions emerge from the literature: the simple-complex dimension and the static-dynamic dimension. The simple-complex dimension refers to the number of factors or variables that influence the environment. The fewer the factors, the more stable the environment; contrarily, the greater the number of factors, the more complex the environment. For instance, if a market has many suppliers and many buyer groups, then the business environment in such a market is considered to be relatively complex.

The static-dynamic dimension refers to the degree of change over time related to the factors or variables pertaining to the internal and external environments. The lesser the change, the more static the environment and vice versa. Duncan (1972) refers to two subdimensions of the static-dynamic dimension: the degree of change over time (stability/instability) in the factors that the firms' managers consider during the decision-making process, and the frequency with which the decision makers consider new or different factors.

Environment Types

The environment is classified into various categories so it could be comprehended, analyzed in terms of the forces that emanate from it, and used as part of the firm's decision-making framework. The literature identifies the categories of the environment to consist of the general, the task, and the firm environments. Whereas the general environment is macro in terms of its effect on the firm, the task environment, which is more immediate, is the business environment within which the firm operates. The industry environment, which is an integral part of the task environment, consists of categorizing firms based on the industry structure, and it is derived from the incumbent firms' positioning strategies. The firm environment, as discussed earlier, is its internal environment that consists of personnel and functions. These environmental categories are discussed in more detail in the following sections.

UNDERSTANDING THE MACRO ENVIRONMENT

The firm is located in an environment that influences its customers and stakeholders. The immediate environment that affects the firm is the micro environment in which it operates. Beyond this environment lies the macro environment, which influences the firm from sociocultural, economic, technological, political (including legal), and ecological perspectives. It should be noted that there are no clear demarcations between environment categories, but the boundaries are imaginary for the purpose of conceptualization and comprehension. These categories form the five major subcategories of the macro environments (Figure 3.1). They are discussed in more detail in this section.

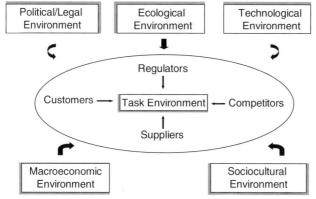

FIGURE 3.1 *Environment Types—General and Task Environments.*

The Political/Legal Environment

The political and regulatory factors have been instrumental in defining how firms can maneuver, succeed, and expand in local and international markets. Transparent legal and political systems, especially in the West, have enabled firms to use franchising as a mode of development in the international context. Firms are impacted by regulations related to human resources management, ecology, technology, copyright- and patent-related issues, and market-related factors and issues, including handling customer-related issues. The regulations related to how tourism businesses are formed and how they need to be operated from human resources and ecological viewpoints are important to consider from local and global perspectives. From the employees relations perspective, due consideration should be given to legal issues related to human resources from different ethnic backgrounds as well as gender-related issues. Changes in rules, regulations, and laws in the business environment that impact the firm must be tracked.

In fact, the political environment is equally important to consider because it influences the policies and decisions that impact all other environmental categories. Policies in terms of terrorism-related issues, including safety, security, ecology, and so forth, are politically driven, so they impact the laws and the regulatory environment of businesses. They must be considered in order to track changes in the environment. For instance, from an ecological perspective, what is considered acceptable in the U.S. context may not be acceptable in the German or Canadian contexts, given the political, legal, and social norms in these geographic domains. In the same vein, what is acceptable in the Chinese context may not be acceptable in the U.S. context. Table 3.2 lists the key variables and issues that are part of the political/legal environment.

Table 3.2   General Environment—Key Variables/Issues to Track and Analyze

General Environment	Variables/Issues to Track and Analyze
■ Political/Legal	■ Regional policies
	■ Change in government
	■ Terrorism
	■ Wars
	■ New regulations impacting businesses, including minimum wage, manufacturing and consumption of indigenous products, and so on
	■ Policies related to protectionism
	■ International trade-related policies
	■ Health-related policies

Table 3.2 General Environment—Key Variables/Issues to Track and Analyze *continued*

General Environment	Variables/Issues to Track and Analyze
	■ Labor law and hiring workforce locally versus from abroad
	■ Policies related to the ecology including global warming, greenhouse gas emissions, and so on
	■ Policies related to corporate and personal taxation
Economic	■ Interest rates
	■ Inflation rate
	■ GDP growth rate
	■ Cost of input factors
	■ Consumer price index
	■ Consumer confidence
	■ Price of oil and commodities
	■ Stock market
	■ Mortgage rates
	■ Balance of trade/exports and imports
	■ Exchange rates and purchasing power parity
	■ Corporate, personal, and capital gains taxes
	■ Availability of credit
	■ Unemployment rate
Sociocultural	■ Demographic changes
	—Birth and death rates
	—Immigration
	—Emigration
	—Age-related changes
	—Gender-related changes
	—Education-related developments
	■ Psychographic changes
	—Life style of the baby-boomer generation
	—Life styles of generations X and Y
	■ Cultural changes
	—Multiculturalism
	■ Other factors
	—Spread of diseases
	—Work–life balance
	—Terrorism
	—Religion
	—Nationalism
Technological	■ New technology-related hardware
	■ New technology-related software
	■ New technology applications
	■ Development of new products

Table 3.2	General Environment—Key Variables/Issues to Track and Analyze *continued*
General Environment	**Variables/Issues to Track and Analyze**
Ecological	■ Investments in technology-related R&D ■ Safety and security related technological developments ■ Demand for "green" products ■ Supply of "green products" ■ Global warming and greenhouse gas emissions ■ Disposal of waste ■ Recycling paper and landfills ■ Deforestation and climatic changes ■ Protecting the natural environment/flora and fauna

The Economic Environment

The economic environment relates to the forces that emanate from the economy, which includes variables such as the GDP growth rate, interest rates, mortgage rates, stock market performance, foreign direct investment, consumer confidence, and inflation rates. These variables depict the state of the economy and the prospects of business in that economy. Firms would need to track changes in the economy so they will be aware of the impact of these changes in terms of cause and effect. The business cycles need to be considered in the analysis in terms of economic cycles as well as industry-related impacts of these cycles. An upturn in the economy would have an impact on businesses in terms of opportunities for enhancing their profitability, which would in turn have an effect on the tourism industry in terms of business and leisure travel. For instance, the greater the business opportunities, the greater the number of managers who would be willing to travel for business to tap those opportunities. In fact, the more the business succeeds, the more their managers would earn bonuses, which in turn would also impact the propensity to consume products and services for leisure.

These factors affect the hospitality and tourism businesses significantly, as seen in the current financial downturn (from Q4 2008 to the present), where many airline, hotel, restaurant, and other hospitality and tourism firms globally are reducing their fares and rates in an attempt to stimulate demand and fill capacity. Key indicators of economic performance have all been affected, and there has been a slide in the inflation rate, interest rates, mortgage rates, the GDP growth rate, and consumer confidence, all of which have affected the stock market. In fact, some of the developed countries are even predicting that the economy would deflate in the immediate future.

The opposite effect was seen in the preceding years (especially from 2007 to mid-2008), when the economy was booming and firms were growing at an unprecedented rate. The fares and rates offered for tourism industry–related products and services had reached very high levels due to the state of the economy. It should be noted that while the GDP was growing in many developing and developed countries, other key economic variables such as mortgage rates, the inflation rate, consumer confidence, interest rates, and oil price were at an all-time high in some of these countries. Since firms, including tourism and hospitality firms, were succeeding in making a profit, they were more revenue driven than cost driven in terms of the impact of these key variables on the costs related to the factors of production.

Therefore, the importance of scanning the economic environment is essential to finding out how the business is being affected from an economic perspective. However, it is essential to get a more comprehensive view of the environment by considering the mutual effects of each environment category on the business. In the following sections, we provide such an analysis and discuss other environmental categories (see Table 3.2).

The Sociocultural Environment

The sociocultural environment pertains to the geographic, demographic, and psychographic description of markets and the emerging trends in them. The geographic locations of markets in particular zip codes, counties, states, regions, and national contexts have an influence on the business. For instance, the sociocultural factors that influence businesses in New England would be considerably different from those in California. There could also be significant differences between regions in the same state, such as Los Angeles, California, and San Francisco, California. These differences are based on demographic and psychographic factors that are influenced by generational differences. Needless to say, sociocultural differences across national contexts—for example, the United States and the United Kingdom, the United States and Turkey, or the United States and China—could be significant. Therefore, in the context of the business, it is essential that the factors related to the sociocultural environment be tracked to comprehend the cause-and-effect relationship.

For instance, a sociocultural shift could occur in terms of demographic and psychographic factors if a restaurant business has been in business for the past 50 years. Regardless of whether it is a blue-chip company like McDonald's or a small family business, a significant shift in demographic and psychographic factors over five decades of the restaurant company's existence is in itself is a major factor that would impact the firm's task environment. Companies like this would need to track down the age, gender, income, occupation, race, and other demographic factors to find out how much of a change has happened. Age group, gender, income, occupation, birth/death rate, and race-related factors could easily shift the product market to such an extent that businesses might find it difficult to operate if this change has not been considered in terms of its impact on the strategic orientation of the firm. These changes are gradual and incremental, something that could easily escape the scrutiny of the manager if a more formal and comprehensive process of screening the environment is not in place. The foregoing is applicable to businesses in the eastern and western provinces of China and the northern and southern regions of India, making it even more important for a firm like McDonald's to formalize the scanning process.

Included in the sociocultural environment–related factors are psychographic factors that are influenced by generational differences like those between the baby boomers and the X and Y generations. The psychographic factors that influence the lifestyle of the groups of consumers who belong to different generations are important to consider when analyzing the sociocultural effects of the environment. Conceptualization and development of products and services in the tourism industry should in fact be based on how these different groups' idiosyncratic needs and wants are unique and how they would impact the business.

Note that the business also must deal with a multicultural society and their impact on the resource and capabilities of the firm. The workforce is diverse, and firms' managers need to not only understand the psychographics of their customers but also the employees' behaviour and orientation. Education is another aspect that firms have to deal with in the knowledge economy. It is becoming more important for hospitality and tourism firms to hire experienced, qualified employees, even if it means recruiting help from other countries.

Other variables that are part of this environment include multiculturalism, the spread of diseases, the work–life balance, terrorism, religion, and nationalism, which all impact a company's task environment (see Table 3.2).

The Technological Environment

Whereas the economic and sociocultural environments have a significant impact on the firm, it is equally important to consider the impact of the technological environment that has had a major influence on businesses over the past two decades. Technology has played a major role in the way products and services are consumed, how they are produced, and even how they are marketed and distributed. Significant changes have taken place in the post–World War II era in terms of the role of technology in science, engineering, and business. In the past two decades, the advent of computer technology has revolutionized how markets and businesses connect with one another and how linkages among business units are established across national contexts. The thrust to globalization of businesses during the past three decades has been propelled by technological advancements in the eighties and nineties, which is continuing at a rapid pace today.

Hospitality and tourism firms have been impacted in a major way that includes demand- and supply-side-related effects. Consumers have accessibility to products using the online medium in a way that has driven businesses to create market interfaces that are purely technology based. Operations have been impacted to the extent that efficiency and productivity have improved. In fact, employees have become multitask oriented, while addressing ecological issues by being more environment friendly in handling day-to-day transactions.

Safety and security issues have been addressed through technology (air and water quality and securing the tourism business from security-related threats), and consumers have been increasingly engaged in co-creating product-service experiences using the technology interface. Technology has helped managers to operate global business units more efficiently, while connecting to international markets with more ease and efficiency. Smart rooms, smart cars, and the "chip" technology have driven firms to redefine the service transaction (see Table 3.2).

The Ecological Environment

The ecological environment has had a major impact on businesses in recent years, with more and more firms becoming socially responsible in how they deal with increasing threats related to the environment. These threats have emanated because of degradation of the environment and depleting natural resources, including global warming. Key variables/issues include demand for and supply of "green" products, global warming and greenhouse gas emissions, disposal of waste, recycling paper and landfills, deforestation and climatic changes, and protecting the natural environment.

Table 3.2 lists the variables and issues that are part of the ecological environment. Tourism businesses have had to redevelop and/or redesign their systems, processes, and procedures to become more pro-environment in their orientation. Consumers in turn have become more eco-friendly in their lifestyle and orientation toward tourism products. Eco-certifications have become the norm to identify best practices in the tourism industry. Technology has influenced firms in how they can become more eco-friendly in an efficient and timely manner. The technological developments have been a major force in improving the standards set for firms to become ecologically driven.

THE TASK ENVIRONMENT AND INFLUENCE OF INDUSTRY STRUCTURE

Firms are influenced by the more immediate business or task environment, which, according to Dill (1958), consists of customers, competitors, suppliers, and regulators. These four components of the task environment influence the firms in the industries. Here, *industry* is defined as consisting of firms that offer similar products and services that could be considered close substitutes.

Customers or buyers form an important component of the task environment, comprising different groups with different needs, wants, and buying power. Customer groups with similar needs are defined as part of a segment, and their buying behavior influences firms to position their products and services accordingly. Based on this, from a tourism business perspective, business and leisure travelers could be considered major customer groups, in which subsegments could be defined. Note that these customer groups could be categorized based on propensity to consume various products and services (e.g., luxury versus economy hotel products and services), propensity to consume standardized versus customized products and services (e.g., major hotel chains versus boutique hotels), and propensity to consume products and services based on location (e.g., airport hotels versus city hotels), or it could be a combination of all three (e.g., a midpriced downtown business hotel versus a luxury beach resort hotel).

Competitors form an important element of the task environment. The positioning strategy of the firm defines with whom it competes within the market segments. In the tourism industry, examples of competitor hotel firms in a given market segment include Ritz Carlton and Four Seasons, Marriott and Hilton, Radisson and Ramada, and so forth. The competitive dynamics in a given industry depend on the industry and the product life cycles.

Suppliers form an important component of the business or task environment by supplying raw materials and finished products and goods to the firm. Quality-related issues come to the fore when suppliers are not able to deliver goods and finished products to the firm as agreed. The efficacy with which firms connect with suppliers is of paramount importance if they are to respond to customers' needs and wants. In fact, firms should request frequent feedback from suppliers on how prospective goods and raw materials can be made available so future opportunities can be tapped. This is essential for firms to be able to sustain a competitive advantage in the long term.

Regulators are an extension of the legal environment that set policies, rules, and regulations so firms in a given economy or in industries are engaged in healthy competition. Regulators set the tone for competing firms in markets through policies that ensure that there are no copyright or patent infringements, that antitrust-related issues are not a problem, that price fixing or other such issues do not give unfair advantage to firms, and that there are no infringements related to codes and other regulations. Regulators are constantly screening firms and practices in industries to ensure that norms are adhered to by all firms to level the playing field—in other words, no firm or group of firms has an unfair advantage when it comes to antitrust law–related issues.

The Five Forces Model

Based on the competitive forces that emanate within the industry environment, Porter (1979; 1980) developed the five forces model (Table 3.3), which can be summarized as follows:

1. Potential competitors

2. Competitiveness among industry incumbents

3. Buyer's influence

4. Supplier's influence

5. Substitute products

These forces are assessed from the perspective that the stronger these forces, the fiercer the competition in a given industry and the more difficult it is for firms to earn a profit. The impact of each force is examined following.

Potential Competitors

An industry that has the potential for new competitor firms to enter and establish themselves in a relatively short period of time is said to have low barriers to entry with a high exposure to risk of potential competitors. Firms in such markets are exposed to risk in terms of eroding profitability.

Table 3.3	Porter's Five Forces Model Characteristics

Task Environmental Forces	Characteristics
Potential Competitors	■ This threat is high when industry barrier to entry is low. ■ Established firms hold their position and discourage firms from entering their market through price and margin reductions. ■ This threat is low when firms have established best practices in marketing, management, production, and administration. ■ High brand loyalty enables firms to mitigate this risk.
Competitiveness among Industry Incumbents	■ This threat is high when the industry growth rate has slowed down. ■ It is low if the environment is liberal, seen especially in growing markets. ■ Firms avoid direct competition in mature markets.
Buyers' Influence	■ Is a threat when buyers' buying power and influence on the firm are high. ■ Buyers' influence comes in the form of price discounts, demand for better quality and level of service, especially after-sales service. ■ Buyers could switch to other products and services quite easily when switching costs are low.
Suppliers' Influence	■ The threat from suppliers is high when they can charge higher prices for raw materials and finished goods. ■ Threat arises when few suppliers can provide customized goods with access to unique raw materials, technology, and other relevant resources. ■ Threat is high when suppliers can control the quality and price of raw materials. ■ When the supplier has higher influence, incumbent firms have no choice but to accept or switch suppliers, which is difficult when only a few suppliers exist.
Substitute Products	■ Fads, trends, and consumer buying behaviour influence markets to pursue alternative products. ■ Substitute products are considered when markets are exposed to threats—for example, health-related and so forth.

Source: Summarized from Porter (1980).

Typically, firms that are established in a given market try to hold their position and discourage firms from entering their market by being able to reduce prices and decrease margins so new firms will have difficulty sustaining their profitability in the short term. But if this doesn't discourage firms from entering the market, it only indicates that the firms in such markets are exposed to higher risk. Needless to say, raising prices in such markets is not an option. The opposite scenario leads firms in a given market to raise prices and increase their level of profits.

Incumbents can also benefit from cost advantages due to the adoption of best practices in production, delivery, and management practices, which leads to a lower level of threat of entry from potential competitors. In fact, firms that have larger production capacity based on the product markets they serve usually benefit from economies of scale. The threat of entry is further reduced if the incumbents have created brand loyalty over a sustained period of time. When markets are loyal to firms, it makes it even more difficult for potential competitors to enter the market.

For instance, hotel firms in the luxury market segment have high barriers to entry owing to higher start-up costs. Therefore, firms in this market segment can sustain their profitability through higher rates during high-peak seasons and, to some extent, shoulder seasons. Coupled with this is the brand loyalty effect, which prevents new entrants from moving in with any level of optimism. But this is not true for the economy segment where the barriers to entry are relatively low due to lower start-up costs and the brand loyalty effect. Moreover, the cyclical nature of the business also creates a barrier to entry. Firms need to establish loyalty during high seasons to sustain their business through low seasons. Above all, market segments in which large chain hotels have been able to sustain their brand effects over a period of time, thereby creating loyalty, would have lower threats of new entrants.

Competitiveness among Industry Incumbents

Rivalry among industry incumbents is fierce in a market that has many players that are all dealing with slowing growth rates. This is a result of demand-related factors that lead firms to compete to capture a higher market share. On the other hand, if the environment is liberal in that few firms are competing for a market share and the demand is high or good enough for the major players to sustain their business model, the level of rivalry will shrink, and firms will forbear in order to increase profitability. It should be noted that the industry structure and life cycle have a direct impact on the level of rivalry among firms in markets. In markets where maturity has set in owing to some level of consolidation that has resulted due to slowing market growth rate, firms will avoid competing directly with one another, as such an approach will erode the level of profitability they could sustain otherwise. Since major players emerge in markets that are consolidating, the need to compete directly with other players decreases as firms establish themselves in such markets in terms of brand loyalty and best practices. Fierce competition is evident in markets when firms engage in price wars and marketing campaigns that include "ad wars."

Contrarily, in growing markets, firms use vehicles of growth to enter and move quickly to establish market share. Franchising and management contracts are some market entry vehicles that firms use in the hotel and restaurant business markets globally to enter quickly and spread their brand in a relatively shorter period of time as opposed to the own-and-operate model. Hilton and Holiday Inn were pioneers in using management contract and franchising agreements, respectively, to grow aggressively during the post–World War II era.

Note that the industry structure prevailing in markets is also influenced by the life cycle. In a growing market, as firms enter and try to occupy space, a fragmented structure results. During consolidation, bigger firms take over smaller firms, and a more oligopolistic structure emanates, which sets in as the market matures. The upscale hotel market segment in the United States is a good example of a mature market where major chain operators have established themselves. On the contrary, at the present time, the China upscale market is a growing market where domestic and international players are trying to establish brand identity and loyalty while using vehicles of growth.

Buyers' Influence

This is considered a threat when consumers can put pressure on firms in terms of buying power and influence on the firm's well-being. Buyers' influence comes in the form of price discounts and demands for better quality and levels of service, especially after-sales service. Buyers can also influence the firm when they might choose to switch to other products and services, especially if switching means lower costs. This is often seen in the hotel and restaurant product markets, especially in the midpriced to the lower end of the market. When buyer groups form a significant portion of the market, their influence on firms could be high, thereby increasing their power. The opposite is true when firms are able to influence markets when buyer groups are small. Firms can influence buyer groups by charging higher prices and even providing minimum services at moderate-quality levels.

Suppliers' Influence

Suppliers have more influence on firms when they can charge higher prices for raw materials and finished goods. This happens when the few suppliers can provide customized goods with access to raw materials, technology, and other relevant resources that are unique and have potential for value generation. When suppliers are able to control the quality and price of raw materials based on their power, incumbent firms have no choice but to accept or switch suppliers. But in a market where suppliers have the power, finding a supplier who is able to meet the needs of the firm may be difficult. In the hospitality and tourism business context, suppliers' influence is seen in the case of raw materials supplied to restaurant businesses, especially in emerging markets where quality could be an issue. Many upscale restaurants face challenges when they cannot meet the standards because of the inferior quality of raw materials. The few suppliers who are able to meet the standards have higher power in such a situation.

Substitute Products

This threat pertains to industries and markets where alternative products could replace existing products based on fluctuating demand related to fads, trends, and market buying behaviour. Substitute products are considered when markets are exposed to threats. For example, sales of chicken were up when mad cow disease was at its height. Similarly, chicken products were consumed less when bird flu emerged during the winter months of 2006–2007 in regions where there was more exposure to the disease. The price of products can go up significantly due to increased demand, as seen in the case of chicken and pork products when mad cow disease was rampant.

THE DYNAMICS OF COMPETITION AND STRATEGIC GROUPS

Competing firms engage in rivalrous actions in markets where customers have higher bargaining power. As firms compete among themselves for market share, they develop similarities and differences in terms of strategic posture and market orientation. Essentially, these firms that are similar in terms of strategy could be grouped based on certain firm characteristics. Hatten and Schendel (1977) observed this in the brewing industry and the same phenomenon has been documented in other industries including the restaurant and hotel industries.

Firms that are part of a given strategic group are almost the same in terms of products and services, competing directly against each other. These firms' products and services are close substitutes for one another, often part of the options that customers choose among during transactions. Since the competition among firms in a given group is direct, firms often fight for a position in these groups, including access to resources and supplier/buyer contacts. It should be noted that the similarities among firms in a given strategic group leads to differences across groups as the firms in each group have different traits and behaviours. Firms need to consider their position in groups based on which companies they want to compete against based on their strategic orientation in those markets.

For instance, in the hospitality industry, hotels like Marriott and Hilton offer similar products in global markets based on their positioning strategy. These hotels that are part of a strategic group have similar firm character-istics, including target markets, product-service bundles, core competencies, and the type of contractual arrangements used as vehicles of growth in global markets. In fact, Hyatt Hotels (e.g., Hyatt Regency) also belong to this group in terms of characteristic traits. Another example of strategic groups is fast-food restaurant firms like McDonald's and Burger King that offer similar products and services in global markets. They have similar positioning strategies, products and services, and competencies required to succeed in their product markets.

Based on characteristics of firms in terms of the markets they serve and the products and services they offer, a clearer segmentation of the product-market comes about. In these segments, strategic groups emerge based on the positioning strategies of firms. For instance, in the hotel industry, the market segments include luxury, upscale, midmarket, economy, and budget hotel market segments. In these segments, hotels offer distinct products and services for unique markets, which gives rise to strategic groups as firms vie for positions in a competitive setting.

ENVIRONMENTAL SCANNING AND THE HOSPITALITY/ TOURISM FIRM

Firms' managers constantly scan the environment to keep abreast of devel-opments in the external environment. The process of constantly keeping track of changes in the firm's external environment to assess the trends that create opportunities or pose threats to the firm is called environmental scanning. As discussed earlier, the trends in the general environment impact a firm's task environment. Owing to this, firms' managers should track down the macro environment trends and their impact on the task environ-ment. The effect of these forces on the firm needs to be further tracked to determine how they impact the business.

From a historic perspective, environment scanning was considered the responsibility of top management. The literature (e.g., Jogaratnam and Law, 2006) refers to such managers as boundary spanners, who constantly seek, assimilate, and disseminate information so the firm can process and use it in its key decision-making frameworks. Whereas such an approach would work in a stable environment, given that firms are internationally exposed in a global market, leading to an uncertain and dynamic firm environment, the need for managers at all levels of the firm's hierarchy to scan for relevant information is extremely important. Moreover, the type of information required by managers at different levels varies, giving rise to the notion that environment scanning is required at all levels of the firm's hierarchy, including frontline employees. Owing to this, managers and employees at various levels of the firm's hierarchy are required to be information seekers or boundary spanners so they can immediately spot and assess trends and guide their units in the value-creation process. This notion is supported by hospitality researchers as well (Okumus, 2004).

Many firms are aware of the importance of scanning, but they do not formalize activities related to scanning. Scanning largely remains an informal activity, which is seen in the case of hospitality and tourism firms (Costa and Teare, 2000; Jogaratnam and Law, 2006). Based on the need to seek information, managers may use one of the two approaches: the outside-in approach or the inside-out approach, as defined by Fahey and Narayanan (1986) and supported by Jogaratnam and Law (2006). The former approach is about scanning the environment to seek information about the various trends from a macro perspective. The latter is more about scanning the environment to seek specific information about the trends to address a specific need or situation that has been internally defined. Methods used to scan include individualistic and collectivistic approaches (Mintzberg et al., 1998). The individualistic approach involves managers who need information to make decisions as the case may be, whereas the collective approach involves all managers at various levels of the organization's hierarchy.

It must be noted that the frequency with which scanning is carried out depends on the level of the job and the nature of the task at hand. Also, in a job that includes scanning as an integral part of the activities (e.g., sales and marketing manager), the frequency would be much higher compared with a job that is operational and task oriented (e.g., front desk manager). Needless to state, information technology has made the scanning task easier in terms of the level of scanning and the frequency with which it is carried out. In fact, Jogaratnam and Law (1996) state that all managers included in the sample at the strategic, tactical, and operational levels "indicated that they utilized computer systems to aid the process of scanning the business environment" (p. 183).

The scanning process includes tracking down trends that have both positive and negative impacts on the firm. Yet, managers might be influenced by the type of information during the scanning process. Based on their personal preferences and biases, some managers may be inclined to consider more positive pieces of information than negative ones, leading to strategic myopia. Managers who encourage this lead their firm into a situation where they find themselves caught in a web due to the impact of the threats emanating from the firm's task and general environments. Therefore, perceptions of managers play a defining role during the scanning process. To ensure that the scanning process is devoid of personal preferences and biases, managers should include both objective and subjective information on the environment as part of objective and subjective impact analyses.

The availability of information might be an issue that managers may have to deal with. In such cases, it is essential that proxies are used that are close substitutes for the information they are intended to replace. In many cases, managers rely on data and information from consulting firms to substitute information that may not be accessible or available. It is imperative that the information available through any source be scrutinized before it is used in the impact analysis. The greater the sources of data, the more comprehensive the analysis. In fact, the more sources of a given type of data, the more verifiable it is and, therefore, the more the accuracy with which the analysis is carried out.

THE EXTERNAL ENVIRONMENT IN THE INTERNATIONAL PERSPECTIVE

The environment in international markets has become more liberal with the emergence of the global market economy. This liberalization is particularly seen in emerging economies as they have deregulated banking, telecommunication, and other sectors, while opening up their economy to firms from developed countries to set up operations in their markets. The flow of capital from Western to Eastern markets and the flow of raw materials and goods in the opposite direction have led to interdependence among economies. Both this and the technological developments have created the knowledge economy, with firms being driven toward knowledge management practices so the focus is on the development of core competencies using a resource-based perspective.

The transnational economy, along with the demand for specialized labor, has led to the flow of labor from developing economies to developed economies. The relocation of firms from domestic to international markets has led to the flow of managerial expertise in the opposite direction. All of this has led to the creation of interdependencies among economies, leading to an era in which global firms and global markets are the order of the day. State-of-the-art technology has also helped firms to create intra- and interfirm networks that have made information flow across national boundaries more effective. Globalization has increased the risk exposure of the firm, as resources are stretched to capture growth. The negative aspects of globalization and the exposure to risk have been in display during the current financial meltdown, which has led firms to seek assistance from governments to survive the unprecedented crisis.

The global hospitality and tourism industry includes firms that have operations in various national contexts. These firms range from hotels, restaurants, and airlines to casinos, cruises, and travel-related businesses. Given the cyclical nature of the business in the international context, firms are able to effectively balance the upturns and downturns by pursuing an international strategy. For instance, Marriott International can manage business cycles related to leisure travel by operating hotels in the Northern and Southern Hemispheres. When leisure travel is down in the winter months in Europe, the firm could balance this downturn by benefiting from the summer months in Australia. But with internationalization comes an increased risk of exposure, which could be effectively managed by using various modes of development (franchising, management contracts, and ownership).

SUMMARY

This chapter provided conceptualizations of the external environment and described its characteristics, dimensions, and types. Understanding the external environment is essential so firms' managers can formulate strategies while taking into consideration the various forces that emanate from its categories. The general and task environments impact the firms in it, and comprehending the origin of these forces in the general environment and corresponding impacts on the task environment is essential. Porter's five forces model provides a clearer understanding of the business environment and its immediate impact on the firm. Likewise, understanding the industry structure, strategic groups, and market segments in the industry is essential to being able to comprehend the strategy formulation and implementation process.

STUDY QUESTIONS

1. Why do we need to analyze the external environment?

2. How can we classify the external environment?

3. What is the task environment, and how does it influence the firm?

4. How can Porter's five forces model be used to analyze the task environment?

5. What are the potential challenges in analyzing the external environment?

6. Who should analyze the external environment and how often?

7. What is strategic myopia, and how it can be overcome?

REFERENCES AND FURTHER READINGS

Bourgeois, L.J. (1980). Strategy and environment: A conceptual integration. *Academy of Management Review*, 5, 25–39.

Brotherton, B. and Shaw, J. (1996). Towards an identification and classification of critical success factors in UK Hotels Plc. *International Journal of Hospitality Management*, 15(2), 113–135.

Child, J. (1972). Organization structure, environment and performance: The role of strategic choice. *Sociology*, 6, 1–22.

Costa, J. and Teare, R. (2000). Developing an environmental scanning process in the hotel sector. *International Journal of Contemporary Hospitality Management*, 12 (3), 156–169.

Dess, G.D. and Beard, D.W. (1984). Dimensions of organizational task environments. *Administrative Science Quarterly*, 29, 52–73.

Dill, W.R. (1958). Environment as an influence on managerial autonomy. *Administrative Science Quarterly*, 2, 409–443.

Duncan, R.B. (1972). Characteristics of Organizational Environments and Perceived Environmental Uncertainty, *Administrative Science Quarterly*, 17(3), 313–327.

Gerloff, E.A., Muir, N.K., and Bodensteiner, W.D. (1991). Three components of perceived environmental uncertainty: an exploratory analysis of the effects of aggregation. *Journal of Management*, 17 (4), 749–768.

Emery, F.E. and Trist, E.L. (1965). The causal texture of organizational environments, *Human Relations*, 18, 21–32.

Fahey, L. and Narayanan, V. (1986). *Macro Environmental Analysis for Strategic Management*. St. Paul, MN: West Publishing.

Hamel, G. and Prahalad, C.K (1989). Strategic intent. *Harvard Business Review*, 63–74.

Hamel, G. and Prahalad, C.K. (1994). Competing for the Future, Boston, Mass.: Harvard Business School Press.

Harrington, R. (2001). Environmental uncertainty within the hospitality industry: Exploring the measure of dynamism and complexity between restaurant segments. *Journal of Hospitality and Tourism Research*, 25(4), 386–398.

Hatten, K.J. and Schendel, D.E. (1977). Heterogeneity within an industry: firm conduct in the U.S. Brewing industry 1952–71. *Journal of Industrial Economics*, 26 (2), 97–113.

Jogaratnam, G. and Law, R. (2006). Environmental scanning and information source utilization: Exploring the behavior of Hong Kong hotel and tourism executives. *Journal of Hospitality and Tourism Research*, 30(2), 170–190.

Jurkovich, R. (1974), A core typology of organizational environmen*⌐ Administrative Science Quarterly*, 29, 380–394.

Lawrence, P.R. and Lorsch, J. (1967). *Organization and Environment*. Cambridge, MA: Harvard University Press.

Litteljohn, D. (1999). Industry structure and strategic groups. In Brotherton, B. (Ed.), *The Handbook of Contemporary Hospitality Management Research.* John Wiley & Sons Ltd.

Mintzberg, Henry, Ahlstrand, B. W., and Lampel, J. (1998). Strategy safari: A guided tour through the wilds of strategic management, New York: The Free Press.

Okumus, F. (2004). Potential challenges of employing a formal environmental scanning approach in hospitality organizations. *International Journal of Hospitality Management*, 23, 123–143.

Olsen, M.D. (1980). The importance of the environment to the food service lodging manager. *The Journal of Hospitality Education*, 4(2), 35–45.

Olsen, M.D. (1991). Environmental scan: Global hospitality industry trends. *World Travel and Tourism Review*, 120–124

Olsen, M.D. and Cassee, E. (1995). The international hotel industry in the new millennium: Visioning the future IHRA White Paper, 52–70.

Olsen M.D. and Zhao, J. (1995). Accommodation: New management practice in the international hotel industry. *Travel and Tourism Intelligence*, 52–70.

Porter, M.E. (1979). How competitive forces shape strategy. *Harvard Business Review*, March/April 1979.

Porter, M.E. (1980). *Competitive Strategy*. New York: The Free Press.

Porter, M.E. (1985). *Competitive Advantage: Creating and Sustaining Superior Performance*. New York: The Free Press.

Thompson, J.D. (1967). *Organizations in Action*. New York: McGraw-Hill.

Venkatraman, N. (1989). The concept of fit in strategy research: Toward verbal and statistical correspondence. *Academy of Management Review*, 14, 423–444.

West, J.W. and Olsen, M.D. (1988). Environmental scanning and its effect upon firm performance: An exploratory study on the foodservice industry. *Hospitality Education and Research Journal*, 127–135.

CHAPTER 4

The Organisational Context

Learning Objectives

After reading this chapter you should be able to:

- Identify different elements of an H&T organisation's internal environment.
- Discuss the complexity of H&T organisations' internal environment.
- Analyze an H&T organisation's internal environment.
- Evaluate the influence of organisational variables/factors on strategy formulation and implementation, and provide recommendations to overcome potential challenges in this process.

CONTENTS

Opening Case

The case study organisation that is known as a U.S.-based company has set the goal of becoming a key force in main European markets, including the United Kingdom, Germany, Spain, and Italy. This was to be achieved through organic growth—by opening new hotels. This case study describes how the case study organisation plans to achieve its goal in Europe.

Country managers, who are usually local nationals or people who have lived in the area for a long time, are given the responsibility of establishing a network of contacts and identifying project opportunities in different country markets. These country managers are based in country markets in different countries. Since they know the sociocultural and business environments of the country in which they work, these country managers are kept responsible for the international expansion process. They have the role of evaluating international projects that have been developed in their regions. Interestingly, however, people get involved in the country manager's area of responsibility and assess the potential merits of projects for the whole company. For example, senior members from the marketing discipline ensure that the project serves the long-term benefits of a specific brand in a particular market. Operations people assess the profitability of the project. Business support managers ensure that the risks associated with the project are reasonable and that the project will contribute to the shareholder value. The physical condition of the hotel properties and the safety issues are controlled by the technical services. The legal experts ensure that the legal framework of the partnership is properly set.

In the case study organisation, the expansion process at first may seem logical and rational: Decision makers follow a specific route and make their decisions based on the organisation's strategy, procedures, and standards. The decision-making process is guided by strict stages and guidelines. This structured approach to decision making, however, is only one facet of the activity. Decisions are not simply the outcome of an ordered and rational process but are more dynamic. Besides company strategy and standards, different decision makers with diverse views and interpretations contribute to decision making and influence the final decision.

International expansion is a multidiscipline process. Therefore, the case study company takes advantage of the knowledge of different experts of organisational members. This suggests that there is a considerable amount of empowerment to the experts, who could bring their subject knowledge and experience to the decision-making process. This, however, does not mean that the case study organisation relies entirely on a decentralised structure for decision making. There is a certain element of "centralisation" of decision making. For instance, hotel project ideas that emerge from different countries have to be "filtered" through "rational" processes. This process consists of the assessment of projects against certain standards and decision-making criteria. Moreover, although the projects are continuously evaluated by the experts as they go through the process, they still must be approved by a committee. Additionally, the same details of the hotel projects are discussed and assessed many times by different disciplines.

Decision making is so centralised that the country managers' decisions can always be overridden by senior decision makers. This suggests that they have only limited power. In addition, country managers have to work within the financial parameters that have been set for them, as well as the framework of guidelines that outlines the case study organisation's priorities for market expansion. Moreover, country managers are expected to use both formal and informal channels to update the senior decision makers with their ongoing activities. Based on these interactions and discussions, they are advised as to whether they should pursue a project idea.

Such a control-oriented approach to decision making has a number of implications for international expansion. It both hinders the case study organisation's ability to take advantage of international expansion opportunities and it demotivates the country managers. In particular, the increase in bureaucracy slows down the decisions made with regards to different opportunities and makes the country managers feel that their views and knowledge are not acknowledged and appreciated by the senior decision makers.

Development and implementation of the strategy is highly dependent on placing country managers in different countries where expansion opportunities emerge. However, both senior decision makers and country managers need to better understand each other in order to be able to make healthy decisions about different country markets. Country managers should be fully aware of the key priorities of their organisation, and senior decision makers need to understand that the way business is conducted is different in each market. Top management might need to delegate more responsibility to country managers in order to facilitate organisational learning about different country markets and thus help to improve the company's international expansion performance.

Case Study Questions

1. How would you describe the management structure of the case study organisation? Please provide evidence to illustrate your answer.
2. Please identify different control tactics used by the case study organisation to ensure that the strategy is properly implemented.
3. What is the importance of country managers in implementing strategy in different country markets?
4. What are the implications of a tight, centralised management structure?

INTRODUCTION

In the preceding chapter we explained and discussed how to analyze the external environment of H&T organisations. This chapter will help you to evaluate the influence of an organisation's internal environment on strategy formation and implementation. In particular, the importance of organisational structure, organisation culture, and leadership as key considerations is discussed in the context of the international H&T industry. The chapter also explains how different factors in an organisation's external environment influence the internal environment and the functioning of an organisation.

IDENTIFYING DIFFERENT STAKEHOLDERS

One of the main concerns of today's H&T organisations is how to manage the interests of different stakeholder groups in its environment. If managers are to act strategically and plan their actions, they must have some ideas about how key players both in the external environment and in their organisations will act and respond to changes and challenges. Therefore, identifying and analyzing stakeholders' needs, expectations, and predicted responses become important.

A stakeholder is any group or individual who can affect or is affected by the achievement of a firm's objectives (Freeman, 1984). To meeting the needs of these groups, you need to answer three general questions about stakeholders:

- Who are they? (This question concerns their attributes.)
- What do they want? (This question concerns their ends.)
- How are they going to try to get it? (This question concerns their means.)

Many of the answers to the question "Who are they?" are long lists of different types of stakeholders. These include customers, shareholders, employees, suppliers, bankers, and community and pressure groups, including environmental groups or employee unions. These key actors affect the strategic direction of any hospitality and tourism organisation, and they may control critical resources with varying interests and may attract the attention of senior executives.

In response to "What do they want?," we can generate numerous lists of their interests. Each of the preceding groups may have different expectations. For example, the ultimate interest of shareholders is economic welfare. The sustainable growth of any organisation will depend on creating value for its owners. If no value is generated to owners, then the organisation will not be able to survive. It is, however, worth noting that an organisation's ability to offer a return on the shareholders-owners' investment depends on their ability to meet the expectations of other stakeholder groups. Value would not be delivered unless customer expectations are met and employees were kept motivated and productive with the appropriate salary ranges and a pleasant working environment. In addition, the required service/product output would not be delivered if a good working relationship is not developed with the suppliers and bankers. Otherwise, we would not fulfill our responsibilities to the community groups and the other stakeholders with an ethical and socially responsible manner.

Finally, answers to the question "How are they going to try to get it?" require careful analysis of different stakeholder groups' influence on the organisation and their means to achieve their needs and expectations. Shareholders monitor the activities of the organisation, exert power and influence on top executives, and/or withhold the flow of the firm's resources. Customers, community, and pressure groups could boycott the products and services in order to force the organisation toward a certain direction. Employees could go on strike or lobby in order to influence the managers.

Stakeholder interests are the foundation of corporate strategy itself, representing "what we are" and "what we stand for" as a company. Organisations therefore need to establish certain fundamental principles that guide how it does business—particularly with respect to how it treats stakeholders—and use those principles to drive decision making. Although different stakeholders exist in H&T organisations, shareholders interests come first. Hospitality and tourism organisations should respond to the interests of shareholders because they are the most closely watched and monitored by these important stakeholders. It is the shareholders who control resources that can facilitate or enhance the implementation of corporate decisions.

It is therefore critical that organisations understand and always keep in mind the shareholders' influence. Agency theory suggests that senior executives and managers in organisations may make decisions and allocate resources to strengthen their positions and gain personal benefits. These decisions, initiatives, and resource allocations may not always be rational and beneficial for organisations. Alternatively, these executives may not support new projects and initiatives that may be essential and beneficial for the company, but they may create threats to the executives' positions. Following the agency theory, one other important group of stakeholders in H&T organisations is executives and managers. When analyzing the internal environment of an H&T organisation—as well as its decisions, investments, and future projects——it would be helpful to look at strategic issues from the perspective of senior executives and managers.

EXERCISE

Please identify the stakeholders of an H&T company, discuss what each stakeholder may expect from this company, and explain how they can try to achieve their expectations. You may compare and contrast different stakeholders' influences on this company's direction in terms of their power and interest.

ORGANISATIONAL FUNCTIONS

Organisational functions influence an organisation's ability to respond to the changes in the dynamic external environment. They can be divided into four main areas:

1. The *operations function* deals with the day-to-day operations of the system in order to ensure that the organisation has the appropriate

systems and procedures in place and delivers consistent quality of service and products.

2. The *marketing function* deals with the management of demand by developing and implementing appropriate pricing policies and running marketing campaigns and programmes through various channels, including television, magazines, and the Internet.

3. The *human resources* function carries out a careful analysis of how human assets of an organisation add value to the organisation and contribute to sustainable competitive advantage. The human resources function responds to the employee selection and recruitment issues and addresses the needs and wants of employees by monitoring pay and reward systems, training, and empowerment policies.

4. The *finance function* is concerned about identifying the main sources of funding and financing the operations of an organisation in a cost-effective way. This function carries out a systematic analysis of how different financial resources add value and contribute to competitive advantage.

When carrying out an internal analysis of an H&T organisation, it should be essential to analyze each functional area to identify strengths and weaknesses coming from these functional areas. In some cases, strengths and weaknesses may result in a combination of factors emerging from different functional areas rather than one functional area.

Resources, Core Competencies, and Distinctive Competencies

Hospitality and tourism organisations should first identify their tangible and intangible resources. Tangible assets of an organisation can be seen in the form of a plant, equipment, and/or land. The building itself is a good example of a tangible asset for a hotel company. Intangible assets are associated with the company knowhow and skill sets. They have no physical presence but represent real benefit to the organisation. They include company reputation and brand, product reputation and brand, employee/leadership skills/experience and knowhow, culture, networks, databases, supplier knowhow, distributor knowhow, public knowledge, contracts, intellectual property rights, and trade secrets.

Core capabilities and distinctive competencies are built on tangible (what the company has) and intangible (what the company can do) assets. Core capabilities refer to those areas that an H&T company does exceedingly well, whereas distinctive competencies refer to those areas and activities that an H&T company excels at and is better than its competitors (Wheelen and

Hunger, 2006). Core capabilities are the most critical and most distinctive assets an organisation possesses, and they are the most difficult to copy when effectively linked with appropriate strategic targets in a value chain that begins and ends with the company's key stakeholders (Brownell, 2008). H&T organisations should amalgamate their core competencies, including their special knowledge, skills, and technological knowhow, that distinguish them from others with business processes that they use to deliver information in the form of products, services, and other results. In essence, the kind and degree of coordinated and leveraged skills and assets of an organisation can lead to developing core capabilities and, eventually, distinctive competencies.

As the speed of comparable tangible asset acquisition accelerates and the pace of imitation quickens, H&T organisations need to protect, exploit, and enhance their unique intangible assets. While competitive advantage is obtained by appealing to customers in targeted markets, sustainable competitive advantage is the result of developing and combining several distinctive competencies, which are eventually difficult to imitate and substitute by competitors.

To better explain this issue, we need to refer to the research-based view (RBV) in the strategic management field. The RBV suggests that competitive advantage comes from a firm's unique tangible and intangible resources (Barney, 1991). In order for a resource to be a competitive advantage, it must be *valuable*, *rare*, *inimitable*, and *nonsubstitutable*, and the firm should be organized in a way that it can effectively and efficiently exploit the resource (Barney and Wright, 1998).

If a resource is to be considered valuable, it should contribute to the company's performance in the areas of finance, HRM, marketing, operations, and innovation. For example, a hotel company may own a piece of land that may have some financial value, but if it does not contribute to the company's bottom line, it may not be considered as a strategic resource. In terms of a resource being rare, only one company or a few companies should have it. The unique shows and attractions of the World Disney can be considered rare resources, since only very few companies have them.

To protect your valuable assets from being imitated, H&T companies need to do well in different areas and connect all their resources and competencies with one another. This will create barriers for competitors to imitate not only all of the key resources but also to create connections among them. For example, Pfeffer (1994; 1995) noted that Southwest Airlines' competitive advantage greatly comes from several closely related areas: very well-trained, productive, and dedicated workforce and managers; a positive and caring organisational culture; a relatively flat organisational structure; and a strong service delivery culture. Over the years, Southwest Airlines has managed to use fewer employees per aircraft, fly more passengers per employee, and supply more available seat miles per employee. The company has won the Triple Crown award for fewest lost bags and fewest passenger complaints (Barney and Wright, 1998; Pfeffer, 1994). In other words, a combination of great organisational culture, well-trained and dedicated employees, a healthy organisational structure, and a high level of customer service has created a sustainable competitive advantage for Southwest Airlines that is considered rare, difficult to imitate, and unique.

Many of the competencies in this company have evolved over many years and are shaped by the organisation's unique culture, history, and founders, and therefore their competitors have not been able to easily duplicate the history and culture in which those practices are embedded (Harrell-Cook, 2002). For example, Continental Airlines, United Airlines, and Delta all have attempted to compete with Southwest Airlines by providing low-cost service to a number of destinations. However, they have not been able to deliver superior performance. Herb Kelleher, the cofounder of Southwest Airlines, stated that even if their competitors achieve the same level of cost structure and quality service, they cannot create the spirit of Southwest employees' attitude toward service (Barney and Wright, 1998).

THE INFLUENCE OF ORGANISATIONAL STRUCTURE

Organisational structure can be defined as the coordination of workflow and communication, and management of authority relationships in an organisation (Altinay and Altinay, 2004; Hall, 1991; Mintzberg, 1979; Ritchie and Riley, 2004). It is a critical antecedent to decision making. This is concerned with where the decision-making power lies, who makes the decisions, and how the decisions are made. Organisational structure influences the way tasks, duties, activities, coordination, communication, and resource allocation procedures are organized.

Several types of organisational structure can be seen in H&T organisations, which can include functional, multidivisional, and matrix:

1. A *functional structure* is based on functional activities undertaken by an organisation, such as operations, marketing, human resources, and finance. The responsibilities of an organisation are divided in this type of structure according to the organisation's primary roles. For example, in a small hotel, there may be several functional departments that include the front office, food and beverage, security, marketing, human resources management, and finance and security.

2. A *multidivisional structure* refers to having separate divisions based on products, services, and geographical areas. Under each division or geographical region are functional areas such as operations, marketing, human resources, and finance. For example, some hotel groups structure their organisations based on brands or geographical region, such as North America Division, Europe Division, Middle East Division, and Asia Pacific Division.

3. In a *matrix structure*, functional departments such as marketing, human resources management, finance, research, and development are assigned to work with one or more product or geographic business units. For example, large hotel groups such as Marriott Hotels and Resorts and InterContinental Hotels and Resorts have this matrix organisational structure, where functional departments and specific business units work together, and there are multiple reporting lines.

Certainly, each type of organisational structure has its advantages and disadvantages in developing and implementing strategies. For example, in the functional organisational structure, it would be easy to make decisions, communicate with subordinates, and closely control the processes and outcomes. However, in large organisations, functional structure would not work, since cooperation and input from multiple divisions and units would be needed. In the divisional structure, each division may be able to develop and implement its own strategies, but it may not allow input and cooperation from other business units and regions if each division is independent. Again, some business units may go into different initiatives that may not support the corporation's overall mission and vision. Finally, the matrix type of organisational structure would facilitate input and cooperation from multiple business units, as well as from functional areas. However, it may be complicated, bureaucratic, and time consuming to get input and to buy in from different units and functional areas. Therefore, managers in H&T organisations should first assess the limitations of their type organisational structure in strategy development and implementation.

The other issue that H&T organisations need to assess is whether their organisation has a centralized or decentralized organisational structure. If an H&T organisation has a centralized structure, this means that the decision-making power and responsibility are held by the top management. There is a tendency toward a standard strategy formation with a rigid, control-oriented implementation. On the other hand, where the management structured is decentralised, organisational members at the lower levels of hierarchy are given the responsibility to make decisions. Strategy development is the responsibility of the people from different levels and might require adaptation to certain conditions. Implementation of the strategy is carried out based on a free flow of communication and performance-related incentives.

Developing an appropriate organisational structure to facilitate the strategy development and implementation process has been highlighted as a precondition of exploiting market opportunities. Bureaucratic obstacles and control-oriented approaches to decision making demotivate organisational members and thus hinder proactive organisational behaviour. In particular, it discourages the expression of novel and innovative ideas, teamwork, and, more important, it negatively impacts "organisational learning" about customers and competition. Therefore, in order to be able to take advantage of the opportunities in the market by acting swiftly before the competitors, H&T organisations need to adopt a decentralised structure with an open and transparent communication.

A decentralised organisational structure would facilitate communication and the development of trust between top management and their employees. Such a management structure would facilitate decision making, as employees would be able to express their ideas without going through unnecessary levels. This would enable a faster recognition of feasible ideas in decision making. In addition, a decentralised structure would lead to wide participation of organisational members to strategy formulation and implementation, and thus they would take the ownership of the strategy process. With a decentralised structure, strategy development and implementation would be smoother, as organisational members at different levels will have more knowledge and awareness of issues about different markets and take more ownership of the process.

Although H&T organisations may enjoy the advantages of decentralised structure, it is not wise to stretch the limits of decentralisation. Sometimes, decentralisation leads to confusion about the strategic focus of company among the employees, resulting in ad hoc approaches to organisational behaviour. This is usually the case with large international hospitality organisations. As they become larger and more complex, they find it difficult to inspire and empower innovative employees while still encouraging accountability and responsibility.

Simons (2000) introduced a model called the Levers of Control that aims to strike a balance between formality and flexibility in an organisation (Table 4.1). This model suggests that control systems should be used in such a way that rather than inhibiting innovative behaviour, they set a clear direction and focus for the employees and inspire them to respond to the strategic priorities of the organisation. Boundary systems ensure that employees work within the acceptable domain of organisational activity. For example, an

Table 4.1	Four Levers of Control
Control Systems	**Specifications**
Diagnostic Systems	■ Focus attention on goal achievement for the business and for each individual in the business. ■ Give the opportunity to the managers to measure outcomes and compare results with preset profit plans and performance goals.
Interactive Systems	■ Give managers tools to impose consistency and guide creative search processes. ■ Managers use one system interactively such as profit planning systems that report planned and actual revenues and expenses and the intelligence systems that report information about social, political, and technical business issues. ■ Tactical day-to-day actions and creative experiments can be connected into a cohesive pattern that responds to strategic uncertainties.
Belief Systems	■ A belief system is the explicit set of organisational definitions formally communicated by senior managers through mission statements and credos that give basic values, purpose, and direction. It tells how the organisation creates values and the desired level of performance and how to manage internal and external relationships. ■ Management's vision, expressed in the mission statements and credos, motivates organisational participants to search for and create opportunities to accomplish the overall mission of the organisation.
Boundary Systems	■ These systems ensure that organisational members' activities fall within the acceptable domain of activity. For example, these systems ensure that business activities occur in defined product markets at acceptable levels of risk. ■ Without boundary systems, creative opportunity-seeking behaviour and experimentation can dispel the resources of the organisation.

Source: Adapted from Simons, R. (2000). *Performance Measurement and Control Systems for Implementing Strategy.* Prentice-Hall, London.

international hotel organisation's list of the United Kingdom, Germany, Italy, and Spain as strategically important countries in which the organisation would look for opportunities for growth and expansion would give organisational members a clear idea of where the organisation would like to establish a presence. Diagnostic control systems are the benchmarks used to measure the outputs of employees against preset goals and targets. For example, through setting a target of ten hotel openings every year and giving incentives to those organisational members responsible for growth and expansion in the United Kingdom, Germany, Italy, and Spain, senior decision makers measure organisational members' performance on expansion.

Managers may also use one system interactively, such as profitability and revenue reports, in order to be able to discuss the ongoing performance interactively and to influence and encourage the activities of employees. If we elaborate on the hotel expansion example, organisational members use growth and expansion-related decision-making criteria interactively in order to assess the long-term value of the hotel opening projects. More specifically, they evaluate the impact of an international expansion proposal on the organisation's position in a particular market and the extent to which it will create a competitive advantage over competitors. They ask the organisational members questions and exchange ideas about the market potential of the related country, the extent of competition, and market trends.

In addition, managers use belief systems such as mission statements to guide and inspire employees. These systems are usually used to give a sense of belonging to an organisation and pride in what employees strive to achieve. For example, in most of the international hotel chains, the importance of working for internationally recognised brands and adding value to their image is communicated in the mission statements and decision-making criteria and also frequently suggested to the organisational members during discussions. These approaches make organisational members feel proud of being part of an organisational network, and they also reemphasise the importance of protecting and enhancing the image of the brand further. The successful usage of this model depends on leadership's ability to create a supportive culture with a clear sense of direction and guidance.

A final issue related to organisational structure is the informal organisational structure, as well as politics and conflicts. The informal organisational structure refers to groups being formed by managers and executives from different functional areas and management levels based on their friendships, hobbies, political views, religious affiliations, and other reasons. Managers and executives in such groups may support their group members' decisions and interests even if they are not beneficial to the organisation. It is also possible that there may be ongoing politics and conflicts among functional areas as well as among different divisions, which can influence strategy development and implementation.

INFLUENCE OF LEADERSHIP

Every H&T organisation has key individuals—leaders with skills, ability, and vision to nurture and enable the organisation to develop a business strategy, identify the resources required, and nurture other employees to turn their ideas into business reality (Pittaway, Carmouche, and Chell, 1998; Testa, 2007). Leaders in H&T organisations should have a broad vision, the ability to think creatively and intuitively, and the skill to influence others. They are sometimes seen as exceptional individuals who can come up with a creative idea, drive change in an organisation, and implement it. Organisations need the input of such "leaders" because they are usually very capable of introducing innovative solutions to solve the organisation's problems. They therefore act like initiators of continuous change.

Leaders can facilitate organisational learning by bringing business opportunities to the attention of other organisational members and networking externally with both suppliers and customers. They have the ability to sense the dynamic changes in the internal and external environments and therefore can act like a hinge between the internal environment of their organisation and the external stakeholders such as customers and suppliers.

The outcome of their efforts is innovative solutions to the organisation's problems and new and imaginative means to deal with changes in their environment. Their entrepreneurial skills and attributes are particularly critical in introducing innovation solutions to their organisation's problems across borders. They are creative and good reflectors. They assess the risks involved in working with foreign operations. They employ a "hands-on" management style in bringing a business idea into successful creation by considering the cross-cultural obstacles in different country markets. While identifying business opportunities, they take ownership and are accountable for their activities. They utilise their creative and flexible thinking, risk-taking, and, ultimately, risk-reducing skills.

The different leadership styles are authoritative, persuasive, consultative, and participative decision making, and these can facilitate or hinder effective decision making. Regardless of the leadership style adapted, to a large degree success in decision making and the implementation of strategy depends very much on the background, skills, and abilities of the leader. Ideas and strategy must be supported and appreciated by leadership, both by their physical presence and by making sure that the company resources are available to support the employees in their business endeavours.

Leaders should make a personal commitment to support innovative ideas. Leadership should undertake the role of creating a "supportive culture" where new ideas are nurtured and encouraged, and they should also see themselves as supporters of their subordinates. In addition, while developing and implementing new ideas and managing change in organisations, leaders need to employ persuasive communication, negotiation, and listening skills in order to discover the interests, needs, and commitment of others.

It is worth noting that there is relatively high turnover in leadership positions in H&T organisations. For example, Burger King had over 12 chief executive officers from the early 1990s to 2006. When a new CEO begins working, it is possible that there will be changes in organisational direction, structure, and culture. Another issue is that many H&T organisations employ managers who come from operations, and they prefer to work on day-to-day operations rather than strategic planning and analysis. It may therefore be essential to educate them in strategic management practices.

INFLUENCE OF ORGANISATIONAL CULTURE

Organisational culture is another important factor that shapes the strategic direction of an organisation and thus the behaviours of the employees (Guerrier and Deery, 1998; Kemp and Dwyer, 2001; Roper, Brookes, and Hampton, 1997). It is a holistic, historically determined, socially constructed, shared organisational variable made up of symbols, heroes, rituals, and values. Symbols are words, gestures, pictures, or objects that carry particular meaning in a culture. Heroes are persons, alive or dead, real or imaginary, who possess characteristics highly prized in the culture and who thus serve as models for behaviour. Rituals are collective activities that are technically superfluous but are socially essential within a culture (Brown, 1998). Symbols, heroes, and rituals can be subsumed under the term *practices* because they are visible to an observer, although their cultural meaning lies in the way they are perceived by insiders. The core of culture is formed by values in the sense of broad, nonspecific feelings of good and evil, beautiful and ugly, normal and abnormal, rational and irrational—feelings that are often unconscious and rarely discussed and that cannot be observed as such but are manifested in alternatives of behaviour (Schein, 1985). Values describe what the employees in an organisation believe *should* be, whereas practices describe what they feel at the moment.

Organisational culture fulfills four important functions. First, it conveys a sense of identity for the organisational members. It can even constitute a source of pride in an organisation. Second, it facilitates the generation of commitment to something larger than itself. Third, it enhances social system stability. It is a social mechanism that shapes and guides people's thoughts, values, and beliefs and ultimately controls their behaviour. Culture becomes the source of control through messages contained in rituals, stories, and ceremonies that relay to the organisational members the desired behaviours. Thus, culture is not only a context for the design of control systems but, in certain organisations, it may itself be a mechanism of control.

Finally, culture serves as a sense-making device that can guide and shape behaviour. Through its components, elements, and dimensions, it dictates the organisational structures adopted, the organisational behaviour, and the cognitive functioning of individuals in such a way as to ultimately affect their judgement/decision-making processes when they are faced with an environmental phenomenon. In other words, organisational culture is the main guide that shows individuals how to interpret and respond to the environment. In particular, it determines the efficiency of one person or an organisation in receiving information and then analysing and interpreting it.

An organisation's culture is likely to be especially influenced by key characteristics of the industry in which it operates (Tepeci and Bartlett, 2002). Organisations are founded on industry-based assumptions about customers, competitors, and society that form the basis of the organisational culture. From these assumptions, certain values develop concerning the "right things to do," and consistent with these values, management develops the strategies, structures, and processes necessary for the company to conduct its business (Tepeci and Bartlett, 2002). In the hospitality industry, being customer focused or centred and developing market-oriented practices appeared to be a widely shared value among the international hospitality organisations. Similarly, as a result of pressure from the community, customer groups, and society, hospitality organisations have adopted socially responsible values in their management practices and daily operations.

Founders and key leaders' values also undoubtedly shape organisational cultures. The cultural backgrounds of these strategic decision makers underlay their strategic beliefs. There may be beliefs about what the firm's financial goals should be, in what business it can succeed, what types of risks are acceptable, its strategic vision, capital market expectations, and so on. These beliefs are transposed to the ordinary organisational members through shared practices, the company's mission, and policies.

For example, InterContinental Hotels is described as a control-oriented company that is run by accountants, and the appointment of individuals with financial management backgrounds as presidents and CEOs has been seen to have followed this same rule due to his financial experience and expertise. Similarly, Marriott is seen as an American company because historically the firm's members on the Board of Directors have tended to be dominated by executives from one national state, often the country of origin of the firm. Therefore, American culture gives rise to different philosophies for and approaches to organisational design and planning and the control systems in Marriott.

Company heritage is another determinant of organisational culture. The history of the organisation reflects itself on the practices of organisation as a tradition and accumulated experience. For example, Kemons Wilson developed the idea of Holiday Inn as a result of what he called "the most miserable vacation of my life." Wilson, while on vacation in the early 1950s, identified a "niche" in the market. He discovered that existing motels were small, expensive, and of unpredictable quality. Therefore, he decided to meet an unmet customer need, a gap in the market for quality accommodation, by creating Holiday Inns. The rationale behind the activities of Wilson was faith in the American Dream.

According to Wilson, America played the central role in the world. The "American business system" is the right system that gives people opportunities to build businesses and by hard work and self-improvement, people can achieve great success. Wilson was considered to be more of a promoter and salesman than an innkeeper, more an entrepreneur than a professional hotelman. From the start, he differentiated his company's product from the competitors' and gained a competitive advantage. A Wilson invention, motel franchising made rapid expansion possible, and the company brought the concept of mass accommodation to America. The Holiday Inn concept was to get entrepreneurs involved in financing and development so the company could expand rapidly. Since then, Holiday Inn became a major exponent of branding and began selling franchises with a strong emphasis on brand standardisation that requires systemwide rules of operation. Today, although its portfolio incorporates different business formats, such as owned properties and joint ventures, Holiday Inn is the main driver of franchising business internationally.

When understood and successfully managed, organisational culture can lead to innovative business practices and sustainable sources of competitive advantage. For instance, successful formation of strategy requires diagnosing the organisational culture and identifying whether it is participative or individual centred. If an organisation possesses a participative organisational culture, there is a strong set of shared core values about what the organisation stands for. Formation of strategy involves setting widely shared objectives, teamwork, and regular communication with a decentralised management structure. Implementation of strategy requires understanding the core values of the organisation, and if appropriately managed, strong culture leads to wide participation and support of organisational members to the implementation of strategy.

In an organisation with an individual-centred organisational culture, rituals dominate the organisational culture rather than the core values. The power and organisational culture are centred around a number of individuals, with a strong emphasis on the performance of these individuals in forming short-term tactics rather than long-term goals. Both the formation and implementation of strategy are exposed to the risk of organisation being too dependent on certain individuals. Although relatively soft culture eases the management of change and enhances the organisation's capability to maneuver, there is always an issue of commitment to and support of strategy by the organisational members that makes strategy implementation difficult.

THE ORGANISATIONAL CONTEXT IN THE INTERNATIONAL PERSPECTIVE

All of the elements that exist outside the boundary of an H&T organisation have the potential to affect all or part of the organisation. As an organisation expands its business outside its national borders, it faces all the influences that exist in the environment of the host country or countries, as well as generalised international environmental conditions. Political risks, economic barriers, cultural differences, and technological drawbacks prevent an H&T organisation from effectively carrying out its strategy (Kim and Olsen, 1993; Zhao and Olsen, 1997). An organisation should therefore understand the likely impacts of international environment on strategy formation and implementation. Otherwise, it may lose opportunities, allocate its resources improperly, take unnecessary risks, and end up losing its assets. These all hinder survival and prosperity.

Risk in a broad sense occurs whenever anyone must make a choice, and the potential outcomes involve uncertainty. In other words, if a manager is faced with a decision, and the alternative choices involve estimated potential gains and losses that are not certainties, the situation involves risk. The three main forms of risk are political, economic, and sociocultural. Political risk is the potential for governmental actions or politically motivated events to occur that will adversely affect the long-term profitability or value of an organisation. It exposes itself through a number of political events including political philosophies that are changing or are in competition with one another, rising nationalism, competing religious groups, and terrorist or anarchist groups operating in the country.

Changing economic conditions are also considered a source of risk. Economic risk in a country is the level of uncertainty about the ability of a country to meet its financial obligations. A country's level of economic development generally determines its economic stability and therefore its relative risk to a foreign organisation. Most industrialised nations pose little risk of economic instability, but less-developed nations pose more risk. Economic risk exposes itself through a number of events, including limits on convertibility of local currency into foreign currency; restrictions on repatriation of capital, profit, and management fees; restrictive labour laws;

unique taxation policies; and licensing agreements. The "cultural distance" between the organisation's home base and the intended foreign market can also be a source of risk. Cultural distance is related to the differences and similarities between home and host country consumer markets. The country risk is perceived to be high when managers lack market knowledge about the target consumers in the host country.

The short-term effectiveness and long-term survival of organisations are determined partly by the actions they take in response to their external environments and risks associated with them. In particular, the organisational members' perceptions and interpretations of the organisation's environment and the response strategies are shaped by the internal organisation's context. For example, a risk-averse organisational culture would discourage risk taking internationally and would not support a strategy that encourages market presence in country markets where political, economic, or sociocultural risks are perceived to be high. In these organisations, decision making is usually centralised and held by the people at the higher levels of organisational hierarchy. There is an intense flow of information, experience, and knowledge transfer from the employees at the lower levels of organisational hierarchy who are usually local with extensive knowledge of and familiarity to the local country market conditions and culture. Without upward communication, senior management teams become out of touch with their staff's attitudes and underestimate or misinterpret emerging problems in the marketplace. In order to minimize the risk of operations, there is a strong emphasis on cross-functional interface such as the cooperation among marketing, human resource, and finance functions that would allow access to a greater pool of knowledge and information and the generation of many alternative solutions.

The risk of involvement in countries with varying social, political, and business conditions can only be minimised by understanding a systematic approach to management internationally. Failing to understand the cultural differences internationally and taking unnecessary political and economic risks due to the inappropriate organisational culture and strategy, management structure, leadership, and workforce might negatively influence the perceptions of the customers, employees, shareholders, suppliers, and other stakeholder groups of the organisations' activities. It may also create anxiety among these stakeholder groups. This is not what organisations want. If managers are to act strategically and plan the actions they want their organisations to take, it presupposes that they have some idea of how others in their environment will act and adopt their organisational contexts according to the changing dynamic conditions of the international environment.

SUMMARY

This chapter characterized the internal environment of an organisation and explained the importance of organisational variables for it to function well. A number of conclusions and summary points can be provided:

- An organisation's environment is comprised of different important factors that have influence on and bearing of its functioning.

- It is essential to identify an H&T company's stakeholders, tangible and intangible assets, core competencies, and distinctive competencies.

- When analyzing the internal environment of an H&T organisation, it is essential to look at four functional areas—operations, marketing, finance, and human resources—and to identify strengths and weaknesses.

- Organisational structure, culture, and leadership are three important factors that influence both strategy formation and implementation.

- Organisations need to manage the centralisation-decentralisation organisational structure continuum in order to have a certain degree of formality in the organisation while leaving room for empowerment to nurture innovative, opportunity-seeking employees.

- When understood and successfully managed, organisational culture can lead to innovative business practices and sustainable sources of competitive advantage.

- It is important that we understand the likely impacts of international environment on an organisation's internal functioning. Otherwise, as managers of the future, we may fail to respond to the opportunities and/or take unnecessary risks.

- When analyzing an H&T organisation's internal environment, it is recommended to look at all of the preceding areas. These suggested analyses are not alternative to others, but they complement each other by each providing a different and complimentary perspective.

STUDY QUESTIONS

1. What are the factors in an organisation's internal environment that have influence on and a bearing on its functioning?
2. How important are these factors for an H&T organisation?

3. How do organisational structure, culture, and leadership influence the strategy development and implementation?

4. What are the implications of a centralized organisational structure for an H&T organisation operating internationally?

REFERENCES AND FURTHER READINGS

Altinay, L. and Altinay, M. (2004). The influence of organisational structure on Entrepreneurial Orientation and Expansion Performance, *International Journal of Contemporary Hospitality Management*, (16) 6, 334–344.

Barney, J.B. (1991). Firms Resources and Sustained Competitive Advantage, *Journal of Management*, 17, 99–120.

Barney, J. and Wright, P. (1998). On Becoming a Strategic Partner: The Role of Human Resources in Gaining Competitive Advantage, *Human Resources Management*, 37 (1), 31–46.

Brown, A. (1998). *Organisational Culture*, Second Edition,, Financial Times Pitman Publishing, London.

Brownell, J. (2008). Leading on land and sea: Competencies and context, *International Journal of Hospitality Management*, 27, 137–150.

Clark, J.J. (1993). Holiday Inn: new rooms in the inn, *Cornell Hotel and Restaurant Administration Quarterly*, (34) 5, 59–67.

Freeman, R.E. (1984). *Strategic Management: A stakeholder approach*. Marshfield, MA: Pitman.

Galang, M.C. (2002). The Human Resource Department: Its Role in Firm Competitiveness. In G.R. Ferris, M. Ronald Buckley, and D.B. Fedor (Eds.), *Human Resources Management*, Fourth Edition. New Jersey: Prentice Hall.

Guerrier, Y. and Deery, M. (1998). Research in hospitality human resource management and organisational behaviour, *International Journal of Hospitality Management*, (17) 2, 145–160.

Hall, H.R. (1991). *Organisations: Structures, Processes and Outcomes*. Prentice Hall International Editions, London.

Harrell-Cook, G. (2002). Human Resources Management and Competitive Advantage: A Strategic Perspective. In G.R. Ferris, M. Ronald Buckley, and D.B. Fedor (Eds.), *Human Resources Management*, Fourth Edition. New Jersey: Prentice Hall.

Kemp, S. and Dwyer, L. (2001). An examination of organisational culture—the Regent Hotel, Sydney, *International Journal of Hospitality Management*, (20) 1, 77–93.

Kim, Y.C. and Olsen, M. (1993). A framework for the identification of political environmental issues faced by multinational hotel chains in newly industrialised countries in Asia, *International Journal of Hospitality Management*, 12 (2), 163–174.

Marriott, J. (2001). Our Competitive Strength: Human Capital, *Executive Speeches*, 15 (5), 18–21.

Mintzberg, H. (1979). *The Structuring of Organisations*. Prentice-Hall International Editions, London.

Nagabhushan, M. and Ganesan, S. (2004). Case Study on Four Seasons Hotels and Resorts, ICFAI Business School, Bangalore, India, Distributed by the European Case Clearing House.

Pfeffer, J. (1994). *Competitive Advantage through People*. Boston, MA: Harvard Business School Press.

Pfeffer, J. (1995). Producing Sustainable Competitive Advantage through the Effective Management of People, *Academy of Management Executive 9*, 55–72.

Pittaway, L., Carmouche, R., and Chell, E. (1998). The way forward: Leadership research in the hospitality industry, *International Journal of Hospitality Management*, (17) 2, 407–426.

Prashanth, K. and Gupta, V. (2004). Case Study on Human Resource Management: Best Practices at Marriott International, ICFAI Center for Management Research, Hydarabad, India. This case study is distributed by the European Case Clearing House.

Ritchie, B. and Riley, M. (2004). The role of the multi-unit manager within the strategy and structure relationship; evidence from the unexpected, *International Journal of Hospitality Management*, (23) 2, 145–161.

Roper, A., Brookes, M., and Hampton, A. (1997). The multicultural management of international hotel groups, *International Journal of Hospitality Management*, 16 (2), 147–159.

Schein, E.H. (1985). *Organisational Culture and Leadership: A Dynamic View*. San Francisco: Jossey-Bass.

Simons, R. (2000). *Performance Measurement and Control Systems for Implementing Strategy*. Prentice-Hall, London.

Tepeci, M. and Bartlett, B.L.A. (2002). The hospitality industry culture profile: a measure of individual values, organisational culture, and person-organisation fit as predictors of job satisfaction and behavioural intentions, *International Journal of Hospitality Management*, (21) 2, 151–170.

Testa, R.M. (2007). A deeper look at national culture and leadership in the hospitality industry, *International Journal of Hospitality Management*, (26) 2, 468–484.

Wheelen, T. and Hunger, J. (2006). *Strategic Management and Business Policy*, Tenth Edition. New Jersey: Pearson Prentice Hall.

Zhao, J.L. and Olsen, M.D. (1997). The antecedent factors influencing entry mode choices of multinational lodging firms, *International Journal of Hospitality Management*, 16 (1), 79–98.

PART III

Strategy Content

The third part of the text is concerned with exploring the varying levels of strategy content?the so-called ?what? strategy. The three levels of strategy content that can be viewed as separate areas of strategic management decision making are explored. The importance of context as an influence on strategy content is highlighted throughout the three chapters in this section.

CHAPTER 5

Business-Level Strategies

Learning Objectives

After reading this chapter, you should be able to:

1. Define competitive strategies.
2. Explain positioning and generic business strategies and their role in a firm's value-creation process.
3. Describe the roles of resources, capabilities, and competencies in strategy formulation.
4. Describe the industry life cycle, and explain the competitive strategies that firms follow during each phase of the life cycle.
5. Assess business-level strategy in hospitality and tourism firms from an international perspective.

CONTENTS

Opening Case

As Jerry met with his executives to discuss the situation (described in the opening case of Chapters 1 and 3), the general manager, Tracy Lee, provided more information. She described the hotel as mainly targeting the upscale and luxury business market segments (75 percent), while also attracting the upscale and luxury leisure market segments (25 percent). The hotel's main competitors are Four Seasons, J.W. Marriott, Shangri La, Mandarin Oriental, Landmark Hotel, and Conrad Hotel, which are all located within a two-mile radius. There is fierce competition among the hotels in this market segment, and firms have resorted to price-cutting tactics during economic downturns before.

The products and services of the Great Eastern Hotel have been unique and of high quality. Guests have been particularly satisfied with the ambience of the hotel given that it has focused only on its core market segments for business. The rooms have been designed and appointed to satisfy its market segments. In fact, there has been a coherence among product (tangible aspects) and service quality (intangible aspects). However, the economic downturn has raised questions about how the hotel would maintain its market.

1. Should the Great Eastern Hotel redefine its market segments? Explain why and make assumptions. What are the pros and cons?
2. What are the hotel's options in terms of changing its current market positioning?
3. How could the hotel go about changing its positioning if it is necessary?
4. What is the current business strategy of the hotel? Is this well defined, and is a change necessary? Explain why and do a pros and cons analysis.

INTRODUCTION

This chapter provides an in-depth account of business-level strategies that are critical for a firm's success in its product-service market domains. It is important to understand what factors must be taken into consideration during strategy formulation and their roles in guiding the organization toward success. Note that strategies are formulated based on environment scanning so there is a link between the environment and strategy formulation at the business level. This chapter provides a detailed account of what constitutes a good strategy and describes positioning and generic strategies and their roles in creating a sustainable competitive advantage.

THE PARAMETERS OF COMPETITIVE STRATEGY

Competitive strategies define a firm's position in relation to its competitors in a given market. These strategies enable a firm to develop its market position while being able to create a sustainable competitive advantage. In other words, by implementing competitive strategies that defend or extend their market position, firms are able to add value to their bottom line in terms of return on investment. In fact, Porter (1980) points out that a firm influences an industry's attractiveness as well as its competitive position. While the attractiveness of the industry is important if the firms are to create and sustain value addition, a firm may not be able to sustain value creation if it chooses a poor competitive position.

A *competitive advantage* is defined as the above-average profits a firm is able to generate from its business operations when compared to its competition or competitive set. A *competitive set* refers to all of the firms in a given market/segment that compete directly against one another. The sustainability of competitive advantage is dependent on the duration of time that the firm is able to generate above-average profits as compared to competition in a given market. To be able to sustain the advantage (Figure 5.1), firms need to ensure that resources and capabilities are in place and that strategies are well defined so as to establish a link among resources and capabilities and strategies.

So how do firms create a competitive advantage? The answer to this question lies in the ability of the firm to serve its market with the same products and services that competition does, but at a lower cost. An advantage could also be created if the firm is able to provide products and services to the market that are superior to the competition's. Both of these approaches create a unique position for the firm that leads to competitive advantage. The firm's ability to create an advantage by using a cost or differentiation basis leads to the conceptualization of positioning strategies.

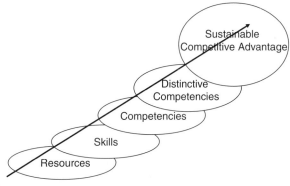

FIGURE 5.1   *Sustainability of Competitive Advantage.*

WHAT IS THE BASIS OF A GOOD STRATEGY?

Before positioning strategies are explored in detail, it is essential to discuss what constitutes a good strategy. According to Porter (1996), a good strategy has to do with the uniqueness the firm is able to create through a course of action, and "the essence of strategy is choosing to perform activities differently than rivals do" (p. 64). Note that there is much confusion about what *strategy* is exactly. Strategy is not action per se; neither is it a mission, a vision statement, nor a goal. Strategy enables a firm to become unique in terms of the position it occupies in the market. A good strategy should be accompanied by a clear definition of the industry and the products and services. In fact, strategy enables a firm to make the right decisions regarding the choices pertaining to the course of action.

Porter (1996) points out that managers often confuse operational effectiveness with strategy. Best practices may not necessarily carve out a unique position for the business, as they are easily imitable in the short to medium term. For instance, in the hotel business, managers often introduce actions that lead to operational improvements, which they mistake for uniqueness at the business unit level. Introducing a system to improve guest service at the front desk of a hotel is not a strategy. Note that the discussions in meetings are usually from the perspective of creating uniqueness at the operating level, which is not sustainable in creating economic value for the firm in the long term. Moreover, strategy needs to have continuity, which many managers fail to consider in their pursuit of operational excellence.

The firm's strategy is developed on market information and analysis. An outside-in approach is based on developing strategy predominantly using a market perspective in terms of tapping opportunities. The firm's resources and competencies are altered based on current and emerging opportunities. On the contrary, an inside-out approach is about developing strategy based on the firm's resources, capabilities, and competencies, while tapping opportunities based on its strengths. A good strategy is one that uses a combination of the two approaches, while leaning more toward an inside-out approach. Since strategy needs to be continuous, the very formulation of strategy should be based on a long-term approach. For this to happen, according to Chandler (1962), a firm needs to clearly define its long-term goals and objectives and how it would attain them through predefined courses of action and resource allocation decisions. We now define *positioning* and *generic strategies*.

POSITIONING AND GENERIC STRATEGIES

Positioning pertains to the market position that firms aim to create. Porter (1996) describes strategic positioning as "based on customers' needs, customers' accessibility, or a variety of a company's products and services" (p. 66). He conceptualizes positioning to be driven by three factors: variety-based, needs-based, and access-based, with the overall objective of "carving out a niche." Yet, positioning could be broad or narrow in terms of the group of customers that the firm would like to target. Positioning is based on a set of activities that are different and unique as compared to competitors. Note that positioning is different from strategy. According to Porter, strategy is "the creation of a unique and valuable position involving a different set of activities" (p. 68).

How do the three types of positioning differ? According to Porter (1996), variety-based positioning relates to the products and services a firm is able to produce based on distinctive competencies and activities. The uniqueness related to products and services is based on what the firm can produce rather than the segment of the market it targets. This is seen in the case of ethnic restaurants and restaurants set up by celebrity chefs such as Paul Bocuse from France and Gordon Ramsay from the United States. Their restaurants are developed on the competencies of the proprietors, which have unique brand value and appeal. On the other hand, needs-based positioning is about targeting customer groups based on their needs. In this case, the company's products and services are produced to meet the specific needs of customer groups in a given market segment. The company would need to develop distinctive activities to meet those needs so they could carve out a competitive position in the market. This is seen in the case of firms such as Marriott International and Hilton Hotels Corp. that have developed various products and services to meet the needs of customers. The competencies are acquired or developed to target the segments in which they position the hotels.

Access-based positioning is based on market segmentation in order to identify customers who could be accessed differently. According to Porter (1996), reaching customers is the essence of this positioning strategy, with firms differentiating themselves on customer geography or customer scale. For instance, motels such as Formule 1 use access-based positioning to take the product to the market. Their products are located only on major highways in France and other countries in Europe and the outskirts of metros. It should be noted that firms do not have to differentiate among customers to come up with an effective positioning strategy. Firms that position based on variety or access do not necessarily focus on customer differences. Porter

(1996) bases his conceptualization of positioning—that is, choosing activities that are different from one's rivals'—on the fact that "if the same set of activities were best to produce all varieties, meet all needs, and access all customers, companies could easily shift among them and operational effectiveness would determine performance."

Generic Strategies

Business-level strategies are referred to as generic strategies, as firms based in any industry, regardless of the products and services they produce and the product-markets they serve, are able to pursue them. They consist of cost leadership, differentiation, and focus. Porter (1980, 1985) derived these types that are closely linked to a framework that uses customer needs, customer groups, and distinctive competencies developed by Abell (1980). The following are the three generic level strategies developed by Porter:

Cost leadership strategy: Firms derive this strategy by maintaining a low-cost position. Low cost refers to the overall cost of producing products and services when compared to competing firms in the same market. If a firm is successful in achieving lower costs as compared to competition over a sustained period of time, it is said to have a competitive advantage. Such products and services meet basic needs and generally come with no frills. To be able to achieve a low-cost position, firms would need to target the products and services to customer groups with the objective of achieving volume sales so the marginal costs related to production could be reduced through economies of scale. The firm typically meets customer needs at the lower end of the market spectrum so a no frills approach can be adopted. The cost leader's market strategy is to meet the basic needs of the average customer through the firm's product-service offerings.

The firm's primary focus is to achieve high efficiency and productivity so the cost of production is optimized. In service firms, the involvement of human resources in the production process is optimized to improve resource-related efficiency and productivity. Many firms have also used technological solutions to manage costs, a case in point being Southwest Airlines. It should be noted that firms that are cost leaders in the market trim down the number of activities involved in producing and delivering the products and services, as seen in the case of Southwest Airlines. Such firms attain a lower per-unit cost of production and service as compared to other firms they compete with. The lower per unit costs are achieved when firms are able to reduce their overhead costs. This, coupled with their ability to lower prices while generating the same amount of profits as compared to the competition, provides them with a competitive edge.

Differentiation strategy: This strategy stems from a firm's objective of providing unique products and services to its customers as compared to competition. The competitive advantage is achieved when firms are able to command premium prices or sell more of a product at a given price as compared to the competition. Moreover, buyer loyalty enables a firm to sustain the advantage during periods of downturn. Porter (1985) states that differentiator firms are able to "gain equivalent benefits such as greater buyer loyalty during cyclical or seasonal downturns" (p. 120), which applies to the hotel industry. Firms such as Four Seasons offer luxury products with the objective of differentiating their offerings from competition.

Note that the customer is not only willing to pay the difference between the prices of such product offerings as compared to the products of the cost leader firm, but he or she is also loyal to them during seasonal downturns. This is driven by the value buyers derive from the product-service offerings of the firm. Porter also points out that "a differentiator cannot ignore its cost position, because its premium prices will be nullified by a markedly inferior cost position. A differentiator thus aims at cost parity or proximity relative to its competitors, by reducing cost in all areas that do not affect differentiation" (p. 14). By doing so, such firms are able to achieve above-average profits in their industry setting.

The differentiator firm does not achieve such a position by reducing unit costs or marginalizing research and development (R&D). Rather, such firms are market driven, so they can offer unique products and services. Owing to this, firms pursuing differentiation invest in R&D more than the average firm while employing cost control–related processes. Cost control does not necessarily indicate a cost-based approach; instead, it would enable such firms to keep costs under check while reducing other overhead costs that do not form an integral part of the "differentiation" process. Therefore, the differentiator firm's cost position would be higher than the cost leader firm. Nonetheless, the uniqueness of the firm would lead to the sustainability of competitive advantage over a prolonged period of time.

Differentiation strategy has been widely pursued by hospitality organizations worldwide. Starwood Hotels and Resorts, with over 400 hotels, is one such corporation that has effectively used an overall differentiation strategy. Strategic business units (SBUs) are created to target various market segments, which are separate units in a corporation that have a unique identity of their own based on resources and capabilities and product-service offerings. SBUs with distinct brand identities in Starwood Hotels and Resorts include St. Regis, Luxury Collection, W hotels, Westin, Le Meridian, Sheraton, Four Points, and Aloft. These SBUs target luxury, upscale, and middle-market segments. Each SBU has a unique positioning strategy.

Focus strategy: This strategy is narrow in scope in terms of the market segment and the product-service offerings. The firm targets a market segment with the sole objective of serving only that particular segment. Note that competitive advantage is derived only from targeting the segment. The firm either develops a cost advantage or it can differentiate itself. Therefore, focus strategies are of two types: cost focus and differentiation focus. Cost focus pertains to seeking a cost advantage in the target market segments. Firms with such an approach are typically narrow in their cost focus. Many standalone, low-end, bed & breakfast economy and budget hotels would fall into this category.

On the other hand, differentiation focus is about differentiating the firm's products and services in the target market segments. The difference between overall cost leadership/differentiation and cost/differentiation focus strategies is that in the case of the former, the firm tries to achieve marketwide cost leadership or differentiation, whereas in the latter, the strategy is limited only to the target market segment. A firm achieves a competitive advantage by focusing on the target market segment. It stems from the inability of competing firms to meet the needs of the customers in the segment and to create uniqueness in terms of cost or differentiation.

Note that the firm's target market segment needs to be different from other market segments; otherwise, the strategy will not be successful. The success depends on how the firm is able to target a unique or different buyer need. An example in the hospitality industry is Four Seasons Hotels and Resorts that offer a unique product-service package to the luxury market segment. They pursue a differentiation focus strategy in that they only have one type of product service offering in one market segment. Ritz Carlton Hotels were also differentiation focus driven as a standalone firm until they were acquired by Marriott International in the late 1990s. Now they are a SBU in the Marriott Corporation and form an integral component of Marriott's overall differentiation strategy.

Stuck in the middle: This situation arises when a firm is not able to pursue generic-level strategies in their pure form but combine cost leadership and differentiation. This combination leads to a confused positioning in their product-service markets, with firms that are cost leaders engaging in activities that should be pursued by differentiators and vice versa. According to Porter, such a situation arises because firms get too caught up in competitive tactics in their markets that drive them out of their strategic orientation. This is despite the fact that such firms start off with a pure generic strategy.

Oftentimes, environmental changes lead firms to take incremental measures, which are not aligned with the firm's generic strategies. Managers lose focus of their firms' generic strategies while attempting to address the environmental factors. For instance, firms that are differentiators engage in cost-cutting measures during economic downturns. Likewise, cost leaders engage in differentiation strategies during economic upturns. Both of these situations drive firms out of their strategic orientation, leading to a situation of being stuck in the middle.

From a historic perspective, a good example of a stuck in the middle firm is Holiday Inn. The firm began by offering a standardized product at a reasonable price that targeted the average customer. The motel concept was new at the time that Holiday Inn entered the market in the 1950s. But over the next two decades, the hotel firm was not able to address a shift in market trends as customers' needs and wants changed in terms of quality, price, and amenities. New hotel firms entered the market, occupying various segments while specializing in those product markets. Holiday Inn was stuck in the middle and was late to react while shifting to a more broad differentiation strategy by offering different products to different markets (e.g., Crowne Plaza, Holiday Inn Express, etc.).

THE INDUSTRY LIFE CYCLE AND COMPETITIVE DYNAMICS

It is essential to introduce the industry life cycle at this stage so the factors that influence a firm's competitive strategies are identified. Essentially, the industry life cycle captures the evolution of firms in an industry over a definite time period. The evolutionary path of firms in an industry is captured in a sigmoid-shaped graphical representation. It consists of five distinct phases: introductory, growth, shakeout, maturity, and decline. In the introductory phase, very few firms invest in unique resources and capabilities to build competencies in tapping a new product-service market. These firms are entrepreneurially oriented as they take a risk in entering a new market. Such firms are in their infancy as customers begin to explore their new product-service offerings. As firms succeed in wooing customers and as market trends lead to increased consumption of their products and services, the demand factor increases significantly. Due to a gap in demand and supply, more firms take notice of the gap and enter the industry.

As the market begins to grow, and as more and more firms enter new markets in the industry, the life cycle enters the growth phase. Competition among firms is not as fierce during this phase, as the environment is munificent and the demand for products and services is high. The objective of firms during this phase is to increase their share while penetrating the market as quickly as possible, using appropriate strategies. Also, firms attempt to enter new market segments in the industry so they can use existing resources and capabilities to expand into these markets. In the hotel industry, franchising and management contracts are used as vehicles to accomplish rapid growth. Distinct business-level strategies emerge during this phase as firms tend to pursue cost leadership, differentiation, or focus strategies. Industries become fragmented during this phase, as both large and small firms are able to grow while being able to occupy niches in the various market segments. Moreover, rapid growth sees the emergence of hotel chains with superior competencies in each of their product-service market segments.

Over time, as the market's growth rate slows down, the gap between demand and supply closes. When supply catches demand and when the rate of growth of firms subsides, firms start to compete directly against one another. Price-based competition increases, and firms try to capture their rivals' markets. The intensity with which firms compete increases to a level where customers benefit from price discounts. Although firms grow during this phase, the industry goes through a shakeout phase. Large firms become larger by acquiring smaller firms that occupy small-niche markets. Small firms that are not able to sustain growth during the shakeout phase exit the market. The industry structure changes during this phase as it goes from a fragmented structure to a consolidated structure.

The changing demand–supply conditions and the competitive forces in the industry give rise to an oligopolistic structure. The industry is comprised of a few firms with resources and capabilities as well as brand loyalty that give them a strong position in their individual product-service markets. Firms recognize one another's strengths and weaknesses, including the generic-level strategies they pursue. They also recognize that the industry has entered maturity. As a result, incumbents avoid direct competition in order to ensure that the level of profitability is maintained. Note that fierce competition between firms leads to price wars, increased marketing expenses, and lower profit margins, even if firms employ cost-cutting measures to squeeze out more profits. There is some level of forbearance between competing firms in a maturing market, and the few firms that occupy strong positions usually have expanded to a level where they occupy various market segments in the industry.

During the maturity phase, supply is almost static with the anticipation that demand would not fall, and if it does, firms enter the decline phase. This phase leads the incumbents to reduce their investments in the markets they occupy in the industry. Declining demand leads firms to trim their product line to the extent that they focus on segments that are profitable. If falling demand is permanent, then firms are forced to exit the segments and, in some cases, the industry.

The preceding concepts related to the industry life cycle and the competitive dynamics can be exemplified while using cases in the hospitality industry. The emergence and growth of Hilton and Holiday Inn brands in the upscale and midmarket segments explain the evolution of the industry structure. Post–World War II saw the emergence of commercial aircraft technology, along which came faster and safer long-distance travel. Since such technology was first put into practice by American airline firms, more American travelers started traveling overseas for business and leisure. With this came the need to stay in hotels that were safe and secure, which provided value for money in terms of the quality-price trade-off.

Domestic hotel brands in the American market, such as Holiday Inn and Hilton, seized the opportunity to locate their hotels outside the United States to tap into this growing demand. These hotels used franchising and management contracts to grow internationally during the 1960s and 1970s and were the leading brands in international markets. In fact, airline firms found it viable to tap this growing demand by entering the hotel product-market. New firms entered the market in the 1970s and 1980s, such as Hyatt, Marriott, and soon the international hotel market was proliferated with hotel brands. Most of these global firms pursued overall differentiation while pursuing multiple-target markets.

Industry shakeout and consolidation occurred in the American market and other international hotel markets as they reached the maturity phase during the early to mid-190s. Major brands in this market included Holiday Inn, Hilton, Hyatt, Marriott, Ramada, and Radisson. Other firms, such as Accor, identified new and emerging markets in the Asia Pacific regions. Note that the upscale Western European hotel market segment reached maturity as well, whereas the midmarket and lower-end market segments in this geographic region were fragmented due to the business ownership structure in this market. Hotels such as the Intercontinental, Holiday Inn, and Forte changed hands a few times. Hilton split into Hilton International and Hilton Hotels Corp as the international markets in the developed world entered the maturity phase of the industry life cycle. Over the past decade, most of these brands have been pursuing aggressive growth in the developing Asian markets as new markets are being explored.

The fast-food industry in the United States saw a similar evolution as the industry grew from one or two firms in the 1950s to several hundred firms in the 1960s and early 1970s, as the industry became fragmented in a growing market. In the late 1970s and 1980s, shakeout and maturity set in as larger firms like McDonald's, Burger King, Wendy's, and KFC emerged, and smaller firms that occupied niche markets segments faded away. These major players have dominated the markets in the United States and other international markets as new products and services have been rolled out due to changing consumer behaviour and market trends.

RESOURCES, CAPABILITIES, AND COMPETENCIES

Resources and capabilities form the backbone of a firm's competitive posture. The development of resources and capabilities should be carried out with the objective of creating sustainable competitive advantage. The resource-based view (RBV), as described by Barney (1991) and others, provides a framework for firms to invest in valuable, rare, and inimitable resources. This is possible only if the focus is on heterogeneous resources that are not perfectly mobile (Barney, 1991; Peteraf, 1993). The more resources are inimitable, the more the sustainability of the competitive advantage. Note that the literature identifies resources as tradable and nonspecific to the firm, whereas capabilities are very much specific to the firm's internal environment and are used in exploiting the firm's resources.

Resources can be tangible and intangible. Tangible resources are physical, financial, and technological, such as plant, machinery, equipment, and other physical assets. Intangible resources include intellectual capital comprising operating, technological, marketing, and financial knowhow, as well as human capital, brand name, goodwill, patents, and so forth. A good example of intangible resources pertains to the Walt Disney Company. The company's brand name and goodwill by themselves are able to create a global competitive advantage.

On the other hand, capabilities relate to a firm's skills, routines, and activities. Inherent in them are also management decision making, creativity, and knowledge building, sharing, and retention-related activities. It should be noted that organizational culture, management style, and practices form an integral component of organizational capabilities. For instance, Marriott's management capabilities are distinctive in how it combines operating and technological knowhow along with knowledge building, sharing, and retention activities. This has played a big role in how the firm has been able to build brand equity internationally over the past few decades. Walt Disney has unique competencies in developing entertainment-based product-service bundles, including filmmaking, especially animation films, making it unique in its product-service market. Competencies are a product of resources and capabilities and are distinctive if the firm is able to combine them to create a unique advantage. Radisson hotels have been innovative in using their resources and capabilities to be able to come up with unique technological innovations pertaining to reservation systems. Likewise, Marriott's reservation system, Marriott's Automated Reservation System for Hotel Accommodations (MARSHA), gives it a unique advantage in developing a global reservation network.

A firm's focus should be on linking resources and capabilities with strategies. The link between resources and capabilities, and strategies is such that the former shapes the latter. Existing competencies would influence the strategies that firms formulate in a given market. However, strategic orientation of firms should be one that builds resources and capabilities to capture emerging or future opportunities. This goes back to the discussion on strategic fit and strategic intent (see Chapter 3). For firms to be able to create sustainable competitive advantage, it is imperative that strategic intent should be at the core of the firm's orientation with its market/environment. This would also provide the firms with sustainable competitive advantage especially for those that rely more on their intangible resources and capabilities. This is exemplified in Hilton's expertise in managing upscale hotel properties and their competencies in executing management contracts, which were used to tap opportunities in the American business and leisure travel markets globally during the 1970s and 1980s. More and more hotel property owners in global markets wanted the American hotel firm to manage their properties, which led to the rapid growth of the firm during this period that included markets such as Puerto Rico, France, Turkey, and Hong Kong. In the past two decades, Marriott, Hilton, Hyatt, and other hotel firms have emerged as leading players in the international market in terms of developing competencies related to managing hotels globally.

Causal Ambiguity, Inimitability, and Sustainable Competitive Advantage

The resource-based view of the firm emphasizes the inimitability of resources and capabilities, which leads to a sustainable competitive advantage. For a firm to be able to sustain its competitive advantage, there should be some level of ambiguity between its competencies and outcomes such as firm performance. This is defined within the realm of causal ambiguity, which is the inability of the firm's managers to explain the exact link between competencies and firm performance and the competitive advantage that results from it (Barney, 1991). Note that the higher the level of causal ambiguity, the higher the firm performance, and thus the higher the sustainability of the competitive advantage.

Why is this so? If a firm's managers cannot explain the link between competencies and firm performance, then there is a low likelihood of managers of competitor firms to explain and subsequently imitate the firm's actions. While this is a source of competitive advantage, there is a flip side. The inability of the firm's managers to explain the causes of firm performance restricts the transferability and leveraging of these competencies, thereby limiting the size and scope of the business.

The inimitability and causal ambiguity are seen in firms such as Walt Disney. The firm has a high level of intangible resources and capabilities that leads to firm competencies that are inimitable. Note that the success of Walt Disney in the United States and Japan did not guarantee success in the European market when Euro Disney was launched in the early 1990s. Despite the fact that Disney's managers were well versed in the functional and administrative aspects of the business, Euro Disney was not successful in generating profits for a prolonged period of time, lasting a good portion of its first decade of operations just outside Paris, France. A repositioning strategy, including a name change to Disneyland Paris, has resulted in an effective turnaround that has made the firm profitable.

The same situation to some extent was seen in Disney's recent expansion to Hong Kong in the mid-2000s, where again the firm was not successful in generating profits in the initial years of business even though the projections suggested otherwise. Note that Disney's main rival in the Hong Kong market, Ocean Park, has been able to fend off the threat from Disney and has been able to sustain its competitive advantage despite being a local player. Ocean Park's managers were not so sure of their ability to sustain their profitability when Disney entered Hong Kong. The fact that Ocean Park has been able to maintain its advantage while sustaining attendance and profit levels despite Disney's market presence is something that could be explained by inimitability and causal ambiguity.

BUSINESS-LEVEL STRATEGY IN THE INTERNATIONAL PERSPECTIVE

Firms face different task environments in domestic and international markets, and therefore their strategy formulation decisions would be influenced by market-related contextual factors. Roth and Morrison (1992) state that the competitive attributes of firms engaged in international and domestic environments would be significantly different. In fact, internationalization is treated as a contingency variable in the firm's strategy formulation framework. Specifically, in terms of variables that affect competitiveness, Roth and Morrison found, among other factors, marketing differentiation and innovation to be key factors in the hospitality and tourism industry. In order to develop marketing differentiation, firms would need to consider brand identification, advertising, promotion, and distribution in the context of international markets.

Note that differentiation has played a key role when firms have launched new products in international markets. For instance, a Radisson hotel in the United States is positioned as a midmarket hotel, whereas in the Asian and Middle Eastern contexts, it could be, and is perceived to be, an upscale property. This is also found in the case of other midmarket hotels such as Ramada, Courtyard by Marriott, and Marriott hotels, which generally are in the lower end of the upscale segment. In Asia and the Middle East, they are considered upscale. This is also seen in the fast-food industry in terms of perception of customers. McDonald's is perceived to be more upscale in France than in the United States (Brannen and Wilson, 1996). Likewise, customers seek a totally different experience from McDonald's in Asia as compared to France or the United States.

Differentiation is based on the perception of consumers as well as the potential to use the brand name to generate more returns in the short to medium term. Market differentiation sometimes creates confusion in the mind of international travelers, which actually reflects the gap between the developed and developing countries in terms of consumers' experience and exposure to goods and services. Firms are required to adjust to market-related differences in an international context, which has an impact on product-service bundles as well as the positioning/generic strategies they pursue in such markets. Note that such differentiation would affect the advertising and promotion strategies in an international context as compared to domestic operations.

Innovation is also another important element of a firm's competitive posture in international markets. Firms would need to provide different product-service offerings in different contexts based on the market's response. In this context, McDonald's product innovation of offering a veggie burger in the Indian market is a good example of the link between market factors and the need to innovate. The fact that the local market needs an international market drove the firm to extend its product line while enabling it to compete with local and other international firms in the Indian market. McDonald's brand name and reputation in providing quality products in the international fast-food industry gave it a competitive advantage in the Indian setting even among vegetarian consumers. Note that such innovations result in the development of new resources and capabilities, which could be extended to other markets where they could put newly acquired competencies to productive use.

SUMMARY

This chapter provided an in-depth review of business strategy, examining positioning and competitive strategies and how they form an essential part of creating and sustaining a competitive advantage. The sustainability of a competitive advantage forms the backbone of how firms are able to add value to the firm through a linkage between its resources and capabilities, and its strategies. Generic strategies are important to conceptualize so firms can pursue overall cost leadership/differentiation or cost focus/differentiation focus strategies. Firms that are unable to do this end up being stuck in the middle, leading to a competitive disadvantage. Resources need to be acquired and capabilities need to be developed so, internally, firms can drive value creation from a resource-based perspective. Yet, firms' managers may not be able to pinpoint how the competitive advantage came about due to the causal ambiguity, which is an integral part of the firm's ability to sustain its advantage over the competition.

STUDY QUESTIONS

1. What is competitive advantage?
2. Differentiate between competitive advantage and sustainable competitive advantage.
3. What are generic strategies? How are firms able to use these strategies at the business level to create competitive advantage?
4. How are overall cost leadership and differentiation strategies different from cost focus and differentiation focus strategies?

5. Differentiate between resources and capabilities. How are competencies defined?

6. What is causal ambiguity? How does this help a firm to sustain its advantage?

7. What is the industry life cycle? Describe the market conditions that prevail at various stages of the life cycle.

REFERENCES AND FURTHER READINGS

Anderson, O. and Kheam, L. (1998). Resource-based theory and international growth strategies: an exploratory study, *International Business Review*, 7, 163–184.

Abell, D.E. (1980). Defining the Business: The Starting Point of Strategic Planning. Englewood Cliffs, N.J.: Prentice Hall.

Barney, J.B., (1991). Firm Resources and Sustained Competitive Advantage, *Journal of Management*, 17(1), 99–120.

Brannen, M., and Wilson III, J. (1996). Recontextualization and Internationalization: Lessons in transcultural materialism from the Walt Disney Company, *CEMS Business Review*, 1, 97–110.

Carman, J. and Langeard, E. (1980). Growth strategies for service firms, *Strategic Management Journal* 1, 7–22.

Chandler, A.D. (1962). *Strategy and Structure—Chapters in the History of the Industrial Enterprise*. Cambridge: MIT Press.

Chathoth, P.K. and Olsen, M.D. (2005). Lodging Industry Competitive Strategies: Developing a Multidimensional Causal Empirical Model to Test the Relationship between Strategy and Performance, *Tourism and Hospitality Planning & Development* 2(2), 67–86.

Chen, J.J. and Dimou, I. (2005). Expansion strategy of international hotel firms, *International Journal of Business Research*, 58, 1730–1740.

Dess, G.G. and Davis, P.S. (1984). Porter's (1980) generic strategies as determinants of strategic group membership and organizational performance, *Academy of Management Journal*, 27, 467–488.

Dev, C.S. (1988). Environmental uncertainty, business strategy and financial performance: a study of the lodging industry, Doctoral dissertation, Virginia Polytechnic Institute and State University, Blacksburg, Virginia.

Dev, C.S. and Hubbard, J.E. (1989). A strategic analysis of the lodging industry, *Cornell Hotel and Restaurant, Quarterly*, 30(1), 19–23.

Dev, C.S. and Olsen, M.D. (1989). Environmental uncertainty, business strategy and financial performance: an empirical study of the US lodging industry, *Hospitality Education and Research Journal*, 13(3), 171–186.

Harrington, R. (2005). The how and who of strategy making: Models and appropriateness for firms in hospitality and tourism industries, *Journal of Hospitality and Tourism Research*, 29(3), 372–395.

Mathews, V. (2000). Competition in the International hotel industry, *International Journal of Contemporary Hospitality Management*, 12(2), 114–118.

Miles, R.E., Snow, C., Meyer, A., and Coleman, H. Jr. (1978). Organizational Strategy, Structure, and Process, *The Academy of Management Review*, 3(3), 546–562.

Miles, R.E. and Snow, C.C. (1978). *Organizational Strategies, Structure and Process*. New York: McGraw-Hill.

Mintzberg, H. (1987). The strategy concept: The five Ps for strategy, *California Management Review*, 30(1), 11–24.

Peteraf, M.A. (1993). The cornerstones of competitive advantage: A resource-based view. *Strategic Management Journal*, 14(3), 179–191.

Porter, M.E. (1980). *Competitive Strategy*. New York: The Free Press.

Porter, M.E. (1985). *Competitive Advantage: Creating and Sustaining Superior Performance*. New York: The Free Press.

Porter, M. (1996). What is strategy?, *Harvard Business Review*, November–December, 61–78.

Roth, K. and Morrison, A.J. (1992). Business-Level Competitive Strategy: A Contingency Link to Internationalization, *Journal of Management*, 18(3), 473–487.

Schaffer, J.D. (1987). Competitive strategies in the lodging industry, *International Journal of Hospitality Management*, 6(1), 33–42.

Whitla, P., Walters, P., and Davies, H. (2006). Global strategies in the international hotel industry, *International Journal of Hospitality Management*, 26, 777–792.

CHAPTER 6

Corporate-Level Strategies

Learning Objectives

After reading this chapter, you should be able to:

1. Understand corporate strategy and identify its components.

2. Evaluate and identify different approaches to corporate strategy development.

3. Understand how organisations can create and sustain the multibusiness advantage.

4. Appreciate how different corporate strategies could add value to a corporation.

5. Appreciate the complexities of developing corporate strategy at the international level.

Opening Case

The case study organisation is one of the largest international hotel chains operating in more than one hundred countries with its internationally recognised brands. However, the company does not have a culturally diverse workforce at the senior level. It usually recruits executives to the key decision-making positions either from the United Kingdom or the United States. In this respect, it is defined as Anglo-Saxon. Some people argue that the company should get the best from other nationalities involved in the development of an organisation's strategy. Different nationalities holding senior positions in the company would not only facilitate the organisation's understanding about foreign markets but would also help the company to start thinking more in a non-Anglo-Saxon way of doing business in different country markets.

Indeed, in this organisation, the U.S. and U.K. activities have been used as benchmarks for doing business in other country markets. There is an attempt to adapt the brand standards to the local market conditions. However, the main goal is to standardise the products regardless of the differences between home and host country markets. Senior decision makers make it clear that the organisation aims to standardise their products and services like McDonald's and Coca-Cola have done in the fast-food and drink industries, respectively. It is a common belief that the organisation should be aiming for a certain degree of standardisation because international customers have a certain perception of the brand and its attributes. The organisation's purpose is to achieve international standardisation and benefit from economies of scale.

There is also a strong desire to force potential partners for franchise, management contracting, and joint venture partnerships to join the standardised network of operations and contribute to the conformity in hotel product standards. The argument usually put to the potential partners is "We have a proven record, and we will be willing to let you benefit from our internationally recognised brand and infrastructure if you acknowledge our inherent superiority and accept our methods and conditions of doing business." Moreover, a certain degree of standardisation is driven by the belief that markets are converging. It is believed that everything is in transition, and cultures are becoming similar. The phrase "If the United States does this and the United Kingdom accepts this, why doesn't Italy or Spain?" clearly manifests the philosophy of strategy dominance in the organisation.

This corporation's overall strategy is facing strong resistance in different country markets due to fundamental differences in the ways hoteliers do business in different country markets. The cultural distance between the organisation's way of doing business and the intended foreign market exposes a threat for the organisation's international expansion attempts in Europe, including Spain, Italy, and Germany. One of the business analysts criticized the company for being financially driven, short-term-oriented, Anglo-Saxon ignorant of issues in the local market. It is apparent that the organisation should try to adapt to the local market conditions rather than trying to rigidly implement the organisation's traditional strategy and standards that were brought from the United States.

Discussion Questions

1. How would you describe the case study organisation's strategy in international perspective? Please illustrate your answers by providing evidence from the case study.

2. What are the organisation's reasons for adopting such a strategy?

3. Do you think it is a feasible strategy to implement given the cultural distance between different country markets? Why or why not?

4. What are the implications of adopting a home country–oriented strategy? What changes would you recommend?

INTRODUCTION

This chapter introduces corporate strategy and its main elements in H&T organizations. It discusses how different corporate strategies could add value internationally. The chapter also reflects on different approaches to corporate strategy—namely, portfolio and competence approaches. Additionally, the chapter explains how H&T organizations can create and sustain the multibusiness advantage, and it illuminates the complexities of developing corporate strategy at the international level. In particular, it explores the potential roles of the corporate centre and its relationship with strategic business units (SBUs). The core tension between coordination and responsiveness is highlighted and discussed.

CORPORATE STRATEGY

Corporate strategy is a firm's overall approach to gaining a competitive advantage by operating in several businesses simultaneously. Gaining a competitive advantage requires setting a clear purpose for the entire organisation and identifying plans and actions to achieve that purpose. At the corporate and headquarters level, H&T organisations need to constantly ask themselves what business they are in, what business they should be in, what their basic directions are for the future, and what their attitude toward international markets is. For example, during its early years, Holiday Inn's purpose was to meet an unmet customer need: a gap in the market for quality accommodations through developing the Holiday Inn brand in United States. With the saturation of the U.S. market, the company decided to expand overseas. The purpose became a broader concept that included hotel properties, international customers, and employees outside of the domestic boundaries.

Later, the decision to expand overseas was taken by the headquarters at that time, and it was also decided that the company would adopt strategies that were shaped by its home-country culture. Holiday Inn set the standards for the rest of the world. This was the right system that gives people opportunities to build business, and, with hard work and self-improvement, people can achieve great success (Nickson, 1997). Holiday Inn was later acquired, and it is now part of InterContinental Hotels and Resorts. However, as it can be seen in the preceding example, the corporate strategy is the overall goal of an organisation that reflects the core values and sets a direction about what business the company is in or is to be in, and what kind of company it presently is or is going to be.

Developing a competitive corporate strategy requires flexibility in terms of being able to reallocate resources quickly and smoothly among different business units in response to changing market conditions. In order to be able to respond to the dynamism in the business environment and enhance competitiveness, organisations should develop flexible corporate strategies and identify effective means in order to achieve this flexibility. The next section describes different corporate strategies employed by large H&T organisations.

THE PORTFOLIO APPROACH

In today's world, the majority of H&T organisations offer more than only one product or service, and many serve more than one customer group. For example, Easy Jet, a budget, no-frill airline company in Europe, not only carries passengers between different destinations in Europe but also rents cars, runs hotels and cruises, and manages cinemas. There are very good strategic reasons for this: Relying solely on one activity would expose the organisation to the risks of a potential downturn in an area of operations. Easy Jet would still run its operations if for any reason one of its products and services fails or if its customers go elsewhere.

Organisations with multiple product lines or business units must ask themselves how these various products and business units should be managed to boost overall performance. Corporate strategy is concerned with decisions about issues such as how much of our time and money we should spend in our best products and business units in order to ensure their continued success and how much of our time and money we should spend developing new products.

One of the most popular aids to developing a corporate strategy that addresses the preceding issues in a multibusiness H&T organisation is portfolio analysis. Portfolio analysis puts the corporate headquarters into the role of an internal auditor. In portfolio analysis, top management views its product lines and business units as a series of investments that will have a return. In the case of Easy Jet, the chief executive officers of the company view airlines, hotels, cruise business, car rentals, and cinemas as separate business units, and they evaluate the return and contribution of each business line to the overall organisation's performance. The product lines/business units form a portfolio of investments that top management constantly assesses to ensure the maximum return on invested money. Two of the most popular portfolio approaches are Boston Consulting Group (BCG) Matrix and the Directional Policy Matrix (GE-McKinsey).

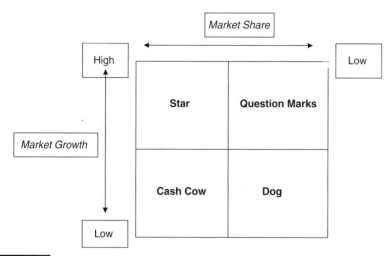

FIGURE 6.1 *The Growth-Share (or BCG) Matrix.*

Using BCG, Figure 6.1 shows the simplest way to portray an organisation's portfolio of investments. Each of an organisation's product lines or business units is plotted on a matrix according to both the growth rate of the industry in which it competes and its relative market share. A unit's relative competitive position (market share) is defined as its market share in the industry divided by that of the largest other competitor. Relative market share is important because in a competitive environment, it is advantageous to be larger than your rivals. Market growth rate is important because markets that are growing rapidly offer more opportunities for sales than markets with lower growth rates. Overall, the matrix assumes that, other things being equal, a growing market is attractive.

The BCG Growth-Share Matrix suggests that as a product moves through its life cycle, it is categorised into one of four types for the purpose of funding decisions:

1. *Stars.* The upper left quadrant represents those products or business units with high market shares operating in high-growth markets. The business units or products in this quadrant may be investing heavily to keep up with growth. However, since they have high market shares, it is assumed that these products will have economies of scale and be able to generate large amounts of cash. Therefore, they are asserted that they will be cash neutral and considered as self-sufficient in terms of investment needs.

2. *Cash cows.* The lower left quadrant shows business units or products with a high market share in low-growth markets. Business units or products in this quadrant are mature, and it is assumed that lower levels of investment will be required. On the other hand, high market share means that the business unit should be profitable. They typically bring in far more money than is needed to maintain their market share.

3. *Question marks.* Sometimes called "problem children" or "wildcats," these are new products with the potential for success but that require much effort and resources for development. Their market shares are less dominant, as competition may be more aggressive. The market growth means that it is likely that considerable investment will still be required, and low market share will mean that such business units or products will have difficulty generating substantial cash. Hence, on this basis, these products are likely to be cash users.

4. *Dogs.* These products or business units have low market share, and since they are in an unattractive industry, they do not have the potential to bring in much cash. Dogs should be either sold off or managed carefully for the small amount of cash they can generate.

EXERCISE

Choose a large H&T organization that operates in different markets with different products or brands. By following matrix in Figure 6.1, analyze each brand's growth and market share, and group each brand accordingly. Please provide specific recommendations for each brand.

The Directional Policy Matrix (GE-McKinsey) is another way to consider a portfolio of business. Originally developed by McKinsey & Co. consultants, this matrix categorises business units or products into those with good prospects and those with poorer prospects. Specifically, it positions business units or products according to (1) how attractive the relevant market is in which they are operating and (2) the competitive strength of strategic business units in that market.

As depicted in Figure 6.2, the GE Business Matrix includes nine cells based on long-term industry attractiveness and business strength/competitive position. In contrast to the BCG matrix, it includes much more data in its two key factors than just business growth rate and market share. For example, at GE-McKinsey, industry attractiveness can be identified by

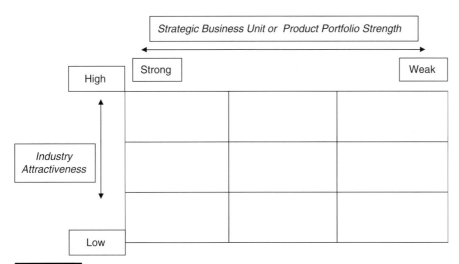

FIGURE 6.2   *The GE Business Matrix.*

PESTE and the five forces analyses (which are explained in Chapter 3), and it includes market growth rate and industry size, among other possible opportunities and threats. Business strength or competitive position includes market share as well as profitability and size, among other possible strengths and weaknesses.

Wheelen and Hunger (2006) propose four steps to plot business units on the GE Business Screen:

1. Select criteria to rate the industry for each product line or business unit. Assess overall industry attractiveness for each product line or business unit on a scale from 1 (very unattractive) to 5 (very attractive).

2. Select the key factors needed for success in each product line or business unit. Assess business strength/competitive position for each product line or business unit on a scale of 1 (very weak) to 5 (very strong).

3. Plot each product line's or business unit's current position on a matrix like that depicted in Figure 6.2.

4. Plot the firm's future portfolio, assuming that present corporate and business strategies remain unchanged. Is there a performance gap between projected and desired portfolios? If so, this gap should serve as a stimulus to review the organisation's current mission, objectives, strategies, and policies.

CORPORATE STRATEGY AND ADDING VALUE

Large organizations that operate in highly dynamic and competitive markets face different types of pressure (Connelly, Hitt, DeNisi, and Ireland, 2007):

1. Pressure to reduce costs

2. Pressure to increase revenue

3. Pressure to increase market share

4. Pressure to be responsive to the markets in which they operate

5. Pressure to innovate and stay relevant

6. Pressure to satisfy shareholders and stakeholders

7. Pressure to transfer information, knowledge, and competencies among business units and functional areas. (p. 564)

In order to respond to some of these pressures, large H&T organizations need to pursue a low-cost strategy at a convenient location where they can benefit from economies of scale. Large H&T organisations may also need to adapt their product and service offerings to the conditions of local markets in order to be able to accommodate the differences between markets. Being able to strike a balance between these competing demands can be seen as a competitive advantage that adds value to the organization's portfolio. The intent is to create and maintain synergy among all business units and functional areas so the whole organization can collectively work together to achieve the corporate goals.

Ghoshal and Barlett (1990) presented frequently used typology to describe the multinational corporate strategy that encompasses the preceding competing demands. They identified four main strategies for the multinational corporations: international, multidomestic, global, and transnational. Table 6.1 outlines the key characteristics of these strategies.

The international strategy creates value through the transfer of core competencies and resources from home to host country markets. An organization pursuing an international strategy adopts a decentralized approach to the management of its resources and capabilities outside the core to subsidiaries (Connelly, Hitt, DeNisi, and Ireland, 2007). In terms of product offerings and marketing, the local networks and competences are exploited, but there is limited adaptation to the local markets. International strategy is appropriate in those markets where although there is a need for local responsiveness it is not urgent. In contrast, a multidomestic strategy strives to

Table 6.1	Multinational Corporation
Organisational Strategy	**Specifications**
International	■ It is a coordinated federation of local companies controlled by a corporate team. ■ The attitude of the parent company tends to be parochial, fostered by superior knowhow at the centre. ■ Its competitive strength relies on its ability to transfer knowledge and expertise to overseas environments that are less advanced.
Multinational or Multidomestic	■ It is a decentralised federation of local companies linked by a web of personal controls. ■ Expatriates from the home country organisation occupied key positions. ■ Its strength lays in a high degree of local responsiveness.
Global	■ The firm makes standardised products and services. ■ It is often centralised. ■ Control of strategic decisions, resources, and information is tight. ■ Its strengths are efficiencies of scale and cost advantages.
Transnational	■ It is made up of a network of specialised or differentiated units. ■ Attention is paid to managing integrative links among local companies as well as with the centre. ■ The subsidiary is a distinctive asset rather than simply an arm of the parent company. ■ Both manufacturing and technology development are located wherever it makes sense, but there is an explicit focus on encouraging local knowhow in order to exploit worldwide opportunities. ■ This organisational form has undoubtedly been held up as possibly the "ideal" organisational structural form.

Source: Adapted from Ghoshal and Bartlett (1990).

achieve maximum local responsiveness. Products and services are designed and developed according to the preferences of local customers (Connelly et al., 2007). The cost of operations according to the expectations could be high, as multidomestic strategy requires leveraging local resources and competencies in each market. Business units are fully responsible and accountable for strategic and operating decisions, as they operate autonomously.

An organisation pursuing a global strategy tends to centralize strategic and operating decisions at the corporate level (Ghoshal and Bartlett, 1990). This strategy also involves standardizing products and services as well as marketing activities in order to benefit from economies of scale. Its strengths are efficiencies of scale and cost advantages. Therefore, the strategy is appropriate when there is a need for cost reduction, and demand for local adaptation is low (Connelly et al., 2007). In the organizations where global strategy is pursued, there is a high degree of cooperation, resource, and competence sharing at the corporate level and learning from the centre (Connelly et al., 2007).

Finally, the transnational strategy aims to strike a balance between lowering costs on one hand and being responsive to local demands on the other. Any organization pursuing this strategy, however, must reconcile conflicting goals: the demand for low cost, which requires global coordination, and the demand for local responsiveness, which requires flexibility and local control (Connelly et al., 2007). Attention is paid to managing integrative links between local companies as well as with the centre in order to resolve this conflict. There is a great deal of sharing knowledge and competences between headquarters and subsidiaries for the company's worldwide operations.

THE CORE COMPETENCE APPROACH

Before we explain the core competence approach for large H&T corporations, we want to refresh your memories about core competencies discussed in Chapter 5. Core competencies are *valuable*, *rare*, *inimitable*, *nonsubstitutable* resources of an organisation that give them a competitive edge in the market. The embedded skills, processes, shadow organisational systems, and culture of an organisation that give rise to the next generation of competitive products are examples of core competencies. A rival might acquire some of the elements that comprise the core competence, but it will find it more difficult to duplicate the more or less comprehensive pattern of internal coordination and learning.

At least three tests can be applied to identify core competencies in a large H&T organisation. First, a core competence provides potential access to a wide variety of markets. Second, a core competence should make a significant contribution to the perceived customer benefits. Third, a core competence should be difficult for competitors to imitate. In the past, corporations could simply point its business units at particular product markets and become world leaders. However, with market boundaries changing ever more quickly, targets are temporary and elusive. In today's dynamic world, the critical task for management is creating products and services that customers need but have not been imagined or experienced yet. This is deceptively a difficult task. Ultimately, it requires radical change in the management of major companies. In particular, it requires top management to oversee the management of core competencies.

Just as they have a portfolio of products and portfolio of businesses, organisations need to manage their portfolio of competencies as well. Most of the time, organisations do not lack the resources to build competencies, but they do lack top management with a vision to build them and the administrative means for assembling resources spread across multiple businesses. Management of core competence is about the organisation of work across business units and the delivery of collective value. Senior managers need to cut across the interests of individual businesses and get them to work toward the achievement of common goals so synergies can be achieved among different business units. They should especially do the following:

- Encourage collective learning within the corporation, especially how to coordinate diverse production skills and integrate multiple streams of technologies.

- Encourage open communication and a deep commitment to working across organisational boundaries by involving many levels of people and all functions across different brands.

For example, world-class research in customer satisfaction and service quality among the customers of an organisation can take place at the corporate level without having an impact on any of the businesses of the organisation. Individuals from different functional areas of an organisation should be able to blend their functional expertise with those of others who carried out research in new and interesting ways in order to benefit from the findings of the project.

According to Prahalad and Hamel (1996), a corporation is like a tree in that it grows from its roots. Core competencies are the roots that nourish core products and engender business units. These scholars believe that senior management should spend a significant amount of its time developing what they called a "corporate-wide strategic architecture." "Strategic architecture" can also be used as a tool in order to decide which core competences to possess or develop. A strategic architecture is a road map of the future that identifies which core competencies to build and their constituent technologies (Prahalad and Hamel, 1996).

First, you must ask yourselves certain questions:

1. How long could we preserve our competitiveness in this business if we did not control this particular core competence?

2. How central is this core competence to perceived customer benefits?

3. What future opportunities would be foreclosed if we were to lose this particular competence?

Second, you use strategic architecture as a template to map out which businesses you are in or you wish to be in and what core competences you already have and/or you need to develop. This template should inform your decision making with regards to the resource allocation priorities to different activities. Such a transparent and consistent approach creates a strong managerial culture, teamwork, a capacity to change, and a willingness to share resources and think long term. Strategic architecture is also a tool for communicating with customers and other external stakeholders. It reveals a broad direction without giving away every step to competitors.

CREATING AND SUSTAINING THE MULTIBUSINESS ADVANTAGE

As explained in Chapter 5, many different views exist on how organisations can create and maintain a competitive advantage. For example, Porter's (1980) five forces industry structure analysis framework and his generic business strategies (cost leadership, differentiation, and focus) are often used to analyze each company's competitive advantage. In some cases, these approaches can be used to analyze each brand's competitive advantage under a corporation. It is assumed that by looking at competition and competitive strategies in an industry, the threat of new entrance and substitutes, and the bargaining power of buyers and suppliers, companies can assess their relative positions in the market. They can then identify their competitive advantage and may choose to follow one of the generic business strategies—cost leadership, differentiation, or focus—in order to gain a competitive advantage.

The research-based view is proposed as an alternative view to analyze the competitive advantage of firms (Barney and Hesterly, 2008). Unlike Porter's positioning view, the resource-based view suggests that a competitive advantage comes from a firm's unique resources. They must be valuable, rare, inimitable, and nonsubstitutable resources possessed both by the corporation and business units, and the corporation should be organised in a way that it can effectively and efficiently exploit these resources (Barney and Hesterly, 2008). Due to globalization and rapid economic, technological, and sociocultural changes, organisations need to be innovative, adaptable, quick, and efficient when using their resources and abilities. Knowledge, experience, and dedication of employees and managers of different business units are often accepted important factors in creating and developing unique resources and competencies. In particular, the kind and degree of coordinated and leveraged skills and knowledge in a global organisation will determine its core capability differentials and its ultimate sustainable global competitive advantage.

Regardless of the approach adopted to sustain and create a competitive advantage, there are issues with which each H&T organisation with multi-business units struggles on the road to developing and maintaining a competitive advantage. There are balances to be struck in the continuing process of developing economies of scale, while at the same time being responsive to the needs of each business unit and its external environment; nurturing diversity while seeking integration; and maintaining flexibility while keeping focused.

Porter (1996) proposes an action program for those organisations with multiple business units to address these issues:

- An organisation should begin to develop a corporate strategy by identifying an existing portfolio of business units in order to find ways to enhance the competitive advantage of existing units.

- It should then select the core businesses that will be the foundation of the corporate strategy. Core businesses are those that are in an attractive industry, have the potential to achieve a sustainable competitive advantage, and have important interrelationships with other business units.

- It should create horizontal organisational mechanisms to facilitate interrelationships among the core businesses. Top management can facilitate interrelationships by emphasising cross-unit collaboration, grouping units organizationally, modifying incentives, and taking steps to build a strong sense of corporate identity.

CORPORATE-LEVEL STRATEGY IN THE INTERNATIONAL PERSPECTIVE

The scope of international strategy is large and involves not only international organisations but also different nations. Some argue that international strategy is a function of a competitive advantage of multinational operations. While reinforcing their competitive advantage or counterbalancing their competitive weaknesses in the international environment, organisations need to consider two central questions: "To what extent are customer needs homogenous worldwide?" and "Can we meet their needs through a standardised one-size-fits-all approach?"

The answers to these questions are vital because standardisation across national markets has an impact on value chain activities. For example, homogenous customer needs may allow economies of scale and a common marketing approach. Heterogeneous needs, by contrast, may require an organisation to adopt different product designs and brand names for each national market. As the managers of the future, you might think that offering globally standardised products will be successful because your organisation will benefit from economies of scale and marketing. On the other hand, you might need to be aware that differences exist among different country markets and consumers in terms of their cultures, values, and styles, so your international strategy should encompass and respond to these differences.

Having recognised the importance of establishing effective mechanisms to coordinate and integrate strategies across national markets, Porter (1990) identified two types of strategies that organisations can follow internationally: multidomestic and global. He defined the multidomestic strategies as country-centred strategies. An organisation exploiting multidomestic strategies will pursue separate strategies in each of its foreign markets. Each overseas subsidiary is strategically independent with autonomous operations and competes independently in different domestic markets. The company enjoys a competitive advantage from a one-time transfer of knowledge from its home base to foreign countries.

The headquarters of the multidomestic company will be responsible for financial and marketing policy and practices, but it will decentralise business strategies and operations. In terms of global strategies, he indicates that an organisation that is exploiting global strategies will see its competitive position in one country as significantly influenced by its position in other countries. An organisation therefore must integrate its activities on a worldwide basis to capture the linkage among countries. The strategy is centralised, but operations may be centralised or decentralised, depending on economies and effectiveness.

Perlmutter (1969) identified four approaches to international strategy: ethnocentric (home country–oriented), polycentric (host country–oriented), regiocentric (regionally oriented), and geocentric (world-oriented). An organisation that pursues an ethnocentric strategy treats foreign markets as an extension of the domestic market. It ascribes superiority to everything from the home country and inferiority to everything foreign. In contrast, a polycentric strategy would acknowledge that there are differences between domestic markets and the other markets, and the strategy would have been designed to maximise local responsiveness. Geocentric strategy recognises that there are global similarities in both cultures and markets. Therefore, it encompasses that best practices are adopted on a global basis and adapted for local conditions where necessary. Regiocentric strategy views region as a potential market, ignoring national boundaries. The organisation develops strategies and organises activities on a regional basis.

These strategies shape the international organisation's mission, governance, and organisation structure. In a hospitality organisation pursuing an ethnocentric strategy, the decision making is centralised in headquarters. Home country standards are applied to evaluate and control the performance of the organisation. You would normally expect a high volume of orders, commands, and advice to the subsidiaries in other countries. People in the home country are developed for key positions everywhere in the world. The implications of a polycentric strategy would have been a decentralised decision-making structure and more authority to the subsidiaries. Home standards would be used to evaluate and control the performance of the subsidiaries. There will be minimal orders and advice to or from headquarters. People of local nationality are developed for key positions in their own country.

In the case of a regiocentric strategy, the decision making is centralised in regional headquarters, and there is a high collaboration among subsidiaries. Standards to measure and control performance are determined regionally. There is little communication to or from headquarters, but it may be high to or from regional headquarters and among countries. Regional people are developed for key positions anywhere in the region.

Geocentric strategy involves collaboration of headquarters and subsidiaries around the world. The standards identified to measure and control performance are universal and local. Communication is both ways from headquarters and subsidiaries and among subsidiaries around the world. The best-qualified people everywhere in the world are developed for key positions everywhere in the world.

SUMMARY

A number of conclusions and summary points can be provided based on the discussions in this chapter:

- Corporate strategy is a firm's approach to how to gain a competitive advantage by operating in several businesses simultaneously.

- Corporate strategy has two main elements: corporate-level strategy and business-level strategy.

- Organizations that operate in a highly competitive international market face two types of pressure: pressure to reduce costs and pressure to be locally responsive to the markets in which they operate. These lead to the development of different corporate strategies: global, international, transnational, and multidomestic.

- There are different approaches to corporate strategy development: the portfolio and the competence approach.

- Portfolio analysis puts corporate and headquarters into the role of an internal auditor. In portfolio analysis, top management views its product lines and business units as a series of investments that will have return.

- T$\eta\varepsilon$ competence approach requires top management to oversee the management of core competencies across business units and manage them to deliver collective value.

- There are balances to be struck in creating and sustaining the multibusiness advantage: developing global economies of scale while being responsive to local environments, nurturing diversity while needing integration, and maintaining flexibility while being focused.

- While reinforcing their competitive advantage or counterbalancing their competitive weaknesses in the international environment, organisations need to consider to what extent customer needs are homogenous worldwide and whether these needs can be met through a one-size-fits-all approach.

STUDY QUESTIONS

1. What is corporate strategy, and why do large H&T corporations need corporate strategy?
2. What is the portfolio approach, and how does this approach group different businesses under a large corporation?
3. How can large H&T corporations create and sustain a multibusiness advantage?
4. What is synergy, and how it can be achieved?
5. What are the definitions of international, multinational, global, and transnational strategies?

REFERENCES AND FURTHER READINGS

Barney, B.J. and Hesterly, S.W. (2008). *Strategic Management and Competitive Advantage*. New Jersey: Pearson Prentice Hall.

Connelly, B., Hitt, A.M., DeNisi, A., and Ireland, D.R. (2007). Expatriates and corporate level international strategy: governing with the knowledge contract, *Management Decision*, 45 (3), 564–581.

Ghoshal, S. and Bartlett, A.C. (1990). *Managing Across Borders: The Transnational Solution*. Random House Business Books, London.

Nickson, D. (1997). "Colourful Stories" or Historical Insight?—A Review of the Auto/Biographies of Charles Forte, Conrad Hilton, J. W. Marriott and Kemmons Wilson, *Journal of Hospitality and Tourism Research*, 21(1), 179–192.

Perlmutter, V.H. (1969). The Tortuous Evolution of the Multinational Corporation, *Columbia Journal of World Business*, 4 (1), 9–18.

Porter, M.E. (1980). *Competitive Strategy: Techniques for Analysing Industries and Competitors*. New York: The Free Press.

Porter, M.E. (1990). *The Competitive Advantage of Nations*. New York: Free Press.

Porter, M.E. (1996). From competitive advantage to corporate strategy. In M. Goold and S.K. Luchs (Eds.), *Managing the Multibusiness Company: Strategic Issues for Diversified Groups*. New York: Routledge.

Prahalad, K.C. and Hamel, C. (1996). The core competence of the corporation. In M. Goold and S.K. Luchs (Eds.), *Managing the Multibusiness Company: Strategic Issues for Diversified Groups*. New York: Routledge.

Wheelen, L.T. and Hunger, D.J. (2006). *Concepts in Strategic Management and Business Policy*. New Jersey: Pearson Prentice Hall.

CHAPTER 7

Network-Level Strategies

Learning Objectives

After reading this chapter, you should be able to:

1. Identify and discuss different motivations for forming strategic alliances.

2. Discuss the advantages and disadvantages of strategic alliances.

3. Evaluate the benefits of franchising, both for franchisors and franchisees.

4. Explain the concept of management contracting and discuss the benefits of this collaboration for both the hotel owners and management companies.

5. Explain the concept of joint venture and identify the benefits of this form partnership for the partners.

6. Evaluate the complexities of strategic alliance formation in the international context.

CONTENTS

Opening Case

When a hospitality and tourism organisation looks for strategic alliance partnerships, it needs to analyse the external and internal environments. Their strategic alliance decisions are influenced by both global economic trends and capital and customer market pressures. Added to these are the influences that exist in the environments of host countries. This case study illustrates how these factors influence an international hotel organisation's choice of forming different strategic alliances. Although its portfolio incorporates different forms of strategic alliances, such as joint ventures, management contracting, and franchising, the organisation is the main driver of the franchising business internationally. Besides franchising, it develops through management contracting, which is another form of nonpartial equity involvement.

The case study company aimed to focus on geographical areas with growth opportunities through which the organisation could create value for its shareholders. The company and analysts pointed out that Europe offers the profitable growth opportunities that the organisation is seeking. It became obvious that economic prosperity, increases in disposable income, and a reduction in the cost of air travel due to liberalisation of the European aviation industry have all resulted in growth in hotel demand in Europe. Moreover, Europe seemed to be a fertile ground, as it generates the highest tourism receipts worldwide. More important, the company has been pushed to expand here due to the maturity of the capital markets in the United States and the organisation's desire to gain brand mass on a country-by-country basis. Analysts have also pointed out that they think the European region should contribute more to the organisation's profitability and do so as quickly as possible.

The organisation perceived Europe as a significant expansion route. However, it has chosen to expand further via franchising and management contracting. The organisation has always been a strong advocator of franchising business internationally, and it continuously looked for partners in order to expand through franchising and benefit from the advantages of employing this business format: fast growth with low risk. The rational reason for choosing to expand via franchising or management contracting can be seen to be as a result of the influence of shareholders and the company's desire to add value to them. International expansion through these strategic alliances provided the security and the fast return that shareholders demand.

Among different markets in Europe, the organisation has its own particular strategic focus: Markets that possess potential in terms of revenue and profit are given more importance. For example, the organisation has set itself the objective of becoming an important force in markets such as the United Kingdom, Germany, Italy, France, and Spain, and these are the markets that have the economic potential for growth. They are among the world's top 12 tourism destinations in terms of the number of visitors.

In addition, the company focuses on markets such as the United Kingdom, Italy, Germany, and Spain and puts large amounts of effort and funding into these countries compared to others. It does not invest unless it is a profitable market and in a region where there is perceived low economic and political risk. For example, most of the organisation's owned and leased properties are in the United Kingdom, Germany, France, and Italy, and the organisation is willing to invest in these markets to accelerate growth. These are the economically stable and growing countries where organisational members believe risk is likely to be low.

On the other hand, the organisation would not be willing to invest in markets such as Russia and Turkey because of the political and economic conditions in these countries. In particular, Russian currency devaluation has a dramatic negative impact on the feasibility of a particular project. Turkey and the Middle East generally are considered to be both economically and politically unstable. In addition, in spite of the economic and political stability in Switzerland, the organisation would not invest in this country because it has strict legal barriers related to human resource issues, particularly related to wage levels, employees' payments, and hiring and firing constraints. Economic and political factors in the host countries, therefore, influence the organisation's choice of using different forms of strategic alliances.

The organisation does not favour direct ownership in countries or markets where there is high political and economic risk and the level of economic development is low. Political instability is a major factor for the wholly owned subsidiaries but may not be a major factor for nonequity modes such as franchising and management contracts. In addition, if the foreign target markets that the organisations plan to enter have high country risk, the organisation will favour strategic alliances with low resource commitments such as franchising and management contracting.

In addition, organisational specific factors, particularly its distinctive characteristics and its members' perceptions of these, can influence their choice of using franchising and management contracting. These are subjective factors that concern an organisation's senior management's perceptions and attitudes toward variables such as branding, central reservation systems, training, management control, and quality. Recognition of the nature of global reservation systems, hotel brands, and international expertise as codified assets supports the organisation's ability to engage in non-equity-based strategic alliance arrangements such as franchising and management contracting.

In the case study organisation, there was an overwhelming view among the organisational members that it is the world's foremost hotel group. Moreover, organisational members emphasised that over the years the organisation has been an active player in the hotel world, particularly as a franchisor, so it has vast expertise and knowledge. These attributes constitute a source of pride among the organisational members. Significantly, this pride seems to be very well grounded. When informants talked about the organisation, they emphasised quality and value, and they believed that the organisation's internationally recognised brands and the support system are "needed and wanted" by the potential franchisees in the market.

Case Study Questions

1. Which factors influence the organisation's choice of using franchising and management contracting?
2. Please group these factors according to internal and external environmental factors.
3. Assess the suitability of international franchising and management contracting for markets such as China and India.

INTRODUCTION

In the preceding chapter, we discuss the extent to which organizations should seek to develop cooperative arrangements when developing strategies. This chapter covers various motivations for entering into a cooperative venture and introduces the advantages and disadvantages of strategic alliances. The chapter also highlights the advantages and disadvantages of different forms of the most popular strategic alliances—namely, franchising, management contracting, and joint ventures in the hospitality and tourism industry. In addition, the chapter explains how the strategic alliances should be formed nationally and in an international context.

STRATEGIC ALLIANCES

The term *strategic alliance* is often defined as an agreement between two or more partners to share resources and knowledge that could be beneficial to all parties involved (Chathoth, and Olsen, 2003). These strategic alliances can be as simple as two companies sharing their technology or marketing resources in order to develop products jointly and market and promote collaboratively. This is a reciprocal relationship in which each partner brings certain strengths, pooling of resources, investments, and risks for mutual gain. In contrast, they can be highly complex, involving many companies located in different countries.

The strategic alliance agreements can also be classified into equity-based or non-equity-based. These agreements range from joint ventures, collaborations, and network arrangements to management contracts, franchising, or licensing and are a result of formal or informal agreements between two or more companies. Various motivations for entering into a cooperative venture include risk reduction, economies of scale, scope and/or learning, market, technology and/or knowledge access, and shaping competition (Chathoth and Olsen, 2003; Crawford-Welch and Tse, 1990). Organisations have specific resource endowments but may also need additional resources to be competitive in particular markets.

Strategic alliances can allow an exchange of tangible assets or intangible capabilities of the firms such as knowledge, skills, financial capital, technical capabilities, managerial capabilities, and other intangible assets such as firm reputation. Less resource-endowed organisations may desire to learn new technical and managerial capabilities, whereas more resource-endowed organisations want to gain knowledge of markets and build relationships to provide access to different markets. Strategic alliances are also intended to maximise market coverage, while also achieving economies of scale and scope and minimizing capital investment.

The first type of alliance occurs at the strategic level of organisations and is exemplified by the growth of consortia-type organisations such as Best Western and Consort. Firms—generally independent operators—are tied together by a common reservation and marketing system. A more complex type of alliance not only brings hotel firms together but also brings other hospitality-related firms, such as travel agencies, as a form of vertical integration. For example, Radisson Hotel company has affiliated with Movenpick Hotel (Swiss), SAS International Hotels (Scandinavian), Park Lane (Hong Kong), Commonwealth Hospitality of Canada, and Pacific Rim Leisure (Australia) in order to better promote its products and services worldwide.

The strength of using strategic alliances as a vehicle of growth is that this approach can rapidly take advantage of the brand recognition of several multinational organisations. Marketing costs can be spread over a larger base, making the effort more efficient and effective through gains in economies of scale. Many of the problems of labour and management expertise are minimised by this growth strategy, as are the problems associated with multicultural differences so often encountered when firms seek to expand into new areas of the world. These partnerships are no longer confined to companies operating in the same industry, and there is an increase in strategic alliances between synergistically related firms such as airlines, car rental, life insurance companies, and lodging corporations.

Those H&T firms involved in strategic alliances seek to achieve organizational objectives better through collaboration than through competition. This results in various mutual benefits. These include higher returns on equity, better returns on investment, and higher success rates. Other benefits include reduction of external environmental and internal uncertainty.

External environmental uncertainty can be overcome partly by reducing demand uncertainty (arising from unpredictability of customers and their behaviour) and partly through reducing competitive uncertainty (caused by competitive interdependence). On the other hand, internal organizational uncertainty can be achieved by reducing operational uncertainty and by gaining access to scarce resources. These all certainly reduce the risk of operations in international markets. A well-managed strategic alliances project helps companies to gain access to those markets that would otherwise be uneconomical. Furthermore, it supports new market entry, as the firms can sidestep governmental restrictions, diffuse new technology, and use existing market leader skills in order to become competent.

Despite having numerous benefits, strategic alliances also have various drawbacks. Alliances provide opportunities to learn new skills and core competencies, but at the same time, alliances create the potential danger of transforming a partner into a competitor. In addition, the dissolution of alliance partnership due to the inappropriate selection of strategic alliance partnership and/or conflicts during the partnerships might result in a poor fit, leading to adverse monetary and strategic effects.

FRANCHISING

Originating in the United States, franchising emerged as a powerful way of facilitating the growth of hospitality organizations. Franchising gives hospitality and tourism industries and organizations an opportunity to form an alliance with partners in different country markets (Lashley and Morrison, 2000). Therefore, from a business perspective, it involves less risk than some other means of expansion, notably direct investment. Grant (1985) defined *business format franchising* as follows:

> *The granting of a license for a predetermined financial return by a franchising company (franchisor) to its franchisees, entitling them to make use of a complete business package, including training, support, and the corporate name, thus enabling them to operate their own businesses to exactly the same standards and format as the other units in the franchised chain. (p. 5)*

Franchising is a partnership between different parties that involves assigning rights by the brand and business system owner (the franchisor) to the franchisee to use the name of the brand and format via a contract. This contract is usually for a fixed period of time with a geographical scope requiring a franchisee to pay an initial up-front fee and thereafter a royalty based on a percentage of actual revenues generated (Taylor, 2000). Franchising offers mutual benefits to both the franchisor and the franchisee. Franchisors prefer franchise partnerships because this business format is seen as a "risk-averse" mode, as it allows fast growth with minimum financial capital input. On the other hand, franchisees benefit from being part of a well-proven and widely recognised brand name and business format associated with managerial assistance and marketing support. Table 7.1 and Figure 7.1 explain this ongoing business relationship of mutual benefits between the franchisor and the franchisee.

Franchising offers the franchisor relatively trouble-free and inexpensive market penetration. This could include not only quicker coverage of a geographical area but also the possibility of penetrating a wider area than would be feasible using existing company resources to support wholly owned and managed properties. In essence, the franchisor is not involved in day-to-day unit problems and therefore needs a relatively small head office staff. Since the day-to-day unit operation is in the franchisee's hands, the franchisee may develop specialist knowledge of the local market, resulting in a better service.

The franchisee benefits from being able to display an established trademark and brand name. Because a franchised product has been used, tested, and proven in a defined market, it saves the franchisee time and cost and minimizes the risk of a new start-up. Another benefit of a franchise is the easy access to the technical and operational expertise from the franchisor. However, there are drawbacks associated with using franchising. Control issues, difficulty in offering adequate support, increased costs, cultural and

Table 7.1	Pros and Cons of Franchising	
	Pros	**Cons**
Franchisor	■ Easier market penetration ■ Access to market exposure and growth ■ Access to local knowledge ■ Saving time in setting up new units ■ Manpower resource allocation by franchisee ■ Sharing legal responsibility with the franchisee ■ Low capital expenditure ■ Personal commitment and motivation ■ Reduced daily involvement	■ Challenges of controlling standardized policies ■ Differing views between franchisor and franchisee about long- and short-term goals ■ Inability to ensure policy of sales maximisation. ■ Losing ownership ■ Dependence on franchisee
Franchisee	■ Designed and tested blueprint operational guidelines ■ A proven track record ■ Initial help and advice in setting up the unit ■ An established name ■ Access to marketing and sales ■ Reduced working capital ■ Support and guidance from franchisor	■ Inflexibility in purchasing decisions ■ Dependence on franchisor for market presence and economies of scale ■ Payments ■ Inflexible rules and procedure ■ Mutual dependence ■ Changes by the franchisor in operating policies and guidelines ■ Too many franchised units in the same region

Source: Developed from Housden (1984) and Maitland (2000).

Franchisor Package
• Trademarks/names
• Copyright
• Design
• Patents
• Trade secrets
• Business know-how

On Going Business Relationship : Mutual Benefits

Franchisee Package
• Initial fee up front
• Continuing franchise fees
• Capital expenditure—plant & equipment
• Recruitment of owner-managers for operations

FIGURE 7.1 *Offerings of Franchisor and Franchisee.*
Source: Adapted from Housden (1984) and Maitland (2000).

language differences, difficulty in assessing local needs, varying governmental regulations, different tax structures, current uncertainties, and difficulty in repatriating royalties are all potential problems (Altinay, 2006).

In addition, franchising entails a high degree of control from the franchisor: being unable to adapt to local tastes and needs without the franchisor's authorisation and payment of a continuing fee. Furthermore, it is quite difficult to ensure that all franchisees retain standard operating methods to achieve uniformity. The franchisor and franchisee may have different objectives regarding turnover and profits, so conflict between the two parties may result. The relationship may also become strained, as franchisees may resent any control by the franchisor (Lashley and Rowson, 2003). When conflicts do occur, however, the franchisor often cannot dismiss the franchisee and is only able to buy the franchisee out. Finally, the franchisor may face competition from the franchisee in the future.

In a franchise partnership, franchisors aim to achieve uniformity across the system by diminishing the likelihood of wide variations in brand standards, which may well lead to dissatisfied customers. On the other hand, franchisees seek autonomy and innovative ways to do business (Connell, 1997). Therefore, in order to create a cooperative environment, franchisors may offer training programmes to franchisees that assist the franchisee to operate in line with the franchisor's guidelines, provide comprehensive details in the franchise manual, and regularly communicate with franchisees.

In addition, franchisors should pay particular attention to the identification and selection of prospective partners in order to avoid the consequences of a possible franchise partnership failure. Improper or poor franchisee recruitment may result in franchisees' lack of initiative, low interest in operations, refusal to follow instructions, and inability to run the system. Franchisors consider a number of selection criteria when recruiting their prospective partners. A franchisee partner should have the financial strength in order to maintain the financial health of the system and a compatible business goal with the franchisor. In addition, there should be a cultural compatibility between the franchise partners. The prospective partner should possess a reasonable level of general business knowledge, including a decent understanding of franchising, hospitality industry experience, and certain personal characteristics like a desire for achievement, self-reliance, and competitiveness in order to be able to contribute to the success of the franchise system.

Franchising can take various forms, but typically it involves satellite enterprises (run by the franchisee) operating under the trade name and business format of a larger organisation (franchisor) in exchange for a continuing fee. Hotel franchising comes in many forms, but the basic premise is that the owner remains in control of the management and property but has the advantages of a large chain in terms of brand name and marketing outreach. The franchisee sets up his or her own business, operating along the lines specified by the franchisor and trading in the product or service previously market tested by the franchisor.

Franchising is an activity that does not necessarily require the conditions of a flourishing economy in order to be successful as long as the product or service that is being franchised is one that meets a demand. Its characteristics, such as facilitating market entry, reducing business failure, utilising economies of scale, and personal motivation of the franchisee, suggest that it is a business method that may be more successful in adverse economic circumstances than traditional forms of businesses.

Franchising has been well appreciated and employed by the hotel industry as well as fast-food chains. Hotel chains see franchising as a form of development strategy, and this is expected to be one of the fastest-growing vehicles for expansion, especially in the international arena. It is particularly attractive for international expansion because it requires substantially less capital than ownership.

There are many different franchising methods (Bradach, 1998). Most U.S.-based international hotel chains have expanded into other countries through one or more of the following methods:

1. *Master Licence:* A company grants a licence to an individual or firm in the target territory so the licencee operates all outlets under its ownership.

2. *Direct Licence:* A franchisor company grants a licence to an operating franchisee and provides direct backup and support.

3. *Branch or Subsidiary Operation:* A firm establishes a direct presence in an area by setting up a branch or subsidiary and then expands into the area by granting franchises and providing direct services to its franchisees.

4. *Joint Venture:* A company establishes a joint company with another one in the target territory and grants the on-site partner licence to operate its own outlets, subfranchises, or both.

A number of factors have encouraged H&T organisations to become internationalised by adopting a franchise system:

■ *Expanded Market:* An increase in population and a rise in disposable income, which can be rapid in some countries, have generated a market for hotel companies. The expanded market size and potential demand of franchised hotels are growing, especially in South East Asia.

- *Demographic Trends:* Trends that favour the increase of franchising in foreign markets are increased educational levels of the local population; technological advancements that facilitate travel overseas; the ability of the younger generation to try new, foreign products; rapid development of rural areas; and concentration of population in urban and industrial areas.

- *Increased Travel and Tourism:* More frequent travel for both business and pleasure has positively exposed successful and fast-growing hotel franchising to visitors worldwide.

- *Quality of Products and Services:* The standardisation process that is used by many franchise concepts has created quality assurance and consumer satisfaction. This is more significant in restaurant franchising. Companies such as Mc Donald's Kentucky Fried Chicken and Pizza Hut are known with a certain level of quality of their products and services.

- *Technological Advancement:* Advanced information technology has led to more sophisticated control and management techniques being implemented in many parts of the world and this has made the concept of a franchise system easier to implement.

MANAGEMENT CONTRACTS

Management contracts can be defined as the management of one company by another, and often, but not always, the two are in different countries. A firm with an established reputation for being an excellent manager will grow by contracting to manage properties for an owner in return for a fee. In the hospitality industry, management contracts have been recognised as one of the quickest forms of expansion strategy with minimal risk (Eyster, 1988). In essence, the rationale behind a management contract is one company managing another's resources with either no or minimal equity. Typically, a management contract involves a three-concerned arrangement in which one company (the operator) agrees with another (the owner) to set up a third (the contract venture) to bring together the operator's expertise and the owner's capital (Eyster, 1993).

Management contract arrangements are favoured in many international settings by international hotel chains such as Hilton and Intercontinental Hotels that have internationally recognised brands and a successful track record of hotel management expertise. A management contract allows hotel chains to establish a presence in different country markets without the investment of ownership. The management contract allows for a separation of ownership and operations. With such an arrangement, the owners act as investors who allow someone else to manage the property.

There are certain things that the owner and the operator have to agree on in a management contract (Eyster, 1997). Typically an owner must agree to the following:

- Provide the property, equipment, furniture, fittings, inventories, and working capital.

- Grant the operator sales and exclusive right to control and operate the property.

- Not interfere with the management of the property, since they have the expertise and responsibility to perform this task.

- Cover the payment of all wages and salaries of employees.

- Carry adequate insurance coverage.

- Pay an agreed contract fee and a percentage of the operator's head office expense, if appropriate.

- Give the operator first refusal on buying the property if the owner sells during the term of contract.

On the other hand, the operator must do the following:

- Select, employ, train, and supervising the staff.

- Install suitable accounting systems and maintain bookkeeping records.

- Negotiate leases and concessions in the property.

- Apply for, obtain, and maintain all licences.

- Negotiate all service contracts.

- Carry out operational purchasing.

- Plan, prepare, and contract advertising and promotion programs.

- Prepare annual budgets.

- Carry out operational purchasing.

- Carry out, at the owner's expense, all necessary repairs, replacements, and improvements.

- Comply with the law.

- Provide the chain's name and central reservation system.

H&T organizations usually choose a management contract because it is a good opportunity to generate more revenue with less risk out of expensively acquired knowledge. Here are some other reasons why an operator might choose to enter into a management contract:

- The operator's expertise is saleable.

- The operator has spare resources, such as management, knowhow, and equipment.

- There is a viable new business that offers low-risk market entry.

- It allows the operator to control the standards of operations.

- The contract can bring additional business in the sale of other goods and services.

From the owner's point of view, the major motivating factor for entering the contract is to acquire expertise or simply to put funds into a profitable project. Here are some other motives:

- Lack of essential and technical management skills that the operator could provide.

- The operator provides technical advice, preopening assistance, marketing support, and management services.

- If the contract is established with an operator who has a good reputation, it can make it easier to obtain financing.

JOINT VENTURES

A joint venture can be defined as the participation of two or more companies in an enterprise in which each party contributes assets, owns the entity to some degree, and shares the risks (Kivela and Leung, 2005; Magnini, 2008). The alliance may be one of equal partners or one where one party is stronger than the other because of the resources or expertise it possesses. Companies enter into joint venture partnerships because they reduce the risk of failure by sharing the burden with a partner, gain rapid market access, and internationally they can have an increase in company and product acceptance by having a local firm serving as the direct interface with the customer.

Joint ventures may permit better relationships with local governments and organizations such as labor unions (Magnini, 2008). Government-related reasons can be the major rationale for joint ventures in less developed countries, particularly if the local partner is the government itself or if the local partner is politically influential. The new venture may be eligible for tax incentives, grants, and government support. The key to a joint venture is the sharing of a common business objective. However, internationally, the issue of an inability to work well with the foreign partner might occur because of the cultural differences. In addition, partners might also feel that they are creating business outlets by the local partner that are in direct competition with the joint ventures. Such a perception might reduce the amount of cooperation and knowledge transfer between partners.

In selecting partners, companies pay attention to the cultural compatibility of the partner. For example, in the case of expanding into Indian and Chinese markets, if you do not have market knowledge, joint venture partnership with a local partner can be a viable option in order to make presence in these markets. However, one needs to pay attention to the cultural differences, including the educational backgrounds and cultural values and how these can be managed between the partners. You might also need to consider the market image, reputation, and the customer association of your partner in order to ensure that the partner has the appropriate competences, support, and service capabilities to add value to your operations internationally.

WHOLLY OWNED SUBSIDIARIES

A wholly owned subsidiary involves the ownership and management of physical facilities for producing goods and services. Hospitality organizations might choose to set up their businesses either from scratch or by acquiring another organization where an organization develops its resources and competences by taking over another organization. Regardless of the route taken, a wholly owned subsidiary enables closeness to the customer and thus improves market responsiveness and the ability to assess future opportunities. It also helps organizations to create a unified strategy and objectives on a worldwide basis. On the other hand, it has the disadvantage of creating heavy fixed expenses and start-up costs. There are also problems associated with managing local operations if you do not possess market knowledge and experience.

Recent years have seen a significant growth in the amount of direct investment and the number of acquisitions by hospitality organizations. These approaches to growth allowed them to buy a quick presence, market share, and expertise. For example, in 2001, InterContinental Hotels set itself the objective of becoming an important force in markets such as the United Kingdom, Germany, Italy, France, and Spain, and these are the markets that have economic potential for growth. They are among the world's top 12 tourism destinations in terms of the number of visitors:

- The United Kingdom is well known for providing the highest operating margins and occupancy rates.

- France is the world's largest tourism destination.

- Spain is the world's number two destination and generates the strongest REVPAR growth in Europe.

- Germany is Europe's number two hotel market and the world's largest generator of international travel.

- Italy is the largest hotel market with the lowest brand penetration.

Bass Company (now called InterContinental Hotels and Resorts), which used to be in the brewery business, managed to become a global player in the hospitality industry in the late 1990s and early 2000s by first acquiring Holiday Inns, which brought entrepreneurial flair and negotiating skills related to franchising as well as a wider knowledge of the international hotel scene. Second, InterContinental Hotels helped Bass to complete its brand portfolio by including an upscale brand. However, with acquisitions, organisations may face the risk of misjudgment in terms of cultural compatibility and fit, and also premium prices may have to be paid.

STRATEGIC ALLIANCE FORMATION IN THE INTERNATIONAL CONTEXT

A strategic alliance partnership is often referred to as a "marriage." Improper partner selection may not only prove to be a bad fit, but it would also result in increased management conflicts, slow decision-making processes, and a lack of communication. Moreover, it may also give rise to issues pertaining to reduced sales volume and profit and would hamper overall implementation of operative strategy. In order to avoid these issues internationally, it is essential to consider critical factors such as selective matching of partners, information sharing, role specification, ground rules, and exit provisions between partners. In addition, the parties involved must develop elements of trust, fairness, flexibility, commitment, open communication, and compatibility both before and after the establishment of the partnership.

Companies sometimes enter into alliances without analysing all of the possible options. It is essential that businesses should have a well-executed plan that includes requirements, expectations, and benefits. In the same manner, the selection of a partner for the alliance should also be well thought out. It is important that the strategic alliance partner be selected based on his or her expertise in operations and cultural fit in the firm.

In their study, Mendleson and Polonsky (1995) proposed a three-step process of partner selection. The first stage involves establishing an alliance objective. There are many reasons why a firm decides to enter into an alliance. The firms may have different objectives—for example, develop a new product or create public awareness for the firm's actions or the development-focused markets. Each firm's situation will result in having a different alliance objective. Thus, a clear understanding about the objectives to be achieved sets the basis for the alliance process.

The second stage of the strategic alliance formation process involves determining appropriate alliance partner characteristics such as a credible local and international reputation, a sound knowledge base, or a good understanding of the business environment. Different strategies will require that the alliance partner possess specific characteristics and abilities. Thus, the firms that are entering into the partnership must determine what capabilities and characteristics an alliance partner must bring to the alliance. Finally, the process of partner selection is complete only after identifying the appropriate partner. There may be number of potential partners available, but some may be considered undesirable. The firm must ensure that the future partner can assist in achieving its objectives.

Lorange and Roos (1991) identified five steps that lead to the selection of an appropriate partner in a strategic alliance. This framework suggests that the formation of a successful strategic alliances involves a clearly laid down internal formation process. This process starts with the firm's own assessment of its needs, wants, and objectives and leads to the initial agreement between parties. These are the key stages of the process:

1. Formulate the firm's strategy

2. Develop a partnership benchmark

3. Eliminate undesirable business sectors

4. Select promising business sectors

5. Choose from potential candidates

This five-step model can be used for a more detailed assessment of prospective alliance partners in relation to the company's strategy and the sectors of operations. The choices and needs involved when selecting a specific framework or selection process depend mainly on the strategic alliance negotiation team, who must use these analyses—which may differ in different organizational contexts—when making their choices.

Pett and Dibrell (2001) proposed a business model of a strategic alliance formation. This model has a long-term orientation and requires organisations to go through a series of stages before making any long-term commitments. Organisations pass through four different stages: exploratory, recurrent, relational, and outcome. The exploratory stage involves the initial process of bringing together two or more firms in order to enable them to assess one another's strengths and weaknesses. This stage also deals with issues such as the assessment of national cultures and political, economic, sociocultural, and technological scanning. Once the initial agreements are made, the organizations then move to the recurrent stage. During the recurrent stage, short-term arrangements are made in order to evaluate the risks and motives of participating organisations, and the organisations engage in a number of trust development strategies. Once the element of trust is established and the risk is assessed, organisations move to the relational contract stage and seek a longer-term alliance. Finally, the outcome stage results in the organisations choosing a partner with mutual goals and expectations. This stage can also lead to a failure in alliance formation when organisations realise there is no meeting of the minds in their long-term goals and expectations.

Organisations consider a number of selection criteria in selecting their strategic alliance partners in international collaborations. Gerringer's (1991) typology of partner-task-related criteria highlights the importance of considering both a prospective partner's characteristics and capabilities. Partner-related selection criteria are the potential candidate's qualifications that are not specific to the type of operation but rather affect possible risks. More specifically, they include what are called "intangible" traits, such as business philosophy, reliability, motivation, commitment, and intellectual property protection approach, as well as some general characteristics like experience, reputation, and political connections (Cavusgil and Evirgen, 1997). Task-related selection criteria refer to those qualifications that are relevant for the venture's viability in terms of its operational requirements (Cavusgil and Evirgen, 1997:78). Hence, these variables are specific to operational resources and skills related to the venture. They include financial, marketing, organisational, production and resource and development resources, and customer service. In the case of international strategic alliances, knowledge of local markets, access to distribution channels, access to links with major buyers, and access to information about the local culture are also important skills.

SUMMARY

This chapter presented an analysis of the different types of network-level strategies:

- The highly competitive and volatile nature of today's global environment motivates organisations to seek alliances with other partners.

- In order to cope with an increasingly saturated and competitive operating environment, H&T organisations are joining forces to ensure that they harness the necessary resources, both financial and nonfinancial, to penetrate the marketplace.

- Franchising is the most popular strategic alliance among H&T organisations. It also allows the franchisors to diversify the risk and to establish economies of scale.

- Management contracting is another form of a strategic alliance that requires little or no capital input from an H&T management company. H&T organisations choose a management contract because there is a good opportunity to generate more revenue with less risk out of expensively acquired knowledge.

- Forming strategic alliances in the international context requires understanding the expectations, the culture of the partners, and the business context in which organisations operate.

STUDY QUESTIONS

1. What are the reasons for forming strategic alliances?
2. Discuss the benefits of franchising both for franchisors and franchisees.
3. What is a management contract, and what are the benefits of this collaboration for both the owners and the management companies?
4. What is a joint venture, and what are the benefits of this form of partnership for the partners?
5. What are the challenges of forming strategic alliances in an international context?

REFERENCES AND FURTHER READINGS

Altinay, L. (2006). Selecting partners in an International Franchise Organisation, *International Journal of Hospitality Management*, 25, 108–125.

Altinay, L. and Wang, C. (2006). The Role of Prior Knowledge in International Franchise Partner Recruitment, *International Journal of Service Industry Management*, 12(5), 430–443.

Bradach, L.J. (1998). *Franchise Organisations*. Harvard Business School Press, Boston.

Cavusgil, T.S. and Evirgen, C. (1997). Use of expert systems in international marketing: An application for co-operative venture partner selection, *European Journal of Marketing*, (31)1, 73–86.

Chathoth, K.P. and Olsen, M. (2003). Strategic alliances: a hospitality industry perspective, *International Journal of Hospitality Management*, (22), 419–434.

Connell, J. (1997). International hotel franchise relationships—UK franchisee perspective, *International Journal of Contemporary Hospitality Management*, 9/5/6, 215–220.

Crawford-Welch, S. and Tse, E. (1990). Merger, acquisitions and alliances in the European hospitality industry. *International Journal of Contemporary Hospitality Management*, 2 (1), 10–16.

Eyster, J.J. (1988). Sharing Risks and Decision Making: Recent Trends in the Negotiation of Management Contracts, *Cornell Hotel and Restaurant Administration Quarterly*, May, 43–55.

Eyster, J.J. (1993). The revolution in domestic hotel management contracts, *Cornell Hotel and Restaurant Administration Quarterly*, 34(1), February, 16–27.

Eyster, J.J. (1997). Hotel management contracts in the U.S., *Cornell Hotel and Restaurant Administration Quarterly*, 38(3), June, 21–34.

Fulop, C. and Forward, J. (1997). Insights into franchising: a review of empirical and theoretical perspectives, *The Service Industries Journal*, (17)4, 603–625.

Gerringer, J.M. (1991). Strategic determinations of partner selection criteria in international joint venture, *Journal of International Business Studies*, (22)1, 41–61.

Grant, C. (1985). *Business Format Franchising: A System for Growth*. Economist Intelligence Unit.

Housden, J. (1984). *Franchising and Other Business Relationships in Hotel and Catering Services*. London: Heinemann.

Kivela, J. and Leung, L. (2005). Doing business in People's Republic of China, *Cornell Hotel and Restaurant Administration Quarterly*, (26)2, 125–152.

Lashley, C. and Morrison, A. (Eds.) (2000). *Franchising Hospitality Services*. Butterworth Heinemann, Oxford.

Lashley, C. and Rowson, B. (2003). Divided by a common business? Franchisor and franchisee relationships in the pub sector, *Strategic Change*, (12)5, 273–286.

Lorange, P. and Roos, J. (1991). Why some strategic alliances succeed and others fail, *Journal of Business Strategy*, (12)1, 25–30.

Magnini, P.V. (2008). Practicing effective knowledge sharing in international hotel joint ventures, *International Journal of Hospitality Management*, 27, 249–258.

Maitland, I. (2000). *Franchising—a Practical Guide for Franchisers and Franchisees.* Chalford: Management Books.

Mendleson, N. and Polonsky, M.J. (1995). Using strategic alliances to develop credible green marketing, *Journal of Consumer Marketing*, (12)2, 4–18.

Pett, T.L. and Dibrell, C.C. (2001). A process model of global strategic alliance formation, *Business Process Management*, (7)4, 349–364.

Taylor, S. (2000). An Introduction. In C. Lashley and A. Morrison (Eds.), *Franchising Hospitality Services.* Butterworth Heinemann, Oxford.

PART IV

The Strategy Process

This part provides discussions about the strategy process and consists of three chapters on strategic planning or strategic intent, strategy formation, and strategy implementation, respectively. These three topics are not distinct subjects. In other words, they are not phases or stages that can be looked at and understood individually. They are strongly linked, and they greatly overlap. We include these topics because they have all been the subject of ongoing debate.

CHAPTER 8

Strategy Formation—
Strategy Formulation and
Implementation

Learning Objectives

After reading this chapter, you should be able to:

1. Define *strategy formation*: strategy formulation and implementation.

2. Discuss the evaluation of different approaches to strategy formation.

3. Evaluate assumptions of different schools of thought about strategy formation.

4. Comment on strategy formation in the international context.

Opening Cases

Case A

After working as an assistant manager for two years, Rebecca Learner was promoted to the manager position. She did not have a degree from a university, but she had over 15 years of experience in the restaurant industry. On her first day as manager, she met with the three assistant managers and all of the frontline employees to discuss ways they could take the restaurant forward. Some of her frontline employees expressed that customers often complained about several things such as hygiene, portion sizes, the appearance of the restaurant, employee uniforms, high labor turnover, and outdated menu items. Rebecca also asked customers what they liked and did not like about the restaurant. Taking all of the comments and suggestions into consideration, she started working with her frontline employees and managers on specific initiatives. They introduced new menu items, some of which were well received and others not so successful. They changed the tablecloths and plates, but the customers did not particularly like them, so they had to change them again. The employees were very happy with the new uniforms. Rebecca managed to get raises for several employees, and when business was slow, they spent time training new employees. They ran TV, newspaper, and radio ads and distributed $10 discount coupons. They later realized that their promotion efforts did not work well on TV and radio, so they decided to concentrate on only one TV channel and two radio stations that seemed to generate more business for the restaurant. She further realized that giving a $10 discount coupon was not beneficial for the restaurant, since this initiative attracted a different customer profile that was not profitable for the restaurant. Surprisingly, she also realized that one particular assistant manager's comments and suggestions were not always helpful. It was apparent that this assistant manager had a personal agenda and clear intentions. In other words, he was not happy that Rebecca had become the manager. After working as the manager for a year, Rebecca was very pleased with the improvements in the restaurant since she took over. Profits were up by 20 percent compared to the previous year, their customer satisfaction ratio was higher than ever before, and they had many more repeat customers. In addition, they managed to reduce their labor turnover substantially. Rebecca and her team were successful in delivering very good business results. Her regional manager was particularly impressed with the results and asked Rebecca to prepare a presentation on her strategic plans since she started working as the restaurant manager.

1. How do you describe Rebecca's management style?
2. Did Rebecca have a formal strategic plan when she first started working as a restaurant manager?
3. What can we learn from this case?

Case B

After successfully completing his master's degree at a leading hospitality school, David Park joined Quality Hotels Group and worked for several hotel units. After working several years, he became the hotel general manager of Starr Inn. Following his strategic management professor's recommendations and several strategic management textbooks, he first analyzed both the external and internal environments and developed a detailed strategic plan for his hotel. He shared the strategic plan with his management team and asked them to follow the specific instructions provided and to implement the strategic plan so the hotel could achieve all of the objectives (mainly financial) that David had set. Under his leadership, the hotel followed the strategic plan and achieved its objectives. Every year, David updated his strategic plan, and his managers and employees implemented it. Starr Inn was the most successful hotel unit for the last three years in terms of key performance measures. After his great success at Star Inn, David was promoted to vice president of strategic planning of the Quality Hotels Group. His success at Starr Inn impressed his executives, and they promoted him to this position so he could develop and implement a strategic plan for the whole company. The hotel group had over 150 hotels in five countries. At the general hotel managers meeting, David talked to all of the hotel general managers about the importance of strategic planning, and he shared the hotel group's vision, mission, overall strategic goals, and objectives that he developed. He further explained what each hotel unit needed to do to participate in this strategic planning process. He asked each hotel manager to develop a strategic plan for his or her hotel unit, explain briefly how they could do it, and provided a 300-page strategic planning manual. During and after the annual general managers meeting, he could see that hotel managers, particularly from the home country, were familiar with the strategic planning process, and they seemed to be supportive. However, David learned that the managers from the other three countries were indeed not very familiar with strategic planning practices, and the hotel group had a decentralized organizational structure where hotel managers could operate their business any way they wanted as long as they delivered good results. In other words, the group gave them the freedom to develop and implement their own strategies.

During the next year, David traveled extensively to talk about the importance of the strategic planning process for the hotel group and worked with each hotel general manager on developing a vision, a mission, and a strategic plan for each hotel unit. Although he had a standard format for developing and implementing a strategic plan, he noticed that each hotel general manager approached this process differently. Some hotel general managers developed a strategic plan by themselves and then handed it over to their subordinates for implementation. Some hotel general managers formed a strategic planning committee to work on the strategic plan, whereas some worked with only one or two managers (mainly finance and operations). Some hotels produced a strategic planning document about 200 pages long, whereas other plans were only 10 pages. Many hotel managers complained about this process and perceived it as a waste of time. Some managers even complained to the CEO of the company that David was interfering with hotel units' operations too much.

The CEO of the company asked David to give the hotel general managers more freedom and flexibility in this process. David asked his CEO to centralize the organizational structure of Quality Hotels Group, but the CEO was not very supportive of David's suggestions. During his visits to hotel units, particularly outside the home country, David realized that hotel general managers found it difficult to apply some of the strategic management tools and models such as PEST, SWOT, industry structure analyses, and generic business strategies into their given context. They claimed that these tools had limitations in terms of understanding and analyzing complexities in the business environment. Hotel managers suggested that rather than relying on these tools, they also needed to collect informal comments and suggestions from customers, frontline employees, supervisors, and hotel managers. Initially, David did not agree with them, but after they provided specific examples, he agreed that they should also incorporate these comments into their strategic plans. The external environment and the industry structure in each country were very different, and often changes happened in the general and task environments so the strategic plans developed by hotel units were not always appropriate or were outdated. Therefore, hotel managers often questioned the top-down strategic planning practices. On the other hand, David claimed that it was working for many hotels, particularly in three other countries, and the reason why it was not successful in two countries was that the hotel managers did not believe in it. The CEO of the company told David that they could perhaps be flexible and combine both top-down and bottom-up approaches to strategic management. He claimed that they could try to start with more of a top-down or bottom up approach, depending on the situation or country, and modify their strategies along the way.

The Quality Hotels Group grew from 150 hotels to 400 hotels in only two years. Their performance in terms of profit, occupancy ratios, labor turnover, and customer satisfaction ratios has been impressive. Many executives and managers believed that David greatly contributed to the company and had an important role in the company's growth and success. For the last two months, David has been working with the CEO on developing a new hotel brand that focuses on families. However, the CEO decided to retire for personal reasons, and the new CEO did not approve David's new brand development project. For the last several years, competition in the market has been intense, and several countries suffered an economic recession. The recession in the home country and rising oil prices worldwide created major concerns for the hotel industry globally. The new CEO asked David to attend the hotel development and investment conference in New York. At the conference, David met several executives from a larger international hotel group. They had informal discussions about how both companies were doing and in which countries they were operating. During these discussions, it became clear that the larger hotel group was not very strong in the countries where Quality Hotels Group was in business.

One month after the conference, the larger hotel group made an offer to acquire the Quality Hotels Group, which the owners happily accepted. The larger hotel group then formed a committee to work on how the Quality Hotels Group could be consolidated with the larger hotel group. The committee suggested that the strategic planning and development department at the Quality Hotels Group needed to be eliminated, since the parent company already had a similar department. David was invited to the head office and informed that his department was going to be eliminated. While he was packing up his office, he thought about his years of hard work and efforts on developing plans and strategies for the hotel group. Certainly, he never planned and expected this outcome.

After David left the company, he applied for several senior management positions at other hotel companies, but his applications were not successful because of the poor economy. One day he saw an ad that a nearby hotel unit that he was familiar with was for sale. He remembered the brand development project that he worked on at the Quality Hotels Group, and he believed that the hotel unit could easily be renovated, and new amenities could be installed. He had enough money for the down payment, and with financing from a bank, he bought the hotel and gradually renovated it. It took him one year to reach the break-even point, but after that, business picked up, and he used all of his connections from the Quality Hotels Group to promote his hotel. During the next four years, he bought four other hotels in the region and created his own hotel brand.

1. How do you describe Rebecca's management style?
2. Did David ever plan to have his own hotel company?
3. What can we learn from this case?

INTRODUCTION

The evolution of strategic management has been influenced by many disciplines, such as biology, history, physics, mathematics, psychology, anthropology, economics, urban planning, political science, and military history (Mintzberg, Ahlstrand, and Lampel, 1998). As the strategic management field has evolved, different views on strategic management have emerged on its nature and characteristics. Since the 1980s, scholars have reviewed strategic management literature and recognised groups of authors who share similar views about strategy and strategic management and how strategic decisions should be formulated and implemented. A number of terms have been used for each trend or development, such as *pattern, method, view, approach,* or *schools of thought.*

This chapter discusses how strategy formulation and implementation (called strategy formation hereafter) is viewed by different schools of thought or approaches in the strategic management field. We will critically evaluate each view and offer suggestions for developing and implementing strategies.

STRATEGY FORMATION—STRATEGY FORMULATION AND IMPLEMENTATION[1]

Strategy formulation involves understanding the underlying bases that guide future strategy, generating strategic options for evaluation and selecting the best options among them (Johnson, Scholes, and Whittington, 2008). Strategy implementation addresses the issue of how to put a formulated strategy into action or practice with limited time and resources (Alexander, 1991). Although strategy formulation and implementation are defined separately and perceived as separate areas, in recent years, strategy formulation and implementation have now been seen as a whole process rather than separate activities. Therefore, it is recommended that they should not be defined alone or separated from each other (Mintzberg, 1994; Mintzberg et al., 1998; Okumus, 2003). In other words, the four main elements of strategic management—strategy analysis, strategy formulation, strategy implementation, and strategy control—are not mutually exclusive; in fact, they are interdependent and dynamic. Therefore, the term *strategy formation* is used here to refer to both strategy formulation and implementation as a single unit (Mintzberg et al., 1998). The next section will look at the different schools of thought of strategy formation.

Schools of Thought in the Strategic Management Field

In the early days, the main emphasis was on the importance of planning, and the terminology used for this approach was the planning school. From the

---

[1] This section is primarily derived from Okumus, F. (2000), Strategy Implementation: A Study of International Hotel Groups, Unpublished Doctoral Thesis, Oxford Brookes University, Oxford, United Kingdom, and Okumus, F. and Roper, A. (1999). A Review of Disparate Approaches to Strategy Implementation in Hospitality Firms,' *Journal of Hospitality and Tourism Research,* 23 (1), 20–38.

mid-1970s, the importance of learning has been recognized, and this approach has been called the learning, incremental, or emergent approach. After observing the limitations of previous approaches, it was decided that there was really no "one best way" to develop and implement strategies. It was decided that the most appropriate way to develop and implement strategies would depend on the situation. This approach has been called the contingency school. Scholars such as Mintzberg and colleagues (1998) and Richardson (1994) combined these three schools of thought under one single dimension called the configurational, or comprehensive, school of thought. However, Mintzberg and Quinn (1996) and Stacey (1996) claimed that even this view has limitations, and they proposed that one should look beyond configurations and evaluate the complexities and dynamics of the strategy process. These authors called this final approach the complexity view (Stacey, 1996). The implications of each school on the process of strategy formation are reviewed and evaluated in the following sections.

The Planning Approach

The planning approach is the oldest and most influential approach in the strategic management field (Whittington, 2001). Its development goes back to the late 1960s, beginning with the writings of Ansoff (1965), Andrews (1971), Chandler (1962), and Sloan (1963). This approach views strategy formation as the outcome of sequential, planned, and deliberate procedures. According to this view, strategic planning consists of four separate elements: analysis, strategy formulation, strategy implementation, and control/monitoring. This approach gives more emphasis to the formal analysis of the issues in both the external and internal environments. It is assumed that with precise calculations, techniques, and analysis, planning can make the external environment more predictable so companies can develop and implement successful strategies to respond to changes in the external environment. Developing strategies or strategic decisions by following strategic planning principles and utilizing PESTE analysis, Porter's Industry Structure Analysis, and SWOT analysis are considered the primary responsibilities of corporate offices, senior executives, or specialised departments such as the strategic planning department or the corporate strategic planning office. Because they are considered to be experts in this area, they can see the whole picture and are better able to analyse the situation than those at lower levels. The issue of implementation is seen as purely tactical, and it is an activity that is carried out by middle and lower management levels (Okumus and Roper, 1999).

In other words, strategies or strategic decisions are developed by senior executives, and apart from minor modifications, these executives should not deal with the implementation part. The role of middle managers and supervisors is to implement the developed strategies. This approach further advocates well-specified plans with clear objectives, timetables, budgets and resource allocations, clear lines of responsibility, limited participation in strategy development, and minimum discretion for all levels of implementers. Finally, profit maximization, cost cutting, high market share, and other tangible outcomes are the ultimate aims of the strategy formation process.

The Learning or Emergent Approach

The learning approach does not see strategy formation as a neat, sequential, and rational process. This school of thought suggests that strategies often emerge from the pragmatic processes of trial and error and that they are often developed and executed in an incremental, trial-and-error way, mainly by middle managers, and that the strategy formulation and implementation stages often overlap (Johnson, 1987; Mintzberg, 1994; Pettigrew and Whipp, 1991; Quinn, 1980). For example, Mintzberg and colleagues (1998) describe it as "crafting" or "emergent" strategy and state that successful companies, as in the case of Honda (Pascale, 1984), achieved their position without going through the process of analysis, formulation, and implementation for which the planning approach implies. When we analyze how Southwest Airlines has started and become one of the most successful airlines in the United States, it is evident that the company did not achieve this success through strategic planning but instead by responding to emerging issues in an incremental way and learning from their experiences.

This approach values the significance of power distribution, politics, and organisational culture in the strategy formation process. Having rational, mainly financial, objectives may not always be practical, as companies often need to consider intangible aspects of the process such as internal politics and culture (Whittington, 2001). This is because organisations are often political entities, comprised of shifting coalitions and powerful internal and external interest groups who may have conflicting demands and objectives (Mintzberg et al., 1998). Therefore, it is not always straightforward to develop and implement strategies without considering internal politics and power structures (Pettigrew and Whipp, 1991). In addition, the strategies should be appropriate to the company's values, traditions, and past experiences, as the culture of an organization (Johnson, 1987) or defensive routines (Argyris, 1989) can be slow or can stop the strategy formation process. Previous research studies (De Geus, 1988; Johnson, 1987) support the appropriateness of the 'learning' school where the strategy formation processes are found to be interactive and incremental rather than rational and top-down.

The Contingency Approach

The contingency school of thought suggests that successful strategies are not developed and implemented by a simple or single set of factors. Instead, their successes depend on many factors in the internal and external environments of the company. This approach was developed as a reaction to the idea of "one best way management." According to Child (1984), the contingency view relates to the design of an effective organisation that must cope with the contingencies of certain factors, such as environment, technology, resources, people, and other elements in a situation in which the firm operates. In other words, the effectiveness of the strategy formation process depends on how multiple factors interact in a situation, and there may be different ways to approach the same issue, depending on the situation. Berman (1980) suggests that strategies can be carried out more effectively if they are chosen to match the situation, especially the extent of agreement about the strategy, the degree of capacity and coordination of the strategy formation process, and the stability/complexity of the environment and the organisation. Put another way, the process of strategy formation cannot be uniform for all situations, invariable over time, and homogeneous across organizational levels, and therefore executives and managers should find suitable ways and switch them when necessary to deploy their strategies successfully.

The Configurational Approach

Attempts were made to combine all of the previous strategic management schools of thought into one single perspective, which is called the configurational view (Johnson et al., 2008; Mintzberg et al., 1998; Okumus and Roper, 1999; Richardson, 1994). It was intended to eliminate the disadvantages of the previous approaches and offer a holistic view. The main difference between the contingency approach and the configurational approach is that the contingency view suggests "it all depends on the situation in the strategy formation," whereas the configurational view is concerned with "combining all previous approaches together." Mintzberg and colleagues (1998) stated the following:

> *The process of strategy making can be one of conceptual designing or formal planning, systematic analysing or leadership visioning, cooperative learning or competitive politicking, focusing on individual cognition, collective socialisation, or simple response to the forces of the environment; but each must be found at its own time and in its own context. In other words, the schools of thought on strategy formation themselves represent particular configurations. (pp. 305–306)*

The configurational approach views the strategy formation process as an episodic process. In other words, it suggests that all of the preceding approaches may be combined and used together, although sometimes one approach may be more appropriate for a certain period of time and another may become more important at another time (Mintzberg et al., 1998). Unlike the previous approaches, this view advocates that in a company, managers at every level of management (top, middle, and lower) should participate and cooperate in both formulating and implementing strategies. Considering key factors in the strategy formation process, such as strategy, structure, leadership, culture, resources, communication, and other variables, as a whole is the key to developing and implementing successful strategies and achieving desired objectives.

Key factors make sense in terms of the whole, so there is no use getting just one or two elements right. Because they are all interdependent, they must all fit together and be consistent with one another. Success can only be achieved through appropriate patterns of action, positions, and performances, which should all fit together and support one another (Mintzberg et al., 1998). Therefore, in order to develop and implement strategies, a number of certain factors should fit together and a comprehensive strategy formulation and implementation framework is needed to analyse and evaluate the fit and interactions among the key factors. To sum up, the central idea of the configurational approach is that focusing on only one or two factors is not enough, and therefore a holistic view should be taken into consideration when understanding and evaluating strategy formation in tourism and hospitality organizations.

The Complexity Approach

This view suggest that organisations are adaptive systems that take the form of nonlinear negative and positive feedback loops that connect the individuals, groups, functions, and processes in an organisation to one another, and connect an organisation to other systems in the environment (Levy, 1994; Stacey, 1996; Theys, 1998). Due to these nonlinear feedback loops, any small change or development, both within and outside the organisation, can have significant and unexpected implications for the firm; this is often entitled the "butterfly effect" (Stacey, 1995). In terms of strategy formation, this means that managers need to identify and evaluate the emerging patterns continuously within and outside the company and then develop and implement strategies rapidly. In addition, they also need to consider the implications of the strategy formation process, not just for a specific part of the company but also for other functional areas and on customers, competitors, and all other stakeholders (Glass, 1996; Stacey, 1996).

This view suggests that successful companies operate in a state of nonequilibrium or "bounded instability," that challenges the status quo continuously and tries to change the external and internal environments (Stacey, 1996). It is perhaps not a good idea for companies to aim to achieve and maintain a "fit" between their external environment and their internal resources, since things are always changing and evolving. Stacey (1995) further suggests that companies should attempt to develop diverse cultures, informal working groups, and networks and allow for the emergence of internal conflicts among departments and groups. These should help challenge and change existing formal and mental models, modes of thinking, and structures and subsequently allow the complexities and dynamics of the strategy formation process to be better understood. Eventually, this will allow, and perhaps force, the company to invent and create new ways of developing and implementing strategies. It is also suggested that there might be some regularities and order in chaos, and therefore managers should look for emerging patterns in chaos and complexities (Stacey, 1996; Theys, 1998).

Contrary to the previous approaches, this view does not recommend having definite aims and objectives for the long-term future. Instead, it is suggested that managers need to understand, evaluate, and interpret the complexities and dynamics of the situation as an ongoing process and respond to emerging patterns rapidly if they are to be successful. This may require continuous modification of a company's vision, goals, objectives, structure, and culture to incorporate new and relevant values and norms (Glass, 1996; Stacey, 1996).

Evaluating the Five Approaches

The differences and similarities among these five schools of thought in relation to strategy development and implementation are summarized in Table 8.1. In reality, there is a hierarchical and integrative relationship among these schools of thought in the strategic management field, and they are rarely found in their pure form (Chaffee, 1985; Mintzberg et al., 1998; Okumus and Roper, 1999). The development of these approaches should be interpreted as a chronological evolution of the strategic management literature, as scholars have advocated new approaches in order to eliminate the limitations of previous views (Okumus and Roper, 1999). For example, after the recession and the oil crises in the early 1970s, the planning school was heavily criticised by scholars, particularly Quinn

Table 8.1 Propositions of the Five Schools of Thought in Relation to Strategy Formation

	Planning School	Learning School	Contingency School	Configurational School	Complexity School
Strategy Development	Formal and analytical	Crafted and emergent	Can be formal and crafted	Episodic	Episodic and complex
Focus on	Planning, formulation, internal resources, and environment	Politics, culture, resources, and implementation	It depends on the situation (environment)	Everything	Speedy response to emerging patterns and implications of the process on the company, customers and competitors
Aims	More on financial results and market share	More on political and cultural issues, as well as financial results and market share	It depends on the situation	All kinds of objectives	No need to have clear objectives; along the way new objectives and issues will emerge
Type of Implementation	Sequential and revolutionary	Incremental	Can be both sequential and incremental	Quantum	Can be sequential, incremental, and quantum
Implementation Starts	After strategy formulation	With strategy formulation	It depends on the situation	A holistic approach	A holistic approach
Key Variables/ Issues	Analysis, clear plans and procedures, formal structure, leadership, formal and top-down communication, formal resource allocations	Organisational culture, politics, organisational learning, middle- and lower-level managers and employees, bottom-up and informal communication	External environment and the issues and variables stated by the planning and learning views	All key variables and issues stated by previous approaches plus participation, consensus	Informal networks and shadow organisation, external issues
Central Actors in Strategy Formation	Top management	More emphasis on middle and front line management	Can be both senior and middle managers	Every level of management	Anyone within and outside the company can play an important role in the process

Table 8.1   Propositions of the Five Schools of Thought in Relation to Strategy Formation *Continued*

	Planning School	Learning School	Contingency School	Configurational School	Complexity School
Organisation Structure	Mechanistic and bureaucratic	Organic, flexible	It depends on the context	All kinds of structure	Creative, innovative structure and informal groups are important
Environment	Stable	Unstable: complex and dynamic	It depends on how a manager interprets it	It can be stable, complex, and dynamic	Complex and dynamic
Key Words	Intended strategy, planning and rational: man, PEST, SWOT, industry structure analysis	Emergent, incremental, and muddling through	Flexibility and fit	All previous key words and configuration	Chaos, complexity, adoptive systems, and bounded instability
Key Period	1960s and 1970s	1970s and 1980s	1980s	1990s	1990s
Leading Authors	Ansoff (1965) Andrews (1971) Chandler (1962) Grant (1991) Porter 1980 Sloan (1963) Schendel and Hofer (1979)	De Gues (1988) Johnson (1987, 1988) Quinn (1980) Mintzberg (1987) Pettigrew (1987)	Berman (1980) Burns and Stalker (1961) Donaldson (1996) Kay (1993) Lawrence and Lorsch (1967)	Bailey and Johnson (1992) Miller (1986) Mintzberg, Ahlstrand, and Lampel (1998) Richardson (1994)	Glass (1996) Pascale (1990) Stacey (1995, 1996) Theys (1998)

(1980), Mintzberg (1994), Johnson and colleagues (2008), Okumus and Roper (1999), and Whittington (2001). The main criticisms can be summarised as follows:

- It sees the external environment as simple and stable, although it is often complex and dynamic.

- It views the strategy formation process as a planned, linear, rational process, but the strategies generally emerge from pragmatic processes and existing practices.

- It recommends detailed and clear plans for strategy formation, but imposing such precise and detailed plans is not always helpful, in practice these plans may not be appropriate and helpful in dynamic and complex environments.

- It separates strategy formulation from strategy implementation, although in many cases they are not separable.

- It does not contemplate the importance of the involvement of implementers or middle managers in strategy development.

- It does not consider organizational culture and politics, although in many cases these factors can be very influential.

- It tends to focus on financial objectives, but aiming only for high profit and market share may not always be important. In practice, there are other important issues to be considered, such as internal politics, organisational culture, customers, competitors, and employees.

Despite these criticisms, in many respects the planning school still remains the most dominant approach in the strategic management field, perhaps because it puts forward certain guidelines and analytical tools. For example, Glaister and Falshaw (1999) found that most of the analytical tools and models proposed by this planning school are frequently used in many companies.

However, dissatisfaction with the planning school has been widespread among many strategic writers. From the 1950s to the present, it has been criticized that this approach is unrealistic in complex and dynamic environments and organisations. The learning or emergent approach has been advocated in response to the planning approach, but this approach has also received its fair share of criticism. For example, the learning approach is not always helpful, since it many not always offer practical solutions. Accepting the learning school of thought implies that strategies should be viewed as incremental, that the environment is complex and dynamic, and that internal politics and organizational culture are important. However, some could argue that these factors are still not sufficient to offer a solution to developing and implementing a strategy successfully.

Kay (1993) argues that the contingency school is the most appropriate approach, as it allows flexibility in developing and implementing strategies. However, this view has also been criticised due to its apparent inability to resolve persistent theoretical and empirical problems, particularly in more open-ended contexts, where knowledge about possible contingencies is limited (Mintzberg, 1994; Stacey, 1996). The assumption of the contingency view is that similar contexts will lead to identical outcomes. However, it needs to be recognized that small differences can lead to completely different results, and in addition, the scope of change, risk, stability, and the complexity of the environment can be perceived differently by each person involved in the strategy formulation and implementation process. Therefore, managers in two different firms could interpret the same environment in different ways and implement contrary strategies that may both succeed (Stacey, 1996).

The configurational approach has been advocated in order to combine all of the previous schools into a single perspective. However, Mintzberg and colleagues (1998) and Stacey (1996) claim that even the configurational school has limitations. The main argument is that getting all of the contradictory forces together, achieving a "fit" between these contradictory tensions, and sustaining this coherence are almost impossible, especially in dynamic and complex situations. These same authors suggest that scholars and practitioners should consider the chaos and complexity view.

These five approaches are grouped by Stacey (1996) into only two categories: ordinary management, which incorporates the planning, learning, contingency, and configurational views, and extraordinary management, which comprises just the complexity view. Given the limitations of each approach, Pascale (1990) and Stacey (1996) further admit that perhaps all of the approaches should be used simultaneously. In terms of Stacey's categorisation of the five approaches, he claims that a company can employ ordinary management techniques when the internal and external environments of the company are predictable and stable, and it should use the complexity approach when the situation is complex and dynamic in order to challenge and, if necessary, alter the company's existing systems and mental models. This argument is further supported by Theys (1998) as follows:

> *The old approaches are not obsolete; they correspond to [a] particular configuration of problems and they are essential to [a] model of interaction. But in a wired world, decision[s] will become more and*

more complex. This will require interactive support systems allowing a lot of quick trials to anticipate situations emerging from the multiple potential decisions.... Understanding and acting on any form of life will depend more and more on our ability to master the emerging Theory of Complexity, a new paradigm for representing dynamic systems that does not replace the previous ones, but completes them. It will lead to a whole new set of methods. (p. 262)

STRATEGY FORMATION IN THE INTERNATIONAL CONTEXT

The strategic management literature does not clearly explain how far strategy formation differs in international firms than strategy formation does in domestic firms. Some authors do not view the strategy development and implementation process in an international context any differently from that in general strategic management. For example, Lynch (1997) argues that "international aspects of strategy implementation follow the same principles but are complicated by culture, geographical diversity, and other factors" (p. 698).

In return, several scholars use the strategic management literature, particularly the planning school, when discussing strategy formation in an international context (Deresky, 1997; Fatehi, 1996; Hodgetts and Luthans, 1997; Mead, 1998). These authors identify two main dimensions of international strategy: the diversity and size of the company. Although both of these can be important in terms of strategy development and implementation, international management scholars give more emphasis to the diversity of the company. This is because they refer to and emphasise diverse cultures and locations in managing international firms. However, they fail to evaluate and clearly illustrate how these diverse cultures and locations influence the strategy development and implementation processes in international firms. In other words, the strategy formation in international companies is viewed very similarly to the domestic strategy development and implementation process. According to Fatehi (1996), there are no fundamental differences between domestic and international strategy implementation processes:

Irrespective of the nature of the operation, the strategic management process remains basically the same, for the domestic enterprise and MNC. Just because the firm expands abroad it does not mean that there will be a different strategy formulation and implementation process. (p. 44)

Several authors have further discussed strategy formation in international firms and proposed various approaches to developing and implementing strategies in an international context. (i.e., Brooke, 1996; Chakravarthy and Perlmutter, 1985). The main groupings of these approaches and their propositions are explained in Table 8.2. When we compare and contrast the schools of thought in strategic management with the approaches to strategic planning in the international context, it is apparent that there are important areas of commonality between the approaches in both fields. This is not surprising, as the review of Chakravarthy and Perlmutter's (1985) pioneering study indicates that the four approaches were initially adapted to international or multinational firms from Chakravarthy and Lorange's (1984) conceptual study in the strategic management field. Many international management scholars, such as Deresky (1997), Fatehi (1996), Herbert (1999), Hodgetts and Luthans (1997), and Mead (1998), use the strategic management literature in their studies when they explain and discuss issues related to international firms. This is seen as normal by Bartlett and Ghoshal (1991), since these authors argue that concepts and frameworks are often borrowed from the strategic management field and applied into the international management field. In short, scholars in the international management field have applied the concepts of strategy development and implementation from the strategic management field, and therefore four out of the five approaches found in this field also appear in the international management field. There are not many studies that specifically discuss strategy formation in international firms from the perspective of the complexity view. However, the international management literature does emphasise the complex nature of managing international firms. Therefore, one can perhaps argue that the complexity view can also provide further insights for international firms in developing and implementing strategies.

SUMMARY

This chapter reviewed different schools of thought in the strategic management field. Knowing the propositions of these approaches is important to be able to understand and analyze the current thinking on strategy development and implementation in hospitality organizations. One key theme that emerges from this chapter is that all schools of thought in the strategic management field indicate and emphasise the need for critical consideration and the use of multiple issues and factors when developing and implementing strategies.

Table 8.2 A Comparison of the Approaches to Strategy Formation in International Firms

Approach	Centralised	Decentralised	Contingency	Participative or Integrative
External Environment	Stable or similar across subsidiaries Economical imperatives are more important	Different and complex across subsidiaries Political imperatives are more important	Can be different or similar depending on the region	Can be stable, but generally complex and different Economic and political imperatives need to be considered simultaneously
Internal Characteristics	Similar characteristics across subsidiaries	Different characteristics across subsidiaries	Similar or different characteristics depending on the region/location	Can have similar and different characteristics but aim to share and benchmark good practice across the subsidiaries
Strategies Are Formulated by	Head office or parent company	National subsidiaries	It depends on the context	Head office and subsidiaries together
Strategies Are Implemented by	Subsidiaries	Subsidiaries	Subsidiaries	Head office and subsidiaries together
Central Actor(s)	Head office	Subsidiaries	It depends on the context	Both head office and subsidiaries
Organisational Structure	Centralised hierarchical	Decentralised	It depends (centralised or decentralised)	Global network
Resource Flows to Subsidiaries from Head Office	Knowledge, people, and resources	Resources, support, and people	Knowledge, people and resources	Knowledge, people, resources from head office and other subsidiaries
Resource Flows from Subsidiaries to Head Office	Dividends and formal reports	Dividends and formal reports	Dividends and formal reports	Innovations, knowledge, resources, people plus dividends

Table 8.2 A Comparison of the Approaches to Strategy Formation in International Firms *Continued*

Approach	Centralised	Decentralised	Contingency	Participative or Integrative
Advantages	Central control and economic integration	Empowered subsidiaries and national responsiveness	Flexible approach to respond to both economic and political imperatives	Combines all approaches together, plus emphasise on global learning, co-ordination, communication and teamwork
Disadvantages	Strict, does not consider political imperatives in local markets	Lack of global perspective and does not consider economic imperatives world wide	Does not always work, as in some cases economic and politic imperatives can both be important	Dual responsibility, possible conflict. Should be supported with experts, culture and reward systems

As illustrated in Tables 8.1 and 8.2, the strategic management schools of thought found in the literature have their own propositions and suggestions in terms of how these factors should be evaluated and used. However, the key issue here is that all these schools of thought directly or indirectly refer to the same areas and factors such as external environment, organisational structure, culture, people, communication, resource allocation, planning, and monitoring. Incorporating some of these issues and elements, some authors have developed strategy implementation frameworks, and subsequently, a whole body of strategy implementation literature has evolved discussing and presenting strategy implementation issues. In answering the why and how questions, previous studies have developed and proposed these frameworks in order to illustrate key areas and elements when developing and implementing strategies. By proposing these frameworks, they aim to simplify and conceptualise this complex area of the strategic management field and subsequently assist companies and researchers in understanding and evaluating strategy implementation and implementation processes. The next chapter will propose a strategy implementation framework.

STUDY QUESTIONS

1. What is strategy formulation?
2. What is strategy implementation?
3. What is strategy formation?
4. Evaluate main propositions of each school of thought to strategy formation.
5. Which school of thought provides the most appropriate and useful propositions and suggestions to develop and implement strategies in hospitality organizations?
6. Why are the advantages of looking at strategy formation from the perspective of different schools of thought?
7. How easy is it to achieve a coherence (or fit) between the external and internal environments?
8. Why is it not a good idea to achieve a coherence (or fit) between the external and internal environments?
9. Can you think of any H&T companies that have changed the external environment and set new rules and standards? Do they always try to achieve a coherence with the external environment?

10. How does national culture influence strategy formulation (decision making) and implementation in H&T organizations?

11. How can international hotel groups develop and implement successful strategies?

12. Think about a project or an idea that you planned and implemented well. Please (1) explain why your plan went well, (2) identify key success factors in this process, (3) explain what type of challenges you faced, and (4) tell how you overcame them.

13. List several key events and developments in your life that happened with no planning or anticipation on your part. Explain how you handled the situation and what you learned from it.

14. It is often said, "There is no best way of doing things." Give some examples of different ways to make decisions. You can also think about achieving something by following different paths.

15. Think about a situation that had a clear plan to follow, but you had to revise it again and again due to personal and external issues that emerged. Discuss how you revised your strategies and moved forward.

16. Describe a minor event or development that changed your life forever.

REFERENCES AND FURTHER READINGS

Alexander, L.D. (1991). Strategy Implementation: Nature of the Problem. In D. Hussey (Ed.), *International Review of Strategic Management*. Chichester: New York: John Wiley & Sons Ltd.

Andrews, K. (1971). *The Concept of Strategy*. Homewood, Illinois: Dow-Jones Irwin.

Ansoff, H.I. (1965). *Corporate Strategy*. New York: McGraw-Hill.

Ansoff, H.I. (1994). Comment on Henry Mintzberg's Rethinking Strategic Planning, *Long Range Planning*, 27 (3), 31–32.

Argyris, C. (1989). Strategy Implementation: An Experience in Learning, *Organisational Dynamics*, 18 (2), 5–15.

Bailey, A. and Johnson, G. (1992). How Strategies Develop In Organisations. In D. Faulkner and G. Johnson (Eds.), *The Challenge of Strategic Management*. London: Kogan Page.

Bartlett, C. and Ghoshal, S. (1991). Global Strategic Management: Impact on the New Frontiers of Strategy Research, *Strategic Management Journal*, 12, 5–17.

Berman, P. (1980). Thinking about Programmed and Adaptive Implementation: Matching Strategies to Situations. In H.M. Ingram and D.E. Mann (Eds.), *Why Policies Succeed or Fail*. Beverly Hills, California: Sage.

Brooke, M. (1996). *International Management: A Review of Strategies and Options*, 3rd ed. Cheltenham: Stanley Thorne Ltd.

Burns, T. and Stalker, G. (1961). *The Management of Innovation*. London: Tavistock.

Chaffee, E.A. (1985). Three Models of Strategy, *Academy of Management Review*, 10 (1), 89–98.

Chakravarthy, B.S. and Lorange, P. (1984). Managing Strategic Adaptatoin: Options in Administrative Systems Design, *Interface*, 14 (1), 34–46.

Chakravarthy, B.S. and Perlmutter, H.V. (1985). Strategic Planning for A Global Business, *Columbia Journal of World Business*, 20 (2), 3–10.

Chandler, A. (1962). *Strategy and Structure*. Garden City, New York: Doubleday.

Child, J. (1984). *Organisation: A Guide to Problems and Practice*. London: Poul-Chapman.

De Geus, A.P. (1988). Planning as Learning, *Harvard Business Review*, March–April, 70–74.

Deresky, H. (1997). *International Management*. New York: Addison-Wesley.

Donaldson, L. (1996). The Normal Science of Structural Contingency Theory. In S. in Clegg, C. Hardy, and W.R. Nord (Eds.), *Handbook of Organisation Studies*, Thousand Oaks, CA: Sage.

Eccles, T. (1993). Implementing Strategy: Two Revisionist Perspectives. In J. Hendry, G. Johnson, and J. Newton (Eds.), *Strategic Thinking: Leadership and the Management of Change.* Chichester: Wiley & Sons Ltd.

Fatehi, K. (1996). *International Management: Cross-Cultural and Functional Perspectives*. London: Prentice Hall.

Glass, N. (1996). Chaos, Non-linear Systems and Day-to-day Management, *European Management Journal*, 14(1), 98–106.

Glaister, K.W. and Falshaw, J.R. (1999). Strategic Planning: Still Going Strong?, *Long Range Planning*, 32 (1), 107–116.

Grant, R.M. (1991). *Contemporary Strategy Analysis Concept*. Oxford: Basil.

Herbert, T. (1999). Multinational Strategic Planning: Matching Central Expectations to Local Realities, *Long Range Planning*, 32 (1), 81–88.

Hodgetts, R.M. and Luthans, F. (1997). *International Management*, 3rd ed. New York: McGraw Hill, Inc.

Johnson, G. (1987). *Strategic Change and the Management Process*. Oxford: Blackwell.

Johnson, G. (1988). Rethinking Incrementalism, *Strategic Management Journal*, 9 (2), 75–91.

Johnson, G., Scholes, K., and Whittington, R. (2008). *Exploring Corporate Strategy*. London: Prentice Hall.

Kay, J. (1993). *Foundations of Corporate Success*. Oxford: Oxford University Press.

Lawrence, P.R. and Lorsch, J.W. (1967). *Organisation and Environment: Managing Differentiation and Integration*. Boston: Harvard Business School.

Levy, D. (1994). Chaos Theory and Strategy: Theory, Application, and Managerial Implications, *Strategic Management Journal*, 15, Summer, 167–178.

Lynch, R. (1997). *Corporate Strategy*. London: Pitman Publishing.

Mead, R. (1998). *International Management*, 2nd ed. Oxford: Blackwell.

Miller, D. (1986). Configurations of Strategy and Structure: Towards a Synthesis, *Strategic Management Journal*, 7 (3), 233–249.

Mintzberg, H. (1987).Crafting Strategy, *Harvard Business Review*, July–August, 66–75.

Mintzberg, H. (1994). *The Rise and Fall of Strategic Planning*. London: Prentice Hall.

Mintzberg, H. and Quinn, J.B. (1996). (Eds.) *The Strategy Process Concepts, Contexts, Cases* 3rd Edition, London: Prentice Hall.

Mintzberg, H., Ahlstrand, B., and Lampel, J. (1998). *Strategy Safari*. London: Prentice Hall.

Okumus, F. (2000). Strategy Implementation: A Study of International Hotel Groups, Unpublished Doctoral Thesis, Oxford Brookes University, Oxford, UK.

Okumus, F. (2003). A Framework to Implement Strategies in Organizations, *Management Decision*, 41 (9), 871–883.

Okumus, F. and Roper A, (1999). A Review of Disparate Approaches to Strategy Implementation in Hospitality Firms, *Journal of Hospitality and Tourism Research*, 23 (1), 20–38.

Pascale, R.T. (1984). Perspectives on Strategy: The Real Story Behind Honda's Success, *California Management Review*, 24(3), 47–72.

Pascale, R.T. (1990). *Managing On the Edge: How Successful Companies Use Conflict To Stay Ahead*. London: Viking Penguin.

Pettigrew, A.M. (1987). Context and Action in the Transformation of the Firm, *Journal of Management Studies*, 24 (6), 649–670.

Pettigrew, A.M. and Whipp, R. (1991). *Managing Change for Competitive Success*. Oxford: Blackwell.

Prahalad, C.K. and Doz, Y. (1987). *The Multinational Mission: Balancing Local Demands and Global Vision*. New York: Free Press.

Quinn, J.B. (1980). *Strategies for change: Logical Incrementalism*. Homewood: Richard.

Richardson, B. (1994). Comprehensive Approach to Strategic Management: Leading Across the Strategic Management Domain, *Management Decision*, 32(8), 27–41.

Schendel, D.E. & Hofer, C.W. (1979). *Strategic Management: A New View of Business Policy and Planning*. Boston: Little, Brown.

Sloan, A.P. (1963). *My Years with General Motors*. London: Sedgewick & Jackson.

Stacey, R.D. (1995). The Science of Complexity: An Alternative Perspective for Strategic Change Process, *Strategic Management Journal*, 16(7), 477–495.

Stacey, R.D. (1996). *Strategic Management & Organisational Dynamics*, 2nd ed., London: Pitman Publishing.

Theys, M. (1998). The New Challenges of Management in a Wired World, *European Journal of Operational Research*, 109 (2), 248–263.

Whittington, R. (2001). *What Is Strategy and Does It Matter?* London: Routledge.

Strategy Implementation and Change

Learning Objectives

After reading this chapter, you should be able to:

1. Discuss why do we need a strategy implementation framework.

2. Identify and group key factors in implementing strategies.

3. Evaluate strategy formulation and implementation from a holistic perspective.

4. Discuss potential barriers and challenges in developing and implementing strategies.

5. Comment on managing change in the international context.

Please search what type of strategies Southwest Airlines has initiated and implemented since the company was founded, and discuss whether such strategies have made any impact on the company's overall success. Can we claim that this company has a competency in developing and implementing strategies?

You can find information about Southwest at their website as well as through a Google search or through http://scholar.google.com/.

INTRODUCTION[1]

As we discussed in Chapter 8, strategy formation directly or indirectly relates to all facets of organizations, so it is essential to follow a holistic approach when analyzing and evaluating complex issues of strategy formation. Bartlett and Ghoshal (1987) noted that in all of the companies they studied, "the issue was not a poor understanding of environmental forces or inappropriate strategic intent. Without exception, they knew what they had to do; their difficulties lay in how to achieve the necessary changes." Supporting this, Miller (2002) reports that organizations fail to implement over 70 percent of their new strategic initiatives.

There are some commonly used models and frameworks available, such as SWOT, industry structure analysis, and other generic strategies, for researchers and practicing managers in the areas of strategy analysis and formulation in strategic management. By contrast, there is no agreed-upon and dominant framework in strategy implementation (Noble, 1999b and Okumus, 2003). This chapter proposes a framework by identifying key factors and categorizing them into different groups depending on their role and importance. The role and importance of each factor, as well as its relationship with other factors, are explained. The chapter also evaluates the magnitude and pace of strategic change. There will be some discussions on potential barriers and resistance to strategy development and implementation and how they can be overcome.

---

[1] This chapter is primarily derived from Okumus, F. (2003). A Framework to Implement Strategies in Organizations, *Management Decision*, 41 (9), 871–883, and Okumus, F. (2000). Strategy Implementation: A Study of International Hotel Groups, Unpublished Doctoral Thesis, Oxford Brookes University, Oxford, UK.

PREVIOUS IMPLEMENTATION FRAMEWORKS

One of the most cited implementation frameworks was proposed by Waterman, Peters, and Phillips (1980). Based on their research and consultancy work, these authors argued that effective strategy implementation is essentially attending to the relationship between seven factors: strategy, structure, systems, style, staff, skills, and subordinate goals. The conceptual strategy implementation frameworks developed by Stonich (1982), Hrebiniak and Joyce (1984), Galbraith and Kazanjian (1986), and Reed and Buckley (1988) consist of explicit key implementation factors. These were the first implementation frameworks to have appeared in the field of strategic management. These frameworks consist of similar factors, including strategy formulation, organizational structure, culture, people, communication, control, and outcome. In their conceptual studies, Alexander (1991) and Thompson and Strickland (1999) also discussed and referred to similar implementation factors.

Unlike the preceding frameworks, several conceptual studies propose linear implementation models such as Vasconcellos e Sa's (1990) ten-step model, Noble's (1999a) four-stage model, Galpin's (1997) six-stage model, Bergadaà's (1999) four-step model, and De Feo and Janssen's (2001) ten-stage model. There are important similarities among these works in proposing certain tasks to be undertaken or certain aims to be achieved at each stage of the implementation process. These studies also refer to similar implementation factors, including organizational structure, culture, planning, resource allocation, communication, and incentives to be considered or used at different stages of the implementation process.

Several authors have proposed frameworks based on empirical studies and identified similar factors that were noted in many conceptual studies (Bryson and Bromiley, 1993; Hambrick and Cannella, 1989; Hrebiniak, 1992; Okumus, 2001; Pettigrew and Whipp, 1991; Roth, Schewieger, and Morrison, 1991; Schmelzer and Olsen, 1994; Skivington and Daft, 1991). It is apparent that these studies often included strategy formulation as a factor or element in their frameworks.

The balanced scorecard technique has been linked to strategy formation in recent years (Epstein and Manzoni, 1998; Kaplan and Norton, 1996; 2001). The overall idea behind this technique is that organizations are advised to align their performance measures in four perspectives: financial, customer, operations, and learning and growth. In terms of using the balance scorecard approach in implementing strategies, Kaplan and Norton (1996) identified four main implementation factors: (1) clarifying and translating the vision and strategy, (2) communication and linking, (3) planning and target setting, and (4) strategic feedback and learning. However, the balance scorecard technique neither solves all implementation problems nor provides new insights into this area, since these four implementation factors (and subfactors) are very similar to the factors that have been identified by previous studies. Second, as stated by Nørreklit (2000), the balanced scorecard is mainly a control mechanism, suggesting a top-down approach with limited participation from lower levels. In the balance scorecard approach, strategy development and implementation are regarded as separate phases. In addition, the technique does not give much emphasis to or many explanations of problems in the strategy implementation process involving conflicts and power struggles among interest groups, organizational culture, resource allocation, and training.

TOWARD AN IMPLEMENTATION FRAMEWORK

There are important similarities among the previous implementation frameworks in terms of the key factors forwarded and the assumptions made. The overriding assumption of these frameworks is that multiple factors should be considered simultaneously when developing and implementing a strategy or strategic decision. Some frameworks combine several elements under one factor, while others refer to each element as a separate key factor. For example, in the frameworks proposed by Galbraith and Kazanjian (1986), Okumus (2001), Stonich (1982), and Waterman and colleagues (1980), the issues related to managers and employees are incorporated under a separate factor entitled "people" or "staff." In the frameworks developed by Hrebiniak and Joyce (1984) and Schmelzer and Olsen (1994), a manager's style, incentives, and training are presented as individual factors. In some frameworks, such as Stonich (1982) and Waterman and colleagues (1980), systems include planning, resource allocations, budgeting, and rewards.

However, each framework includes different numbers and types of factors, and some frameworks identify more factors than others. In addition, various titles are given to similar factors. For example, communication is also interactions (Skivington and Daft, 1991), information systems (Schmelzer and Olsen, 1994), and selling the strategy (Hambrick and Cannella, 1989). Strategy formulation is referred to as strategy, business strategy, intended strategy, market strategy, vision, new strategy, and strategic decision. Outcome is referred as results and success. A further issue is that some frameworks have a starting point, which is usually the formulation of strategy (Hambrick and Cannella, 1989; Hrebiniak, 1992; Hrebiniak and Joyce,

1984; Galbraith and Kazanjian, 1986; Skivington and Daft, 1991; Stonich, 1982), whereas some other frameworks, such as those proposed by Miller (1997), Schmelzer and Olsen (1994), and Waterman and colleagues (1980), do not specifically point to a starting point when looking at strategy implementation.

From an analysis of the previous frameworks discussed, 11 key factors can be identified that play an important role in the strategy formation process:

1. Strategy development

2. Environmental uncertainty

3. Organizational structure

4. Organizational culture

5. Leadership

6. Operational planning

7. Resource allocation

8. Communication

9. People

10. Control

11. Outcome

Regarding design, characteristics, and use of these factors, each school of thought in the strategic management field has its own assumptions and suggestions (Mintzberg, Ahlstrand, and Lampel, 1998; Okumus and Roper, 1999; Stacey, 1996). Table 8.1 in the previous chapter also provides explanations and discussions about how each factor is viewed by different schools of thought. For example, with the exception of the configurational and the complexity views, each school of thought requires or advocates a standard design for each factor. For example, the planning school advocates a stable environment, a centralized organizational structure, formal and top-down communication activities, and standard formal planning and resource allocation activities, whereas the learning school requires a decentralized organizational structure, bottom-up and informal communication, flexible planning, and resource allocation activities. According to the configurational school, the environment can be both stable and dynamic, the organizational structure should allow flexibility and participation from different levels of management, and the communication systems should allow top-down, bottom-up, and informal and formal modes of communication. Finally, the complexity view states that it is difficult or even misleading to require standard factors for each situation, as strategy implementation is an evolving process; therefore, it may not be possible to have and maintain a certain pattern of factors. Previous studies on strategy implementation did not appear to advocate any specific implementation approach.

Based on their roles and characteristics in the process, the implementation factors can be grouped into a number of categories as follows:

- Context, process, and outcomes (Bryson and Bromiley, 1993)

- Planning and design (Hrebiniak and Joyce, 1984)

- Realizers and enablers (Miller, 1997)

- Content, context, and operation (Dawson, 1994)

- Content, context, process, and outcome (Pettigrew, 1987; 1992; Okumus, 2001; 2003)

- Framework and process components (Skivington and Daft, 1991)

- Context and process (Schmelzer and Olsen, 1994)

- Contextual, system, and action levers (Miller and Dess, 1996)

Four areas of groupings emerge from an analysis of the preceding categories (Okumus, 2003). Considering the role and characteristics of each implementation factor, the 11 implementation factors can further be grouped into four categories: strategic content, strategic context, process, and outcome (Figure 9.1).

1. *Strategic content* includes the development of strategy.

2. *Strategic context* is further divided into external and internal context. The former includes environmental uncertainty, and the internal context includes organizational structure, culture, and leadership.

3. *Operational process* includes operational planning, resource allocation, people, communication, and control.

4. *Outcome* includes the results of the implementation process.

In order to provide further clarification, the role and importance of each factor in the strategy development and implementation process is explained in Table 9.1. In addition, the relationships between each factor

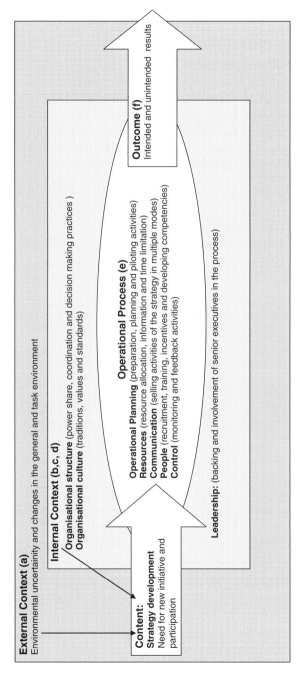

Key

a   Changes in the external environment influence the strategic context and force organizations to deploy new initiatives.

b   Problems and inconsistencies in the internal context require new initiatives.

c   The strategy is implemented in the internal context, and the characteristics of organizational structure, culture, and leadership influence the process factors.

d   Having an organizational context that is receptive to change is essential for the successful implementation of strategy.

e   The process factors are primarily used on a continuous basis to implement the strategy and manipulate the internal context.

f   The characteristics of the context and process factors and how they are used directly influence the outcomes.

FIGURE 9.1   *The Strategy Implementation Framework.*

Source: Okumus (2003).

Table 9.1	Defining Key Implementation Factors, their Roles, and their Impact on the Process

Strategic Content

Strategy development refers to why and how strategy is initiated. Key areas to be considered are:

- The new strategy should be consistent with the overall strategic direction of the company.
- The aims of the new initiative should be clearly identified.
- The expertise and knowledge of strategy developers in managing change are crucial.
- Active participation from all levels of management is recommended.
- The potential impact of ongoing and future projects on the new initiative should be considered.
- The potential impact of the new strategy on other ongoing strategic initiatives should be assessed.

External Context

Environmental uncertainty refers to the degree of uncertainty and changes in the task and general environments. The main issues are:

- Changes, developments, and problems in the general and task environments require a new strategy.
- The new strategy should be appropriate to the market conditions, trends, and developments in the external environment until the implementation process is completed.

Internal Context

Organizational structure refers to the shape, division of labor, job duties and responsibilities, distribution of power, and decision-making procedures in the company. Issues to be considered are:

- The potential changes in duties, roles, decision making, and reporting relationships due to the new strategy.
- Whether the organizational structure facilitates the free flow of information, coordination, and cooperation among different levels of management and functional areas.
- The potential impact of the new strategy on informal networks, politics, and key shareholders.
- The attitude of powerful groups toward this new strategy.
- The potential challenges of using the existing organizational structure when using process variables, including operational planning, communication, and resource allocations.

Organizational culture is the shared understanding of employees about how they do things in an organization. Issues to be considered are:

- The company's culture and subcultures and their possible impact on the implementation process.
- The impact of organizational culture on communication, coordination, and cooperation among different management and functional levels.
- The implications of the new strategy on the company's culture and subcultures.
- Efforts and activities to change the company's overall culture and subcultures and potential challenges.

Leadership refers to the actual support and involvement of the CEO in the strategic initiative. Leadership is crucial in using process factors and also in manipulating the internal context to create a context receptive to change. Key issues to be considered are:

- The actual involvement of the CEO in the strategy development and implementation process.
- Level of support and backing from the CEO for the new strategy until it is completed.
- Open and covert messages coming from the CEO about the project and its importance.

Organizational Process

Operational planning is the process of initiating the project and the operational planning of the implementation activities and tasks. Operational planning has a great deal of impact on allocating resources, communicating, and providing training and incentives. Key issues to be considered are:

- Preparing and planning implementation activities in a detailed format.
- Participation and feedback from different levels of management and functional areas in preparing these operational plans and implementation activities.
- Initial pilot projects and the knowledge gained from them.
- The time scale of making resources available and using them.

Resource allocation is the process of ensuring that all necessary time, financial resources, skills, and knowledge are made available. It is closely linked with operational planning and has a great deal of impact on communicating and on providing training and incentives. Key issues to be considered are:

- The procedures of securing and allocating financial resources for the new strategy.
- Information and knowledge requirements for the process of implementing a new strategy.
- The time available to complete the implementation process.
- Political and cultural issues in the company and their impact on resource allocation.

People refers to recruiting new staff and providing training and incentives for relevant employees. Operational planning and resource allocation have a direct impact on this factor. Key issues to be considered are:

- The recruitment of relevant staff for the new strategy implementation.
- The acquisition and development of new skills and knowledge to implement the new strategy.
- The types of training activities to develop and prepare relevant managers and employees.
- The provision of incentives related to strategy implementation and their implications.
- The impact of company's overall HRM policies and practices on implementing new strategies.

Communication refers to the mechanisms that send formal and informal messages about the new strategy. The main issues are:

- Operational plans, training programs, and incentives that can be used as communication materials.
- The use of clear messages when informing relevant people within and outside the organization.
- The implications of using (or not using) multiple modes of communication (top-down, bottom-up, lateral, formal, informal, internal, external, one-time, and continuous communication).
- The problems and difficulties related to communication and their actual causes.
- The impact of organizational structure, culture, and leadership on selling the new strategy.

Control and feedback refer to the formal and informal mechanisms that allow the efforts and results of implementation to be monitored and compared against predetermined objectives. The main issues are:

- Formal and monitoring activities carried out during and after the implementation process.
- Communication and operational plans are key to monitoring the process and providing feedback about its progress.

Outcome is the intended and unintended results of the implementation process, which can be tangible and intangible. Key issues to be considered are:

- Whether the new strategy has been implemented according to the plan. If not, the reasons for this.
- Whether predetermined objectives have been achieved. If not, the reasons for this.
- Whether the outcomes are satisfactory to those involved in, and affected by, the process.
- Whether the company has learned anything from the strategy implementation process.

Source: Derived from Okumus (2003).

and other elements and their potential impacts on the strategy formation process are also explained. This framework and the explanations given in Table 9.1 can help us when we examine and evaluate complex cases of strategy development and implementation.

The preceding framework both emphasizes the importance of content, context, process, and outcome and explains the potential role and importance of each factor in the process. In the proposed framework, strategy development and implementation is seen as a process that occurs in the strategic context. In other words, we do not view strategy development and implementation as separate phases. The strategic content is viewed as the strategic direction of the company and the need to design new initiatives. Strategies are initiated and implemented in a strategic context, and the factors in this grouping greatly influence the strategy formulation and implementation process.

The process factors primarily utilized in the strategy formulation and implementation process and the outcome are seen as the expected and the unexpected results of the initiated strategy. When considering the strategy development and implementation process in multiple sites, particularly in international firms, the types and characteristics of factors in each region/site should be analyzed, and necessary actions should be taken to prevent or overcome potential barriers and problems.

The factors in these four groupings in Figure 9.1 should not be considered separately because, as we can see in Table 9.1, a factor in one group can influence the other factors in both the same and other groups. It then changes the outcome of the whole process. This means that the strategy formation process needs to be examined and evaluated from a holistic perspective over a long period of time. To understand and evaluate the strategy formation process, researchers and executives need to adapt a more comprehensive view and look at content, context, process, and outcome simultaneously (Okumus, 2001; 2003; Pettigrew, 1987; 1992).

On the other hand, it may not be possible for everyone to understand and evaluate the content, context, and process simultaneously, as more time and resources are required in such an approach (Argyris, 1988; Buchanan and Boddy, 1992). However, the framework proposed in this chapter provides a more comprehensive view for understanding and evaluating the complex transformation processes. Focusing only on the initiated change process and ignoring the wider context produce a very limited scope of understanding about the issues and their actual causes and possible effects. Following a holistic approach can help executives and middle managers to understand the wider implications of the processes of change in their organizations. It will encourage them to not simply focus on a specific part of the company but widen their focus to other functional areas, customers, and competitors.

The overriding assumption in many strategy implementation frameworks is that there must be "coherence" among all key implementation factors if the strategy formulation and implementation process is to be successful. For example, Thompson and Strickland (1999) commented that "the stronger the fits, the better the execution of strategy." Hrebiniak and Joyce (1984) stated that "everything depends upon everything else in strategy implementation" and that therefore there should be harmony among the key implementation factors.

A whole range of questions can be directed at practicing managers concerning how "harmony" can be achieved and maintained. Some sample questions for managers and executives may include whether the environment fits the strategy, culture, and structure, or whether the proposed decision fits the organizational structure, culture, resources, and people. Such questions can assist in assessing and evaluating the implementation process and perhaps help to diagnose potential problems and barriers to the strategy implementation process in advance.

Given the complex, dynamic nature of strategy development and implementation situations, it may be very difficult, or in some cases even impossible, to achieve and maintain coherence among implementation factors. Therefore, it is perhaps essential to understand how strategies can be developed and implemented without having a proper coherence among such factors. In this regard, as explained in the previous chapter, the complexity school of thought in the field of strategic management (Stacey, 1996) provides valuable propositions. According to the complexity view, successful companies are those that operate in a state of nonequilibrium or "bounded instability." It is not good for companies to aim to achieve coherence between the environment and the internal systems of the company, particularly as certain factors such as organizational structure, culture, and the company's environment are constantly changing or evolving. Companies should therefore attempt to develop diverse cultures, informal working groups, and networks, and allow for the emergence of internal conflicts among departments and groups. These mechanisms will help to challenge existing mental models and eventually allow, and perhaps force, the company to invent and create new ways of developing and implementing strategies even if there is no coherence among the implementation factors.

BARRIERS AND RESISTANCE TO STRATEGY IMPLEMENTATION

The following are the main barriers to strategy implementation and change (Alexander, 1985; Kotter, 1995; Noble, 1999a; Okumus and Hemmington, 1998; Strabel, 1996):

- Time limitation or more time needed than originally planned
- Lack of or poor communication
- Lack of resources
- Lack of coordination
- Lack of support from other management levels
- Resistance from lower levels
- Poor planning activities
- Sudden changes
- Fear of losing something valuable
- Lack of skills and knowledge
- Unpleasant previous experiences
- Commitment to previous practices
- Strong organizational culture
- Internal politics
- Trade unions
- Government regulations
- Cost of change
- Financial difficulties
- Other priorities
- Technical difficulties
- Fear of insecurity

We can perhaps add many other items to this list or combine some of them together. Again, one can claim that they are also often interrelated and perhaps be foreseen and overcome by clearly assessing the implementation factors and the relationships among them that are illustrated in Figure 9.1 and explained in Table 9.1.

The identification of potential barriers to strategy implementation is vital. However, it is perhaps more important to decide on and evaluate methods that tourism and hospitality companies can overcome and manage possible sources of resistance to strategy implementation. Kotter and Schlesinger's (1979) pioneering study advocated six strategies: education and communication, participation and involvement, facilitation and support, negotiation and agreement, manipulation and cooptation, and coercion. Similar strategies have been suggested by other scholars and researchers. Interestingly, they further recommend that multiple strategies should be employed that are contingent on the organizational situation rather than relying on only one of them.

Okumus (2001; 2003) claimed that the most important method of understanding and overcoming the barriers to implementing strategy is to examine and evaluate the strategic context in which strategies are developed and implemented. As just explained, strategic context consists of environmental uncertainty, organizational structure, organizational culture, and leadership. For example, Okumus (2003) illustrates how a large hotel group failed to implement a revenue management project because they had major problems in the strategic context matching the external environment, they had frequent changes in the senior management team, and their organizational culture and structure did not facilitate a smooth strategy formulation and development.

STRATEGY IMPLEMENTATION AND CHANGE IN THE INTERNATIONAL CONTEXT

It is important to pay close attention to diversity and cultural differences when developing and implementing strategies in different locations and cultures. There can be major variations in the characteristics of strategy implementation factors in different locations and cultures. Hofstede (1993) provides interesting examples of how leadership styles, organizational cultures, structures, and, subsequently, communication vary among countries. For example, Hofstede claims that matrix organizational structure is commonly accepted in the United States, but in France it is not popular, since employees do not like to report to two bosses. Again, barriers and resistance to strategies may vary depending on the location and culture, which may require the use of different strategies in overcoming these barriers. In some countries, such as the United States, employees may openly express their frustration and difficulties with a new process, whereas in countries like Japan, employees may not show their true feelings openly. In short, developing and implementing a strategy in an international context is more challenging and complicated.

There may be specific national preferences in developing and implementing strategies (De Wit and Meyer, 2004). For example, based on their extensive study, Kagono, T., Nonaka, I., Sakakibara, K., Sakamoto, S., and Johnnson, J. (1985) claim that there are differences between the United States and Japanese companies in managing change. U.S. companies follow a guided, logical, deductive approach to achieve a competitive advantage, while Japanese companies follow an inductive, stepwise gradual approach to build on existing strengths. De Wit and Meyer (2004) suggest that the research on strategy formation and managing change in the international context is limited. However, they tentatively suggest a number of areas to explain why strategy formation may be different in different countries. The first issue they refer to is the difference of mechanic and organic organizations. Mechanic organizational structure is dominant mainly in English-speaking countries and France, where there are clear rules for hierarchy, power sharing, tasks, job descriptions, communication, and decision making. On the other hand, in some countries, such as Japan, organizations often have organic structures where job descriptions are not often clearly defined and there is extensive informal communication and coordination both horizontally and vertically to create a strong common set of beliefs and a shared vision. These authors call such organizations "clan-like firms."

De Wit and Meyer further note that in some countries, like the United States and the United Kingdom, companies value their employees and managers but often try to minimize their dependence on them by implementing formalized systems and procedures. On the other hand, managers and employees may not share all their learning and experience with the company, since they may use their learning and experience to negotiate a better position and salary with the same company or with another company. However, in clan-like organizations, employees have job security and therefore they are more committed. As a result, they share information, better prepare themselves for different tasks and changing conditions, and actively participate in decision making and taking responsibility when necessary.

The third issue raised by De Wit and Meyer (2004) is the role of senior managers. In some countries, new strategies, plans, and initiatives come from (or are expected to come from) the senior managers, and the lower managers are expected to implement them. In some countries, senior managers' leadership style is less direct and less viable. Senior managers are expected to facilitate strategies and new initiatives together with their colleagues from different management levels. In other words, new strategies and initiatives come from within the organization. The fourth issue raised by De Wit and Meyer is the short-term time orientation versus the long-term time orientation. In short-term-oriented cultures, such as English-speaking countries, there is a stronger preference for fast, radical change and to generate quick results. In longer-term-oriented cultures, the focus is on long-term success and therefore they see the strategy development and implementation as a marathon. Certainly, all of these factors can be attributed to Hofstede's (1993) cross-cultural dimensions: individualism versus collectivism, masculinity versus feminity power distance, and uncertainty avoidance and long-term orientation.

SUMMARY

This chapter proposed a strategy implementation framework. This framework does not view strategy formulation and implementation as different phases because strategy formation is far too complex to be explained by prescriptive linear models. In order to understand strategy formulation and implementation issues and make the right choices, it is essential that we should place ourselves in a position where we can make informed judgments about the process of strategy formulation and implementation rather than follow ready-made solutions. To be able to do this, we should employ a holistic approach of viewing the formulation and implementation of strategy and then evaluate how multiple factors interact with one another and how they impact on the strategy formation process.

The chapter provided explanations about the role and importance of each implementation factor and its relationship with other factors. The framework in this chapter can be used for a retrospective analysis of past, current, and future cases of strategy formation. The strategy content, the characteristics of the external and internal context, the operational process, and the outcome can be evaluated for specific implementation cases. Specific questions can be asked about the role and impact of each implementation factor on the process of change and, subsequently, the outcome. The challenges, problems, and difficulties of strategy formation can be predicted and evaluated using the framework and checkpoints in Table 9.1. Finally, when analyzing and evaluating strategy formation in a cross-cultural context, we should acknowledge that there will be variances in approaching strategic management practices in different cultures. The framework developed here should again be used to question where these differences may emerge and how they can be managed.

STUDY QUESTIONS

1. Why do H&T organizations need to initiate new strategies?

2. Why is it difficult to initiate and implement strategies?

3. What are the key implementation factors and how can we group them?

4. Why do strategies fail?

5. Can you give any examples about a company that initiated and implemented a strategy well?

6. Do you think being able to implement strategies well and on time can be a source of competitive advantage? Why or why not?

7. Why do diversity and cultural differences in international H&T organizations pose challenges in developing and implementing strategies?

REFERENCES AND FURTHER READINGS

Alexander, L.D. (1985). Successfully Implementing Strategic Decisions, *Long Range Planning*, (18) 3, 91–97.

Alexander, L.D. (1991). Strategy Implementation: Nature of the Problem. In D. Hussey (Ed.), *International Review of Strategic Management*, (2)1, 73–96. Chichester: New York: John Wiley & Sons Ltd.

Argyris, C. (1988). Review Assay: First- and Second-Order Errors in Managing Strategic Change: The Role of Organizational Defensive Routines. In A.M. Pettigrew (Ed.), *The Management of Strategic Change*. Oxford: Basil Blackwell.

Bartlett, C.A. and Ghoshal, S. (1987). Managing Across Borders: New Strategic Requirements, *Sloan Management Review*, (28)2, 7–17.

Bergadaà, M. (1999). Strategic Decision and Implementation: Prodin™, A Prospective Dialectic Interpersonal Model, *Journal of Business Research*, (45)2, 211–220.

Bryson, J. and Bromiley, P. (1993). Critical Factors Affecting the Planning and Implementation of Major Projects, *Strategic Management Journal*, (14)2, 319–337.

Buchanan D. and Boddy, D. (1992). *The Expertise of the Change Agent: Public Performance and Backstage Activity*. New York: Prentice Hall.

Dawson, P. (1994). *Organizational Change, A Processual Approach*. London: Sage.

Dawson, P. (1997). In at the deep end: Conducting Processual Research on Organizational Change, *Scandinavian Journal of Management*, (13)4, 389–405.

De Foe, J.A. and Janssen, A. (2001). Implementing a Strategy Successfully, *Measuring Business Excellence*, (5)4, 4–6.

De Wit, B. and Meyer, R. (2004). *Strategy: Process, Content and Context, An International Perspective*. London: Thompson.

Epstein, M. and Manzoni, J. (1998). Implementing Corporate Strategy: From Tableaux de Board to Balanced Scorecards, *European management Journal*, (16)2, 190–203.

Galbraith, J. and Kazanjian, R. (1986). *Strategy Implementation: Structure Systems and Process*, 2nd ed. New York: West Publishing Company.

Galpin, T.J. (1997). *Making Strategy Work*. San Francisco: Jossey-Bass Publishers.

Govindarajan, V. (1988). A Contingency Approach to Strategy Implementation at the Business Unit Level: Integrating Administrative Mechanisms with Strategy, *Academy of Management Journal*, (31)4, 828–853.

Hambrick, D. and Cannella, A. (1989). Strategy Implementation as Substance and Selling, *The Academy of Management Executive*, (3)4, 278–285.

Hope-Hailey, V. and Balogun, J. (2002). Devising Context Sensitive Approaches to Change: The Examples of Glaxo Wellcome, *Long Range Planning*, (35)2, 153–178.

Hrebiniak, L. (1992). Implementing Global Strategies, *European Management Journal*, (10)4, 392–395.

Hrebiniak, L. and Joyce, W. (1984). *Implementing Strategy*. New York: MacMillan.

Hussey, D. (1998). Strategic Management: Past Experiences and Future Directions. In D. Hussey (Ed.), *The Strategic Decision Challenge*. –John Wily & Sons Ltd. Chichester.

Kaplan, R.S. and Norton, D.P. (1996). *The Balance Scorecard—Translating Strategy into Action*. Boston: Harvard Business School Press.

Kaplan, R.S. and Norton, D.P. (2001). *The Strategy-Focused Organization: How Balanced Scorecard Companies Thrive in the new Business Environment*. Boston: Harvard Business School Press.

Kogono, T., Nonaka, I., Sakakibara, K., Sakamoto, S., and Johnnson, J. (1985). *Strategic versus Evolutionary Management: A US–Japan Comparison of Strategy and Organization*. Amsterdam: North Holland.

Kotter, J.P. (1995). Leading Change: Why Transformation Efforts Fail, *Harvard Business Review*, (73)2, 59–67.

Kotter, J.P. and Schlesinger, L.A. (1979). Choosing strategies for change, *Harvard Business Review*, (57)2, –106–114.

Lorange, P. (1998). Strategy Implementation: The New Realities, *Long Range Planning*, (31)1, 18–29.

Miller, D. (2002). Successful Change Leaders: What Makes Them? What Do They Do That Is Different?, *Journal of Change Management*, (2)4, 359–368.

Miller, S. (1997). Implementing Strategic Decisions: Four Key Success Factors, *Organization Studies*, (18)4, 577–602.

Miller, A. and Dess, G. (1996). *Strategic Management*, International Edition. New York: The McGraw-Hill Companies, Inc.

Mintzberg, H., Ahlstrand, B., and Lampel, J. (1998). *Strategy Safari*. London: Prentice Hall.

Noble, C.H. (1999a). Building the Strategy Implementation Network, *Business Horizon*, November–December, 19–28.

Noble, C.H., (1999b). The Eclectic Roots of Strategy Implementation Research, *Journal of Business Research*, (45)2, 119–134.

Nørreklit, H. (2000). The Balanced Scorecard—A Critical Analysis of Some of Its Assumptions, *Management Accounting Research*, (11)1, 65–88.

Okumus, F. (2000). Strategy Implementation: A Study of International Hotel Groups. Unpublished Doctoral Thesis. Oxford Brookes University, Oxford, UK.

Okumus, F. (2001). Towards a Strategy Implementation Framework, *International Journal of Contemporary Hospitality Management*, (13)7, 327–338.

Okumus, F. (2003). A Framework to Implement Strategies in Organizations, *Management Decision*, 41(9), 871–883.

–Okumus, F. and Hemmington, N. (1998). Barriers and Resistance to Change in Hotel Firms: An Investigation at Unit Level, *International Journal of Contemporary Hospitality Management*, 10(7), 283–288.

Okumus, F. and Roper A, (1999). A Review of Disparate Approaches to Strategy Implementation in Hospitality Firms, *Journal of Hospitality and Tourism Research*, 23(1), 20–38.

–Pettigrew, A.M. (1987). Context and Action in the Transformation of the Firm, *Journal of Management Studies*, (24)6, 649–670.

Pettigrew, A.M. (1992). The Character and Significance of Strategy Process Research, *Strategic Management Journal*, (13)1, 5–16.

Pettigrew, A.M. and Whipp, R. (1991). *Managing Change for Competitive Success*. Oxford: Blackwell.

Reed, R. and Buckley, M. (1988). Strategy in Action—Techniques for Implementing Strategy, *Long Range Planning*, (21)3, 67–74.

Roth, K., Schweiger, M., and Morrison, J. (1991). Global Strategy Implementation at Unit Level: Operational Capabilities and Administrative Mechanisms, *Journal of International Business Studies*, (22)3, 369–402.

Schmelzer, C. and Olsen, M. (1994). A Data Based Strategy Implementing Framework for Companies in the Restaurant Industry, *International Journal of Hospitality Management*, (13)4, 347–359.

Skivington, E.J. and Daft, L.R. (1991). A Study of Organizational Framework and Process Modalities for the Implementation of Business Level Strategic Decisions, *Journal of Management Studies*, (28)1, 45–68.

Stacey, R.D. (1996). *Strategic Management & Organizational Dynamics*, 2nd ed. London: Pitman Publishing.

Stonich, P. (1982). *Implementing Strategy: Making Strategy Happen*. Massachusetts: Ballinger.

Strabel, P. (1996). 'Why Do Employees Resist Change?, *Harvard Business Review*, (74)3, 86–92.

Thompson, A and Strickland, A. (1999). *Strategic Management Concepts and Cases*, 11th ed. Boston, Mass: McGraw-Hill/Irwin.

Vasconcellos e Sa', J. (1990). How to Implement a Strategy, *Business*, (40)2, 23–32.

Waterman, R.H., Peters, T.J., and Phillips, J.R. (1980). Structure is not Organization, *Business Horizons*, (23)3, 14–26.

Wilson, I. (1994). Strategic Planning Isn't Dead—It Changed, *Long Range Planning*, (27)4, 12–24.

Yip, G.S. (1992). *Total Global Strategy*. London: Prentice Hall.

Synthesis

Part V integrates the key themes and concepts discussed in earlier chapters in an effort to provide readers with the holistic perspective. It summarises main discussions in previous chapters.

CHAPTER 10

Conclusions: Relating Content, Context, and Process

Learning Objectives

After reading this chapter, you should be able to:

1. Integrate the key themes explored in earlier chapters.
2. Discuss the challenges of strategic management for H&T organizations.
3. Provide a holistic perspective of strategic management practices in the H&T context.
4. Evaluate the dynamics of context, content, process, and outcome.
5. Provide discussions about gaining a sustainable competitive advantage.
6. Provide suggestions about turning H&T organizations into learning organizations.
7. Discuss strategic management practices in an international context.

CONTENTS

INTRODUCTION

This book is aimed at senior undergraduate and postgraduate students in travel, tourism, and, hospitality/hotel management programs who are studying strategic management. We have aimed to produce a valuable source for students and practicing managers in H&T organizations. This text combines both prescriptive and descriptive approaches to strategic management that should offer both teachers and students a better educational and applied

191

approach. This final chapter integrates the key themes explored in earlier chapters to provide readers with the holistic perspective that is inherent in effective strategic management practice.

THE CHALLENGE OF STRATEGIC MANAGEMENT IN THE H&T CONTEXT

Strategic management is a process through which a firm is able to set a mission, a vision, goals, and objectives, as well as craft and execute strategies at various levels of its hierarchy in order to create and sustain a competitive advantage so the firm can achieve its goals and survive in the long term. Strategic management provides a holistic view and can help H&T organizations prioritize important choices for them. It has four main elements: strategic analysis, formulation, implementation, and evaluation. Although these four elements are often presented as distinct phases in reality, they overlap and go hand in hand.

Strategic management has evolved over the past 50 years. In the 1960s, it was viewed from a general management perspective, with emphasis on the role of the leader. During the late 1960s and the 1970s, strategic management was viewed more as a strategic planning exercise. In the 1980s and 1990s, more attention was given to competitive advantage and strategy implementation. Scholars focused on firms' competencies to explain strategy, which led to the emergence of the resource-based view of the firm.

In the 1990s, globalization led to the emergence of network strategies, and strategic alliances became the focal point around which researchers developed the literature. More efforts from a resource-based perspective led to the conceptualization of characteristics related to the firm's internal competencies that enabled them to sustain a competitive advantage. The shift toward internal competencies also saw a shift in perspective toward the knowledge-based view and learning at the core of strategic competitive advantage in the late 1990s. There have been continued efforts using the knowledge perspective during the 2000s, with increased emphasis on corporate social responsibility and understanding complexities in business environments.

In line with the preceding developments, several strategic management schools of thought have emerged. As explained in Chapter 1, Mintzberg, Ahlstrand, and Lampel (1998) identified ten schools or perspectives: design, planning, positioning, entrepreneurial, cognitive, learning, power, cultural, environmental, and configuration. As explained by Mintzberg and his colleagues, the first three schools are more prescriptive, with an emphasis on strategy formulation that developed from the 1960s to the 1980s. The next six schools are less prescriptive and more descriptive while emphasizing how strategies are developed and implemented. The tenth school (configurational) conceptually combines and captures the other nine schools into an integrative whole.

In the H&T field, strategic management emerged as a field of study in the mid- to late 1980s that aimed at applying strategic management models and frameworks to H&T organizations. Most of these efforts aimed at applying and confirming theories related to the contingency, strategic planning, and competitive strategies. In the H&T domain, Olsen, West, and Tse (1998) developed the coalignment concept. Later efforts by Harrington (2001), Okumus (2004), and Jogaratnam and Law (2006) in the 2000s focused on environmental scanning in the hospitality industry context, whereas Harrington and Kendall (2006), Okumus and Roper (1999), and Okumus (2001), among others, attempted to develop the strategy implementation framework for H&T firms during this period. More recent efforts in the field have moved toward a knowledge-based view and corporate social responsibility.

Like all other organizations, H&T organizations need to create value for its stakeholders. In order to create value and develop a sustainable competitive edge, it is essential for H&T organizations to employ both strategic planning and strategic thinking so they can engage in a constant assessment of their strategic position and competencies. Many factors in H&T organizations' external and internal environments constantly change. In other words, the complexity and variability associated with creating and sustaining competitive advantage is high. Therefore, H&T organizations need to constantly analyze the external and internal environments so they can identify developments and changes. Then, based on this information, they can formulate and implement their strategies at the corporate, business, and functional levels and finally evaluate their progress and outcomes.

Strategic management entails futuristic thinking and developing a course of action to survive and create a sustainable competitive advantage. H&T organizations need to first of all define their vision, mission, goals, and objectives. The vision can be defined as the desired future state of an organization. The mission statement explains why the organization is in existence. Goals are general statements in terms of what the organization aims to achieve in a certain period of time to fulfill its mission and vision. Objectives are definite and quantifiable so they can be measured. Strategies clearly identify how the objectives will be met in terms of the plan, and tactics are the actions that operationalize the strategy—those that lead to the attainment of objectives.

What is important here is that H&T organizations not only need to develop their vision, mission, goals, objectives, policies, and strategies, but they must also revise them if and when necessary in response to developments and changes in their environments as well as expectations from their shareholders and stakeholders. In other words, vision, mission, goals, objectives, policies, and strategies should not be static but should be questioned and revised if and when necessary.

It is also essential to carefully evaluate the responsibilities of an H&T organization. For example, four responsibilities for a business are economic, legal, ethical, and discretionary (Hunger and Wheelen, 2003):

1. *Economic* responsibilities refer to producing goods and services that will be purchased by customers so an H&T organization can financially survive. This is more related to satisfying shareholders' expectations.

2. *Legal* responsibilities refer to laws and regulations that H&T organizations need to obey. Interestingly, many H&T organizations operate in different countries and cultures or offer services and products from different countries. Thus, their legal responsibilities are complicated.

3. *Ethical* responsibilities refer to following and respecting generally accepted beliefs and values in a society. Similar to legal responsibilities, many H&T organizations operate in different cultures and countries. Therefore, they need to be sensitive to the beliefs and values in different cultures.

4. *Discretionary* responsibilities refer to voluntary obligations in which an organization may like to participate, such as charity events and making donations. We know that increasingly stakeholders, including customers and employees, are paying more attention to whether H&T firms are participating in ethical and discretionary activities.

H&T organizations can be grouped under different categories depending on their primary activities, size, profit motive, and geographic coverage. These broad groups and subgroupings are helpful when analyzing the diverse nature of the industry. Certainly, some of the firms can be placed under multiple groupings. Depending on their functional area, size, profit, and nonprofit motives and geographical coverage, the internal and operational environments, the level of competition, the barriers to entry and exit, and substitutes and resource requirements may vary, and there may be differences in organizational culture, structure, cost structure, competitive strategies, and resource levels. As discussed earlier, such differences have implications on the application of strategic management theories and models in H&T organizations.

On the one hand, one may claim that because of these differences, we should be cautious about making generalizations about management practices in H&T organizations. It can be claimed that regardless of the different services offered by H&T organizations, close attention needs to be paid to the unique characteristics of H&T organizations: inseparability, perishability, intangibility, heterogeneity, cost structure, and labor intensiveness. Ignoring these unique characteristics can lead to unexpected outcomes. We need to acknowledge the differences among H&T organizations in terms of their size, service type, profit motive, and customer segment and at the same time see their common, unique characteristics.

What is evident is that despite the differences and similarities among H&T organizations, most of them operate in dynamic and complex environments. Changes in legislations, regional and global economic and political crises, sociocultural trends, sophistication of customers, stiff competition, terrorism, security, global warming, multiculturalism, globalization, mergers and acquisitions, labor shortages, and advanced technological developments all pose important challenges to the owners and managers of H&T organizations. Managing the firm through a strategic management perspective can help H&T organizations not only in responding to these trends and developments but also in proactively developing strategies to change the rule of the game.

THE DYNAMICS OF CONTENT, CONTEXT, PROCESS, AND OUTCOME

As explained earlier, *content* refers to description, selection, and justification of a certain strategy (or strategies). Content is all about explaining what the strategy is and why it needs to be chosen, developed, and implemented. *Context* refers to the environment in which strategies are developed and implemented. The context can be grouped under the external environment (macro and industry) and internal environment. The *process* refers to development and implementation of strategies in the external and internal contexts. *Outcome* refers to intended and unintended results of the deployment of strategies. We want to emphasize here that rather than seeing strategic management as a step-by-step process, we need to focus more on dynamics and interactions among content, context, process, and outcome. This cannot only help us better understand, what, why, where, and how, but it makes it easier to strategically analyze each H&T firm's situation.

Strategic management is important to H&T organizations regardless of their size and type. However, we should stress that H&T organizations operate in unique external and internal contexts, which makes it particularly important to understand why certain strategies are developed and how they are developed and implemented. For example, the environment in which they operate impacts the firms in it in terms of the strategies they formulate, the investments they make, and the value they generate from such investments. Large corporations such as McDonald's, Marriott, and Hilton and small ones like independent family hotels are all exposed to the same macro environment.

The alignment between the firm and its environment has been emphasized in terms of strategy formulation and implementation over several decades of work conducted by scholars starting from as early as the 1950s. However, on the other hand, if we critically analyze certain H&T organizations strategies such as Disney, Southwest Airlines, and McDonald's, they have not only aligned themselves to the external environment but have also manipulated and influenced the external environment and thus changed the rules of the game in the industry. In other words, H&T organizations should not just try to align themselves with the external environment but should also look at their distinctive competencies very carefully and influence the external environment by putting these competencies to productive use by offering unique products and services.

The H&T industry has experienced dramatic changes in customer expectations and needs. They not only need to develop new products and service concepts on an ongoing basis, but they must also control their costs and manage their human resources wisely. Supporting Pine and Gilmore's (1998) view, many H&T organizations such as Disney World, Hilton, Marriott, and Starbucks refer to their respective services as *an experience*. This requires changing the mindset of managers and employees in their strategic thinking and daily actions. In order to achieve this shift, there is a need to know both the H&T context and how this strategic change can be achieved in that context.

As noted earlier, McGahan and Porter (1997) and Porter (1980) claimed that the industry context does matter because it can influence the strategy formation process. Conversely, Baden-Fuller and Stopford (1994) argued that it is the internal characteristics of firms that matter most, not the industry. These authors claim that successful organizations are able to skillfully ride the waves of industry crises, and less successful ones disappear due to industry misfortunes besetting the industry. For example, Southwest Airlines has been profitable and successful since the early 1970s, while many other major airlines have faced serious challenges, and some of them have even declared bankruptcy. Here, the industry structure and characteristics are considered to be of secondary importance, and the internal distinctive competencies play a crucial role.

Given these conflicting views as to whether the industry context or the individual firm is more important when devising a strategic plan, we propose a different but more holistic view on this controversial issue. In support of McGahan and Porter (1997), we believe that the industry structure and the unique characteristics of the H&T industry do matter and that they can have a clear impact on the strategy-making process and on the productivity and profitability of H&T organizations. Therefore, we need to have a better and deeper understanding of how the external environment affects the H&T industry. We further acknowledge that the industry context is one of the dimensions impacting the management practices in H&T organizations and their performance.

We also need take into consideration the importance of firm-specific factors on performance and to embrace many of the insights derived from the resource-based view. There is an essential need to identify and discuss those factors that arise both externally and internally to influence the performance of H&T organizations. To achieve this, we can use and apply those strategy theories, models, and frameworks and be informed by the propositions developed in the generic field of strategic management in the H&T context. Supporting Lowendahl's (2000) arguments, to do this, we must have a better understanding and in-depth knowledge of both the generic strategy literature and the unique internal characteristics of H&T organizations.

Following Lowendahl (2000), we can claim that service firms are different and therefore many of the strategic management models and frameworks, such as Porter's value chain analysis, and generic strategies may have to be modified or even changed greatly for the context specific aspects of the service sector. In short, the context at both the industry level and the organizational level is crucial to be able to use and apply strategic management theories and models in H&T organizations.

The importance of context to strategy making means that the preceding argument holds across all industrial sectors, not just hospitality and tourism. All issues related to the strategy development and implementation process and the strategy content must always be framed within that specific context. In other words, we cannot meaningfully separate the strategy process from its industry context or from its internal organizational context.

SUSTAINING COMPETITIVENESS

Hospitality and tourism organisations should first identify their tangible and intangible resources. Tangible assets are plant, equipment, and/or land, whereas intangible assets are associated with the company knowhow and skills sets. They have no physical presence but represent real benefit to the organisation. They include company reputation and brand, product reputation and brand, employee/leadership skills/experience and knowhow, culture, networks, databases, supplier knowhow, distributor knowhow, public knowledge, contracts, intellectual property rights, and trade secrets.

Capabilities relate to a firm's skills, routines, and activities. Inherent in them are also management decision making, creativity and knowledge building, and sharing- and retention-related activities. It should be noted that organizational culture, leadership, management style, and management practices form an integral component of organizational capabilities. For instance, Marriott's management capabilities are distinctive in how it combines operating and technological knowhow along with knowledge building, sharing, and retention activities. This has played a big role in how the firm has been able to build brand equity internationally over the past few decades. Walt Disney has unique competencies in developing entertainment-based products and services bundles, including filmmaking (animation), giving it uniqueness in its product-service market. Competencies are a product of resources and capabilities and are distinctive if the firm can combine them to create a unique advantage.

Core capabilities and distinctive competencies are built on tangible (what the company has) and intangible (what the company can do) assets. Core capabilities refer to those areas that an H&T company does exceedingly well, whereas distinctive competencies refer to those areas and activities in which an H&T company excels (Wheelen and Hunger, 2006). Core capabilities are the most critical and most distinctive assets an organisation possesses, and they are the most difficult to copy when effectively linked with appropriate strategic targets in a value chain that begins and ends with the company's key stakeholders (Brownell, 2008). H&T organisations should amalgamate their core competencies, including their special knowledge, skills, and technological knowhow, that distinguish them from others with business processes that they use to deliver products, services, and other outputs.

H&T organizations need to protect, exploit, and enhance their unique intangible assets. While a competitive advantage is obtained by appealing to customers in targeted markets, sustainable competitive advantage is the result of developing and combining several distinctive competencies, which are eventually difficult to imitate and substitute by competitors. To better explain this issue, we need to refer back to the research-based view in the strategic management field, which suggests that a competitive advantage comes from a firm's unique tangible and intangible resources (Barney, 1991). For a resource to be competitively advantageous, it must be *valuable*, *rare*, *inimitable*, and *nonsubstitutable*, and the firm should be organized in a way that it can effectively and efficiently exploit the resource (Barney and Wright, 1998).

If a resource is to be considered valuable, it should contribute to the company's performance in the areas of finance, HRM, marketing, operations, and innovation. For example, a hotel company may own a piece of land that has a certain dollar value, but if the land does not contribute to the company's bottom line, it may not be considered a strategic resource. A rare resource is one that competitors do not possess or that is not easily available. For instance, the unique shows and attractions of the World Disney Parks are products and services that are delivered through a combination of unique resources and capabilities. These products and services are valuable and inimitable due to the efficient exploitation of resources and capabilities.

To protect your valuable assets from being imitated, H&T companies need to do well in different areas and connect all their resources and competencies with one another. This will create barriers for competitors to imitate not only all the key resources but also create connections among them. For example, Pfeffer (1994; 1995) noted that Southwest Airlines' competitive advantage mostly comes from several closely related areas: a very well-trained, productive, and dedicated workforce and managers; a positive and caring organizational culture; a relatively flat organizational structure; and a strong service delivery culture. Over the years, Southwest Airlines has managed to operate fewer employees per aircraft, fly more passengers per employee, and make available more seat miles per employee. They have won the Triple Crown award because of the fewest lost bags and fewest passenger complaints (Barney and Wright, 1998; Pfeffer, 1994). In other words, a combination of a great organizational culture, well-trained and dedicated employees, a healthy organizational structure, and a high level of customer service have created a sustainable competitive advantage for Southwest Airlines that is considered difficult to imitate.

Many of the competencies in this company have evolved over many years and are shaped by the organization's unique culture, structure, history, and founders. Therefore, their competitors have not been able to easily duplicate the history and culture in which those practices are embedded (Harrell-Cook, 2002). For example, Continental Airlines, United Airlines, and Delta have all attempted to compete with Southwest Airlines by providing low-cost service to a number of destinations. However, they have not been able to deliver superior performance. Herb Kelleher, the cofounder of Southwest Airlines, stated that even if their competitors achieved the same level of cost structure and quality service, they could not create the spirit of Southwest employees' attitude toward service (Barney and Wright, 1998).

H&T firms should focus on linking resources and capabilities with strategies. The link among resources, capabilities, and strategies is such that one shapes the other two. A cost-leader firm should be able to develop resources and capabilities that enable it to sustain its position. Likewise, a broad differentiator should be able to use its resources and capabilities to develop an array of products and services for various market segments. Resource development of the firm should complement the competitive strategy so there is alignment between the former and the latter. A misalignment is the reason for failure in many a case, such as Holiday Inn in the 1980s.

It should be noted that existing competencies would influence the strategies that firms formulate in a given market. However, a strategic orientation of firms should be one that builds resources and capabilities to capture emerging or future opportunities. This goes back to the discussion on strategic fit and strategic intent (see Chapter 3). For firms to be able to create a sustainable competitive advantage, it is imperative that strategic intent should be at the core of the firm's orientation with its market/environment. This would also provide the firms with a sustainable competitive advantage, especially for those that rely more on their intangible resources and capabilities. This is exemplified in Hilton's expertise in managing upscale hotel properties and their competencies in executing management contracts, which were used to tap opportunities in the American business and leisure travel markets globally during the 1970s and 1980s. More and more hotel property owners in global markets wanted the American hotel firm to manage their properties, which led to the rapid growth of the firm during this period that included markets such as Puerto Rico, France, Turkey, and Hong Kong. In the past two decades, Marriott, Hilton, Hyatt, and other hotel firms have emerged as leading players in the international market in terms of developing competencies related to managing hotels globally.

MANAGING CHANGE AND CREATING LEARNING ORGANIZATIONS

As noted in Chapter 9, companies often face more challenges and difficulties in managing change rather than analyzing their environment and making strategic choices. As noted by Miller (2002), about 70 percent of efforts in managing change and implementing strategies fail. In relation to this, Okumus (2001; 2003) claimed that failure to analyze and change the strategic context is the main reason why strategies are not developed and implemented successfully. As noted in Chapter 9, strategic context consists of environmental uncertainty, organizational structure, organizational culture, and leadership. It is often the case that organizations cannot adapt to the changes and developments in the external environment and change their structure, culture, and leadership in a timely matter.

After looking at how companies in different sectors managed change successfully and survived and succeeded regardless of developments in the external environment, Pettigrew and Whipp (1993) identified four success factors for organizations to manage change and be successful:

1. Having key actors who champion assessment techniques that increase the openness of the organization to new ideas and changes.

2. The structural and cultural characteristics of the company that facilitate healthy information freely and cooperation among different levels and functional areas.

3. Environmental pressures are recognized in organization, and their potential implications are well received and responded to by the members.

4. Assessment is undertaken as a multifunction activity, and it is seen as an end in itself but is then linked back to prosperity and further development of the business.

H&T organizations should be more adaptive and receptive to new ideas and practices and should be able to implement their strategies successfully and on time. To turn hospitality organizations into learning organizations, responsibility and accountability should be distributed more widely across these organizations. Many H&T organizations, regardless of their size, have rigid mindsets, cultures, and structures. Adaptability is not only a function of size but rather of mindset, leadership, culture, processes, and organizational structure. In order to manage change and create a learning organization, Macmillan and Tampoe (2000) recommend the following:

- Flexible information systems that provide business needs without losing financial or operational control

- Leadership that both mentors and influences appropriate behaviors among members but at the same time makes sure that everything works to exception

- Effective followers who are proactive and willing to learn new skills and to change when necessary

- Flexibility among organizational members in terms of forming and reforming teams
- Sensors that can catch mood swings and alert to emerging challenges
- Senior executives with flexible and open minds to change the organization to current needs
- Systems and structures that *continuously* scan and analyze external and internal environments
- A fast and successful implementation ability to turn new strategies quickly into action
- Valuing and capitalizing on an organization's intellectual capital (p. 270)

An organization's adaptability also reflects its overall posture toward learning and knowledge management. A competitive advantage is sustainable only if firms have effective learning processes in place, and a learning organization is one that is able to develop and sustain an effective feedback loop. This would ensure that firms are able to adjust to gaps that appear in its strategic posture and current as well as emerging market trends. It is imperative that once a firm is able to identify the gap that exists between its present position and current/emerging trends, it should be able to initiate change such that the current posture is adjusted to reflect a shift in orientation in a given market. This is possible only if the firm has an effective feedback loop, which would enable the firm to quickly act on the information it has gathered and the knowledge it has developed.

STRATEGIC MANAGEMENT IN AN INTERNATIONAL CONTEXT

There is limited knowledge available about how far strategic management practices differ in international firms than strategic management practices in domestic firms. Scholars tend to apply strategic management theories and concepts into the international context and suggest that more emphasis should be given to the diversity and size of companies in the international context. It is clear that there may be major variations in leadership styles, organizational cultures, structures, and subsequently communication styles. Therefore, managers working for international hospitality and tourism organizations should be educated and trained not only about such differences but also how they should respond to and manage such differences. As noted in the preceding chapter, Hofstede's (1993) cross-cultural dimensions can assist us better understand differences in management practices among different cultures.

REFERENCES AND FURTHER READINGS

Baden-Fuller, C. and Stopford, J.M. (1994). *Rejuvenating the Mature Business*. Boston: Harvard Business School.

Barney, J.B. (1991). Firms Resources and Sustained Competitive Advantage, *Journal of Management*, 17, 99–120.

Barney, J. and Wright, P. (1998). On Becoming a Strategic Partner: The Role of Human Resources in Gaining Competitive Advantage, *Human Resources Management*, 37 (1), 31–46.

Brownell, J. (2008). Leading on land and sea: Competencies and context, *International Journal of Hospitality Management*, (27), 137–150.

Deresky, H. (1997). *International Management*. New York: Addison-Wesley.

De Wit, B. and Meyer, R. (2004). *Strategy: Process, Content and Context, An International Perspective*. London: Thompson.

Fatehi, K. (1996). *International Management: Cross-Cultural and Functional Perspectives*. London: Prentice Hall.

Hamel, G. and Prahalad, C.K. (1989). Strategic intent, *Harvard Business Review*, 67 (3), 63–74.

Harrell-Cook, G. (2002). Human Resources Management and Competitive Advantage: A Strategic Perspective. In G.R. Ferris, M. Ronald Buckley, and D.B. Fedor (Eds.), *Human Resources Management*, 4th ed. –New Jersey: Prentice Hall.

Harrington, R. (2001). Environmental uncertainty within the hospitality industry: Exploring the measure of dynamism and complexity between restaurant segments, *Journal of Hospitality and Tourism Research*, 25(4), 386–398.

Harrington, R. and Kendall, K. (2006). Strategy implementation success: The moderating effects of size and environmental complexity and the mediating effects of involvement, *Journal of Hospitality and Tourism Research*, 30(2), 207–230.

Hodgetts, R.M. and Luthans, F. (1997). *International Management*, 3rd ed. New York: McGraw-Hill, Inc

Hofstede, G. (1993). Cultural Constraints in Management Theories, *The Executive*, 7 (1), 81–94.

Hunger, J.D. and Wheelen, T.L. (2003). *Essentials of Strategic Management*, 3rd ed. New York: Prentice Hall.

Jogaratnam, G. and Law, R. (2006). Environmental scanning and information source utilization: Exploring the behaviour of Hong Kong hotel and tourism executives, *Journal of Hospitality and Tourism Research*, 30(2), 170–190.

Leibold, M., Probst, G., and Gibbert, M. (2002). *Strategic Management in the Knowledge Economy: New Approaches and Business Applications*. Erlangen: Publicist.

Lowendahl, B.R. (2000). *Strategic Management of Professional Service Firms*. Copenhagen: Copenhagen Business School Press.

Macmillan, H. and Tampoe, M. (2000). *Strategic Management*. Oxford: Oxford University Press.

McGahan, A. and Porter, M. (1997). How Much Does Industry Matter?, *Strategic Management Journal*, 18 (Special Issue 1), 15–30.

Mead, R. (1998). *International Management*, 2nd ed., Oxford: Blackwell.

Miller, D. (2002). Successful Change Leaders: What Makes Them? What Do They Do That Is Different?, *Journal of Change Management*, (2)4, 359–368.

Mintzberg, H., Ahlstrand, B., Lampel, J. (1998). Strategy safari: A guided tour through the wilds of strategic management. New York: The Free Press.

Okumus, F. (2001). Towards a Strategy Implementation Framework, *International Journal of Contemporary Hospitality Management*, 13 (7), Special Issue, 327–338.

Okumus, F. (2002). Can Hospitality Researchers Contribute to the Strategic Management Literature, *International Journal of Hospitality Management*, 21 (2), 105–110.

Okumus, F. (2003). A Framework to Implement Strategies in Organizations, *Management Decision*, 41 (9), 871–883.

Okumus, F. (2004). Potential Challenges of Employing a Formal Environmental Scanning Approach in Hospitality Organizations, *International Journal of Hospitality Management*, 23 (2), 123–143.

Okumus, F. and Roper A. (1999). A Review of Disparate Approaches to Strategy Implementation in Hospitality Firms, *Journal of Hospitality and Tourism Research*, 23 (1), 20–38.

Okumus, F. and Wong, K. (2005). In Pursuit of Contemporary Content for Courses on Strategic Management in Tourism and Hospitality Schools, *International Journal of Hospitality Management*, 24, in press.

Olsen, M.D., West, J., and Tse, E. (1998). *Strategic Management in the Hospitality Industry*, 3rd ed. Prentice Hall.

Pettigrew, A.M. and Whipp, R. (1991). *Managing Change for Competitive Success*. Oxford: Blackwell.

Pfeffer, J. (1994). *Competitive Advantage through People*. Boston, MA: Harvard Business School Press.

Pfeffer, J. (1995). Producing Sustainable Competitive Advantage through the Effective Management of People, *Academy of Management Executive*, 9, 55–72.

Pine, J. and Gilmore, J. (1998). Welcome to the Experience Economy, *Harvard Business Review*, July–August, 97–105.

Porter, M. (1980). *Competitive Strategy*. New York: The Free Press.

Wheelen, T. and Hunger, J.D. (2006). *Strategic Management and Business Policy*, 3rd ed. New York: Pearson-Prentice Hall.

PART VI

Case Studies

CASE STUDY 1

Ocean Park: In the Face of Competition from Hong Kong Disneyland

Bennett Yim

In April 2006, Ocean Park, Hong Kong's only home-grown theme park, launched a syndicated loan to raise HK$4.1 billion for a master plan to revamp the Park.[1] The master plan represented the Park's strategic response to the arrival of Hong Kong Disneyland, which had opened the previous year. Ocean Park had expected attendance to drop significantly with Disney's opening, but attendance at the Park had remained strong. Nonetheless, the competition posed by Disney was not to be underestimated. How would the commercial banks assess Ocean Park's strategic plan? Would they buy the Park's strategy in light of the competition posed by Disney?

THE TOURISM INDUSTRY IN HONG KONG

Tourism was a major pillar of the Hong Kong economy. In 2004, the territory recorded 21.8 million visitors who spent HK$91.85 billion,[2] which was 2.9% of its GDP.[3] China formed the key source market for tourists to Hong Kong, with 56.2% of its inbound visitors coming from China [see **Exhibit 1**].[4] Hong Kong had been a favourite destination for

CONTENTS

---

[1] US$1 = HK$7.80.

[2] Hong Kong Tourism Board. (2005). *A Statistical Review of Hong Kong Tourism 2004*.

[3] Hong Kong Census and Statistics Department. *Hong Kong Statistics, http://www.censtatd. gov.hk/hong_kong_statistics/statistical_tables/index.jsp?subjectID=12&tableID=189* (accessed August 19, 2006).

[4] Hong Kong Census and Statistics Department. (2006). *Hong Kong in Figures*.

Exhibit 1	Inbound Tourists and Mainland Tourists Visiting Hong Kong by Year		
Year	Number of Inbound Tourists (in Millions)	Number of Mainland Tourists (in Millions)	Percentage of Mainland Tourists among Inbound Visitors to Hong Kong
1996	12.97	2.39	31.00%
1997	11.27	2.36	26.60%
1998	10.16	2.67	27.13%
1999	11.33	3.20	28.24%
2000	13.06	3.79	29.02%
2001	13.73	4.45	32.41%
2002	16.57	6.83	41.22%
2003	15.54	8.47	54.50%
2004	21.81	12.25	56.17%
2005	23.36	12.54	53.70%

Source: Hong Kong Tourism Board. (2006). "A Statistical Review of Hong Kong Tourism 2005."

mainland Chinese since the early 1980s, but it had found itself competing increasingly with other Asian destinations in the 1990s as the Chinese government liberalised travel policies toward other countries such as Thailand, Malaysia, and Singapore.[5]

The Asian financial crisis hit Hong Kong badly in 1997 and raised concerns about the structure of its economy, which relied heavily on the finance and real estate sectors.[6] The crisis highlighted the need for Hong Kong to diversify its economic base, and the government began to call for the development of industries based on knowledge and driven by innovation while continuing to strengthen the service industries which were key contributors to the territory's economy, such as finance, logistics, and tourism. Hong Kong was run as a laissez-faire economy under British colonial rule, and the Hong Kong government continued using this system after the territory reverted to Chinese rule in 1997. But the government took a more active role when market forces alone appeared to be insufficient to drive the territory's structural transformation.[7]

---

[5] Zhang, H.Q. and Heung, V.C S. (2001). "The Emergence of the Mainland Chinese Outbound Travel Market and its Implications," *Journal of Vacation Marketing*, 8 (1): 7–12.

[6] Official Record of Proceedings of the Hong Kong Legislative Council, *http://www.legco.gov.hk/yr98-99/english/eounmtg/hansard/981111fe.htm* (accessed November 11, 1998).

[7] Leung, T.K. (2005). "A Review and Outlook of Hong Kong Industry's Restructuring," *http://www.tdctrade.com/econforum/boc/boc050302.htm* (accessed October 29, 2006).

Hong Kong was frequently seen as a business city and associated with deal-making, dining, and shopping.[8] Tourist activities in Hong Kong were biased strongly toward shopping, with tourists spending half of their expenses on shopping as compared with only 3% on sightseeing. Unlike some countries such as China, Hong Kong had few natural scenic endowments and therefore had to develop its own attractions. In 2001, the government announced the development of five tourism clusters to increase the attractiveness of Hong Kong to tourists, the redevelopment of Ocean Park being one of them [see **Exhibit 2**].[9] These projects, together with the construction of a Disney theme park, formed part of the government's plan to turn Hong Kong from a mere business destination into a family destination.

OCEAN PARK

Background

Ocean Park, located at Aberdeen on the south side of Hong Kong island, was opened in 1977. It was Hong Kong's only home-grown theme park. It was also the largest marine-based theme park in Asia and the only Asian park to be accredited by the American Zoo and Aquarium Association. The Park's construction was funded by the Hong Kong Jockey Club and was built on land provided by the government at a nominal premium. In July 1987, the Park was severed from the Hong Kong Jockey Club to become a statutory body incorporated under the Ocean Park Corporate Ordinance. The mandate of the Ocean Park Corporate was to manage Ocean Park as a public and recreational park and to provide facilities for educational, recreational, and conservation activities to the public on a self financing basis.

Ocean Park had enjoyed a surplus in income since it opened until 1997,[10] when the Asian financial crisis hit Hong Kong. The crisis began a spell of losses for the Park that lasted four consecutive years [see **Exhibit 3**]. Through creative special events, aggressive marketing, and heavy promotions on the mainland, the Park returned to profitability with a HK$15.3

[8] Gluckman, R. "Mickey Mouse Meets Mao," *http://www.gluckman.com/HKDisney.htm* (accessed July 25, 2006).

[9] Hong Kong Government. (May 2006). Tourism in Hong Kong, *http//www.info.gov.hk/info/hkin/tourism.pdf* (accessed October 29, 2006).

[10] Anonymous, "Ocean Park," Hong Kong Chamber of Commerce, Member's Profile, Ocean Park, *http://www.chamber.org.hk/info/member_a_week/member_profile.asp?id=36&P=3&KW=&search_p* (accessed March 24, 2003).

Exhibit 2	Hong Kong Tourism Clusters

The Hong Kong government announced in 2001 that it would develop five tourism clusters in order to upgrade the territory's facilities and to attract more visitors. The five clusters included the following:

Yam O on Lantau Island

This cluster, together with Hong Kong Disneyland, the Tung Chung Cable Car, and the Big Buddha, will turn Lantau Island into a tourism area.

Sai Kung in eastern New Territories

Sai Kung, with its countryside and beaches, was to be developed into an area with facilities for outdoor activities, such as hiking and water sports. The development of the Sai Kung cluster also would include world class resorts.

A cultural belt stretching along the West Kowloon reclamation area

This belt would include existing museums and performing arts centres, the former Marine Police Headquarters, and the Tsim Sha Tsui Promenade. It would include a new tourism area with a large-scale, multipurpose stadium and a new cruise terminal in southeast Kowloon.

A heritage, entertainment, and dining area in the heart of Central

This area will cover a number of existing landmarks, such as the Government House, St. Johns' Cathedral, and the city's prime nightlife district, Lan Kwai Fong.

The redevelopment of Ocean Park and the new Aberdeen Harbour tourism node

Ocean Park aside, the Aberdeen Harbour tourism node would include a Fisherman's Wharf, a traditional fishing village, and a leisure and dining node.

In addition to the five above-mentioned tourism clusters, the government also had other tourism projects in the pipeline, including the Hong Kong Westland Park near Mai Po in the northwestern part of Hong Kong.

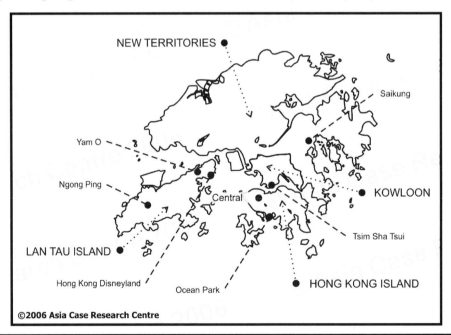

©2006 Asia Case Research Centre

Source: Hong Kong Government. (July 2002). "HKSAR: The First Five Years 1997–2002," *http://www.info.gov.hk/info/sar5/eindex.htm.*

Exhibit 3	Profit and Loss of Ocean Park

Fiscal Year	Profit/Loss in Millions (HK$)
1996–1997	83.90
1997–1998	−85.10
1998–1999	−33.20
1999–2000	−23.70
2000–2001	−62.10
2001–2002	15.30
2002–2003	−4.10
2003–2004	95.70
2004–2005	119.50

Source: Ocean Park Corporation. "Annual Reports" from 1996 to 2004.

million profit in 2001–2002, and a 23% increase in attendance, reaching 3.4 million.[11] But in 2003, the Park was dealt another blow with the outbreak of the Severe Acute Respiratory Syndrome (SARS). As tourists shunned Hong Kong and Hong Kongers stayed home as much as they could, attendance at the Park fell by about 70%, with only a few hundred visitors each day instead of the usual thousands.[12] Consecutive years of loss, coupled with the heavy blow of SARS, threatened Hong Kong's only home-grown theme park with the possibility of closure.

In response to the economy spiralling downward from the impact of SARS, the Chinese government launched the Individual Visit Scheme (IVS), lifting restrictions on the travel of mainlanders to Hong Kong. The scheme allowed mainlanders from designated cities to travel to Hong Kong in an individual capacity rather than only on a business visa or in a group tour as before. The scheme brought a flux of mainlanders to Hong Kong, and Ocean Park, long a Hong Kong icon in China, rebounded quickly, returning to profitability in 2003–2004 [see **Exhibit 4**].

Allan Zeman

In 2002, a government-led task force began charting long-term plans for Ocean Park. One year later, the government also reshuffled the Park's board of directors and appointed new members to replace half of the board. Hong

---

[11] Ocean Park. (2002). "Annual Report."

[12] Ocean Park Corporation. (2003). "Annual Report."

Exhibit 4	Historical and Projected Attendance of Ocean Park
Fiscal Year	**Total Visitors (in Millions)**
1996–1997	3.3
1997–1998	4.1
1998–1999	3.0
1999–2000	3.1
2000–2001	2.8
2001–2002	3.4
2002–2003	3.0
2003–2004	3.7
2004–2005	4.0
2005–2006	4.38
2006–2007	*
Projected Figures	
2007–2008	3.4
2008–2009	4.2
2009–2010	4.6
2010–2011	5.0
2011–2012	5.5
2012–2013	5.8
2013–2014	6.1
2014–2015	6.2
2015–2016	6.3
2016–2017	6.4
2017–2018	6.5
2018–2019	6.7
2019–2020	6.8
2020–2021	6.9
2021–2022	7.0

Sources:
Annual Reports. Ocean Park Corporation.
Crawford, B. (November 30, 2006). "Foul Air HK's No. 1 Worry, says Zeman," *South China Morning Post.*
Eng, D. (August 29, 2006). "Ocean Park Numbers Hit the 1 Million Mark over Summer Period," *South China Morning Post.*
Hong Kong government. Government presentation CB(1)406/05-06(1).
Hui, S. (September 10, 2006). "Hong Kong Disneyland Facing Unexpectedly Tough Competition from Local Fixture Ocean Park," *Associated Press.*
* Attendance at Ocean Park surged past the 1 million mark between July 1, the beginning of the fiscal year, and the end of August 2006. (source: Eng D, 2006; see above).

Kong's chief executive Tung Chee-hwa also appointed Allan Zeman, a Canadian entrepreneur who had made Hong Kong his home, chairman of the board. Somewhat a maverick in business, Zeman had been compared to

Richard Branson of the Virgin Group.[13] Zeman had moved to Hong Kong in 1970, had started his own business exporting garments to Canada the same year, and made his first million by the time he was 20.[14] His company, the Colby International Group, was one of the first supply chain management companies to source garments from China. Colby grew rapidly in the early 1990s and expanded to 36 offices worldwide over the next ten years. In 2001, Zeman sold the company to Li & Fung Limited, a public company listed on the Hong Kong Stock Exchange in the territory, for HK$2.2 billion.[15]

Within Hong Kong, Zeman was more widely known for his role in developing the territory's prime nightlife district, Lan Kwai Fong [see **Exhibit 5**]. When Zeman came across Lan Kwai Fong, a rundown street on

| **Exhibit 5** | Lan Kwai Fong |

---

[13] Crawford, Barclay. (July 31, 2006). "Mr. Enthusiasm", *South China Morning Post.*

[14] Jung, S. (April 13, 2002). "Action Central," *South China Morning Post.*

[15] *Hong Kong Trader.* (February 1, 2004). "'Mr. Lan Kwai Fong' Has the Golden Touch."

Exhibit 5   Lan Kwai Fong *Continued*

the periphery of Hong Kong's central business district in the early 1980s, he envisioned it as a place for expatriates to gather. He opened a restaurant there, the first of more than a dozen themed food and beverages outlets he owned in the neighbourhood, and eventually transformed Lan Kwai Fong into a bustling centre of activity. "To sustain your products, you need to create excitement and make customers buy it," Zeman said with regard to his success with Lan Kwai Fong. "I have created different products in Lan Kwai Fong that draw different people 24 hours a day, from breakfast, brunch, lunch, happy hours, dinner, and after dinner."[16]

A few years after he opened his first restaurant in Lan Kwai Fong, he bought an office building on the same street and boosted the value of the building by renting the office space to retailers and restaurateurs. The venture launched Zeman into the property business, and he eventually bought about 65% of the properties in the neighbourhood.[17]

Thomas Mehrmann

When Zeman became chairman of Ocean Park, he hired Thomas Mehrmann to replace Randolph Guthrie as the Park's CEO. Guthrie had retired after serving for $4^1/_2$ years at the Park. Mehrmann was a theme park industry veteran and had almost 30 years of experience behind him. He had held executive positions at Knott's Berry Farm, which was located only seven miles from Disneyland, and at Six Flags Marine World in California. Prior to joining Ocean Park, he was involved in building Warner Bros. Movie World in Madrid. When Mehrmann first visited the Park, he immediately saw various opportunities (he described as "low hanging fruits") for the Park's performance to be improved. However, he also realised that the Park needed a major enhancement in order to compete shoulder-to-shoulder with its new and formidable rival, Hong Kong Disneyland.

COMPETITION

Walt Disney Company

The Walt Disney Company, founded in 1923, was one of the largest media and entertainment companies in the world, with revenues of

---

[16] Hong Kong Institute of Marketing. (December 11, 2004). "Lan Kwai Fong—Over Two Decades of Success," *http://www.hkim.org.hk/event_20041211.html* (accessed October 29, 2006).

[17] Jung, S. (April 13, 2002). "Action Central," *South China Morning Post*.

HK$248.82 billion in 2005. The company's business was divided into five business segments: media networks, studio entertainment, theme park and resorts, consumer products, and Internet and direct marketing. Among Disney's activities, the theme park and resort segment, with annual revenues growing 10% to HK$70.2 billion in 2005, was a strong growth driver.[18] Disney operated seven out of the top ten theme parks in the world,[19] and its parks were widely considered as the benchmark in the theme park industry.

International expansion was one of Disney's strategic platforms, and it had already opened two other international theme parks, one in Tokyo in 1983 and one in Paris in 1992, when it decided to open a third international theme park. Investors in the theme park industry had increasingly turned their eyes to Asia, since North America, the long-time market leader in the industry that made up half the global market,[20] showed signs of maturation in the 1980s.[21] Analysts forecasted industry growth for Asia at 5.7%, as compared to 3.9% in North America, between 2005 and 2009.[22] "Considering that Asia has a population of more than 3.7 billion, you can see the opportunity," said Jay Rasulo, president of Walt Disney Parks and Resorts. "In particular, China is poised to be the biggest market of all."[23] Hong Kong, with a population of 6.9 million and a strong tourism base, provided the critical mass to support a Disney theme park. In addition, Hong Kong was no more than a five-hour flight for half of the world's population and was located strategically at the gateway to China, where Disney had set the goal of becoming the number one entertainment company,[24] so opening the next theme park in Hong Kong was a natural choice.

---

[18] Walt Disney Co. (2005). "Annual Report," *http://corporate.disney.go.com/investors/annual_reports.html.*

[19] Whaley, F. (2001). "Move over Mickey," Asian Business, 37 (5): 28.

[20] Yoshii, C.L. (April 29–30, 2002). "International Theme Park Development and Trends: Implications and Lessons Learned for China," Presentation by Economic Research Associates in Shenzhen, China.

[21] Jones, C.B. and Robinett, J. (June 1995). "The Future Role of Theme Parks in International Tourism," ERA Issue Paper, Economic Research Associates.

[22] Banay, S. (May 31, 2006). "Wild Ride for Amusement Parks," *http://www.forbes.com/home/travel/2006/05/31/world-amusement-parks_cx_sb_0601feat_ls.html* (accessed October 17, 2006).

[23] Koranteng, J. (April 6, 2005). "Europeans Intrigued by China Pattern," Amusement Business.

[24] Transcript of Hong Kong Disneyland Investor Event—Final, Fair Disclosure Wire, September 8, 2005.

Hong Kong Disneyland

Hong Kong Disneyland was built and operated by Hong Kong International Theme Parks Ltd. (HKITP), a joint venture between Disney and the Hong Kong government. The park, located at Penny's Bay on Lantau Island, was 126 hectares in size, with another 54 hectares reserved for further expansion. The total project development cost was HK$27.67 billion, of which HK$2.3 billion was covered by a commercial loan. The government contributed HK$3.25 billion in return for a 57% equity interest in HKITP, and another HK$6.1 billion in loans for the project. In addition, it also invested HK$13.57 billion on site formation and infrastructure building to prepare Penny's Bay for the park's construction. By comparison, Disney invested HK$2.45 billion in return for a 43% equity interest in HKITP.[25] It earned royalty payments between 5 and 10% on revenues generated from admissions and money spent in the park, and received a 2% base fee plus a variable fee based on the theme park's performance for managing the park.[26]

Since the theme park was a commercial project, negotiations between Disney and the government were kept under cover, and the deal was announced only after it was finalised. The government's disproportionate share of investment in the project gave rise to strong responses from the local community. The government defended itself on the grounds that in contrast to Disney, which assessed the project on its commercial rate of return, it assessed the project on the basis of its economic benefits to Hong Kong.[27] The government projected that the Disney theme park would bring net economic benefits of HK$148 billion to the territory over 40 years and would create 54,200 jobs by 2020.[28] The government also saw the Disney theme park as a strategic infrastructural project that would help turn Hong Kong into a "world city"[29] and a family destination

[25] Hong Kong Tourism Commission, Economic Services Bureau. (November 1999). "Briefing Paper: Hong Kong Disneyland," *http://www.legco.gov.hk/yr99-00/english/hc/papers/brief.pdf* (accessed October 29, 2006).

[26] Transcript of Hong Kong Disneyland Investor Event—Final, Fair Disclosure Wire, September 8, 2005.

[27] Transcript of Press Conference on Hong Kong Disneyland Project by the Hong Kong government, November 3, 1999.

[28] Hong Kong Tourism Commission, Economic Services Bureau. (November 1999). "Briefing Paper: Hong Kong Disneyland," *http://www.legco.gov.hk/yr99-00/english/hc/papers/brief.pdf* (accessed October 23, 2006).

[29] Hong Kong government. (November 4, 1999). "Chief Executive's Speech," Press Release, *http://www.info.gov.hk/gia/general/199911/04/1104231.htm* (accessed October 20, 2006).

for tourism.[30] While Hong Kongers generally welcomed the benefits of the park, the controversial co-operation between the government and Disney generated much debate within the community.[31]

Acculturation in Park Design

When Disneyland Paris opened in 1992, Disney banned wine from the park's restaurants, as it saw wine as incompatible with family entertainment. Rides were named in English, and its working conditions led workers to walk off in protest days after it opened. Disney's cultural insensitivity caused uproar among the French public, driving one critic to call the park a "cultural Chernobyl."[32] Having learnt its lessons, Disney worked hard to be culturally sensitive in planning Hong Kong Disneyland. The layout of the park was rotated several degrees at the early design stage at the recommendation of a *feng shui* master. In line with Chinese tradition, auspicious dates were picked for the commencement and completion of all the park's buildings. The number eight, which signified prosperity in Chinese culture, abounded in the park, while the number four, which was associated with death, did not appear even on lift buttons. Park signs and explanation for rides were written in both Chinese and English for the convenience of the Chinese tourists.[33] The park also offered both local music and food, including the first Chinese eatery on Main Street. Taking into account the Chinese's unfamiliarity with Disney's stories, Disneyland opened with only 16 attractions, compared to 52 at Disneyland Paris. At 126 hectares, Hong Kong Disneyland was the smallest among the Disney theme parks—it took only 30 minutes to walk through the park.[34] Aware of Chinese tourists' strong liking for taking pictures, Disney introduced Fantasy Garden, the first in any Disney theme park, for visitors to take pictures with Disney characters.[35]

---

[30] Hong Kong government. (November 3, 1999). Transcript of Press Conference on Hong Kong Disneyland Project, *http://www.info.gov.hk/gia/general/199911/03/disney-e.htm* (accessed September 20, 2006).

[31] See cases "Hong Kong Disneyland (A): The Walt Disney Perspective," "Hong Kong Disneyland (B): The Walt Disney Perspective," and "Hong Kong Disneyland (C): The Joint Venture Negotiation," published by Asia Case Research Centre, University of Hong Kong, 2000.

[32] Wiseman, P. (November 10, 2005). "Miscues Mar Opening of Hong Kong Disney," *USA Today.*

[33] Ho, D. (February 6, 2006) "Hong Kong Disneyland—It's a Small World," *http://www.brand-channel.com/features_profile.asp?pr_id=269* (accessed September 20, 2006).

[34] Ibid.

[35] Schuman, M. (May 8, 2006). "Disneyland Hong Kong's Headache," *Time Asia.*

Unprepared at Opening

Despite its efforts, Disney failed to fully appreciate the gap that existed between the American brand and Chinese culture. With little idea about Disney's stories and their characters, many mainland visitors were unsure what to expect or how to enjoy the park. Some left after wandering around the park for a couple of hours.[36] "We need to take visitors almost by the hand and tell them what to expect," said Joseph Wang, vice-chairman of Ogilvy & Mather China, Disney's marketing company.[37] Disney had already focused its marketing campaign on educating people about core Disney stories prior to the park's opening,[38] but it acknowledged in hindsight that its marketing was not aggressive enough. John Ap, associate professor of Hong Kong Polytechnic University's School of Hotel and Tourism Management, said: "Disney knows the theme-park business, but when it comes to understanding the Chinese guest, it's an entirely new ball game."[39]

One such example was when Disney launched a discounted one-day ticket in early 2006 that allowed ticket holders to visit the park anytime within six months aside from special days designated by the park. Disney designated the four days that Hong Kongers enjoyed as public holidays during Chinese New Year as special days. It was unaware that mainland China enjoyed seven days instead.[40] So it was totally unprepared when crowds of mainland tourists swamped its gates, demanding access to the park. In order to control the crowds, park staff shut the gates repeatedly despite the fact that visitors held valid tickets.[41] The commotion that arose was captured by local TV stations, leading to strong criticisms from the local press [see **Exhibit 6**]. The embarrassing blunder led to an emotional public apology from Bill Ernest, the park's executive vice-president and managing director. "We regret that anyone may have been disappointed. No one is

---

[36] Fowler, G.A. and Marr, M. (February 9, 2006). "Disney and the Great Wall: Hong Kong's Magical Kingdom Struggles to Attract Chinese Who Don't 'Understand' Park," *The Wall Street Journal*.

[37] Marr, M. and Fowler, G.A. (June 14, 2006). "Hong Kong Disneyland Tries to Bridge Gap," *The Wall Street Journal*.

[38] Transcript of Hong Kong Disneyland Investor Event—Final, *Fair Disclosure Wire*, September 8, 2005.

[39] Schuman, M. (May 8, 2006). "Disneyland."

[40] Bradsher, K. (February 3, 2006). "Disney Magic a Long Wait Away in Hong Kong," *The New York Times*.

[41] Fowler, G.A. and Marr, M. (February 9, 2006). "Disney and the Great Wall."

Exhibit 6   Media Criticism of Disney's Chinese New Year Ticketing Blunder

Media Comments	Source
"The apology struck the right note. So did the promise to learn from mistakes and consult more with the tourist industry about expected demand. But sentiment only goes so far. The press conference was conspicuously lacking in frankness about what went wrong, why mistakes were not identified sooner, and about how Disney plans to avoid a repetition. Even in the moment of mea culpa, the lack of transparency and accountability that has marked Disney's management of one of Hong Kong's biggest public assets was on show. Communication was minimal, commercial confidentiality carried to absurd lengths."	*South China Morning Post.* (February 5, 2006). "Disney Must Come Clean on Ticket Fiasco."
"The chaos at Hong Kong Disneyland has turned it into the laughingstock of the international community. The foreign media, which widely reported the incidents, said it was unbelievable."	*Xin Pao.* (February 10, 2006). "Disney Is a Shame to the Family."
"Following the chaos on the third and fourth of the Chinese New Year, some mainlanders visiting Hong Kong on the Individual Visit Scheme have gone to queue up outside the gates of Disneyland at two or three o'clock in the morning to avoid not being able to get in. Some children can be seen shivering in the cold night on television, and some adults have baggage lying all around them. It is hard to relate this scene to Disneyland. It looks more like an evacuation or people waiting for relief."	Guan, Z. (February 6, 2006). "Waiting Overnight to Get into Hong Kong Disneyland Is a Shameful Scene," *Da Gong Bao.*
"... Disney theme parks have operated for dozens of years; when have the parks ever seen such fierce and violent 'customers'? You don't want to let me in? I just have to get in. You close the gates? I will climb over the wall. Disneyland is not a sealed compound, and it was surrounded by travelers from the Individual Visit Scheme who fought each other to climb over the walls. Chinese people were never worth a dime; they were sent to filling dugouts and block gunshots in wars. Why would Disney not wreck them?"	Li, C.E. (February 6, 2006). "Go Forward, Go Forward," *Apple Daily.*
"Hong Kong Disneyland got into trouble again. It closed the gates to people who spent a lot of money to buy its tickets and came all the way over the mountains and across the water. The foreigners who managed the park actually ignored these people who were crying and jumping up and down as if they did not exist. These foreigners abuse us Chinese without blinking an eye. How can that be?"	Gu, T.L. (February 6, 2006). "One Must Be Disrespectful toward Oneself Before Another Will Insult Him," *The Sun.*

more disappointed than we are. As a father, I understand how frustrating it is to disappoint your children," he said.[42]

Disney also ran into problems with travel agencies and tour operators. Most mainlanders took packaged tours when they went on vacation, so travel agencies and tour operators played a key role in funnelling tourists to the park. Hong Kong Disneyland Hotel and Disney's Hollywood Hotel required Chinese travel agencies to reserve a guaranteed number of rooms weeks in advance when in fact most mainland tourists finalise their plans only a few days before they take off.[43] In addition, Disney was unaware that the places which package-tour guides took their clients to depended on the commission they got from each venue. Hence it failed to give adequate commission to entice mainland travel agencies to market the theme park.[44] "They started off doing business the American way, so they have encountered problems," said Victor Yu, general manager of Beijing's China CYTS Outbound Travel Service.[45]

Though Disney had purposely kept down the size of the park during the initial phase, local visitors expressed disappointment at the size of the theme park and its failure to measure up to its counterparts in the United States, while some mainland visitors opted for Ocean Park because the admission price for Disney was too high. Visitors also complained about long queues for rides and at restaurants.

On the labour front, dissatisfaction among local staff also gave rise to a multitude of complaints and disputes. Within three months of Disneyland's opening, 120 complaints were lodged with the Confederation of Trade Unions by Disney staff. Twenty of the complaints were related to occupational sickness, ranging from back pain to damaged voices[46] and serious muscular problems from standing too much.[47] Cast members complained that they were only entitled to a 15-minute break every four hours, compared to every two hours at other Disney theme parks. They also complained of the underhanded manner in which Disney handled overtime pay. Many staff at Hong Kong Disneyland did not work the same number of hours every day,

---

[42] Eng, D. and Wu, H. (February 7, 2006). "Trouble at the Park," *South China Morning Post*.

[43] Schuman, M. (May 8, 2006). "Disneyland."

[44] Fowler, G.A. and Marr, M. (February 9, 2006). "Disney and the Great Wall."

[45] Schuman, M. (May 8, 2006). "Disneyland."

[46] Leung, W. (November 30, 2005). "Disney Staff in Row with Supervisors," *Hong Kong Standard*.

[47] Lam, A. (November 30, 2005). "Disgruntled Staff Set up Disney Union," *South China Morning Post*.

and they received overtime pay only when their work hours exceeded 195 hours monthly, compared with other Disney theme parks, where overtime pay was calculated based on an eight-hour workday.[48] Cast members also complained that Disney's middle management blocked their views from being heard by the top management.[49]

Other mishaps included the park staff's refusal to let government food inspectors enter the park to do their job unless they hid their identity by taking off their caps and badges. Pop stars who agreed to act in free promotional videos for the park complained about being bossed around in the park, and Kelly Chen, one of the most popular singers in Hong Kong, vowed she would never return.

Disney's blunders were further accentuated by its failure to communicate openly with the Hong Kong public, such as its consistent refusal to disclose Disneyland's attendance figures. Disney's refusal, which was in line with Disney's corporate policy, failed to take into account that Hong Kong Disneyland, though a commercial operation, was built largely with the tax money of Hong Kong residents who expected a reasonable degree of accountability. A poll conducted locally showed that the opinion of 70% of the respondents toward Hong Kong Disneyland took a downward turn following the opening of the park, and 95% of the respondents indicated that Disney should improve its communication with the public.[50]

Crisis Management

Disney moved to remedy their mistakes quickly. It added subtitles in simplified Chinese characters to its Broadway-style shows and provided crash courses for visitors in the form of day-trip guides that explained how they could enjoy the park, highlighting how the park's experience could improve family relationships.[51] It also changed its advertising campaign from showcasing the park to showing visitors' experience in the park and how families could share the Disneyland experience together to help potential visitors understand the park.[52] When it

---

[48] Lam, A. (October 12, 2005). "Mountain in Hong Kong," Associated Press.

[49] Leung, W. (November 30, 2005). "Disney Staff."

[50] Hong Kong Polytechnic University. (April 4, 2006). "Local Residents Have Mixed Views towards Disney", *http://www1.polyu.edu.hk/hotnews/details_e.php?year=2006& news_id=950* (accessed October 14, 2006).

[51] Fowler, G.A. and Marr, M. (February 9, 2006). "Disney and the Great Wall."

[52] Marr, M. and Fowler, G.A. (June 14, 2006). "Hong Kong Disneyland."

prepared for the summer peak season in 2006, it spent three times the amount on marketing than it had up to that time.

Disney learnt to be more flexible with travel agents and tour operators, reducing the advanced notice required for booking hotels.[53] It offered tour operators a 50% personal discount if they visited the park and its hotels to encourage them to bring their customers to the park. Commission for tour operators was increased by HK$2.50 per adult ticket, and tour operators were offered open tickets instead of fixed-date ones to give them more flexibility in bringing visitors to the park.[54] Nonetheless, Disney offered only 10% discount to local travel agents, compared with the 20% offered by Ocean Park.[55] Disney also gave away 50,000 free tickets to Hong Kong taxi drivers so they could share their personal experience of Disney with their passengers. Disney hoped that this move would boost attendance and help the park to meet its target of 5.6 million visitors during its first year of operation.[56]

IMPACT OF COMPETITION ON OCEAN PARK

Ocean Park expected its attendance to drop by as much as 25% when Hong Kong Disneyland opened,[57] but Disney's opening did not wield a major impact on the Park. September was traditionally a low season for the Park, since schools resumed, and the Park saw an average attendance of 10,000 visitors a day during Disney's opening period,[58] compared to a daily average attendance of 11,000 visitors the previous year. A local poll showed that 80% of the respondents found the experience at Ocean Park comparable with Disneyland, and two-thirds disagreed that most people would like to visit Disneyland more than Ocean Park.[59]

---

[53] Schuman, M. (May 8, 2006). "Disneyland."

[54] Fowler, G.A. and Marr, M. (February 9, 2006). "Disney and the Great Wall."

[55] Einhorn, B. (February 6, 2006). "Disney's Mobbed Kingdom," *BusinessWeek Online, http://www.businessweek.com/bwdaily/dnflash/feb2006/nf2006026_2086.htm* (accessed October 8, 2006).

[56] Schuman, M. (May 8, 2006). "Disneyland."

[57] Lam, A. (May 29, 2006). "Ocean Park Record Dispels Fears of Disney Challenge," *South China Morning Post.*

[58] *South China Morning Post.* (April 29, 2006). "No Secrets at Reborn Ocean Park. ..."

[59] Hong Kong Polytechnic University. (April 4, 2006). "Local Residents."

OCEAN PARK'S POSITIONING

Market Position

In 2003, Ocean Park, with its aging facilities, was facing increased competition from a range of other areas: from local shopping malls to the growing tendency for families to spend long weekends on the mainland or other parts of Asia.[60] The entrance of Disney also meant the Park had to face one of the most formidable competitors in the theme park industry. Zeman had never visited Ocean Park until he was appointed chairman, and he was blown away by the scenic view of the cable car ride on his first visit. "I knew we not only had to save the park but make it more relevant to everyone," he said.[61] Zeman and his team began immediately formulating a plan for the future of the Park.

The up side of Disney's entrance for Ocean Park was that it would bring more visitors to Hong Kong and turn the territory into a family destination. The down side was that the local park now had to compete against the leader in the global theme park industry. Ocean Park studied theme parks around the world, especially those located near Disney, and found many of them refrained from competing head to head with the latter. Knott's Berry Farm in California focused on younger children, while SeaWorld in San Diego flourished on an aquatic theme.[62] In Japan, despite the closing of some theme parks after Universal Studios Japan opened, those with a strong focus on children or animals survived.

While Disney was a fantasy operation based on its movie products and intellectual properties, Ocean Park, with its focus on animals and nature, was about reality. Playing on that difference, the Park decided to use the theme of connecting people with nature through the "Ocean" and "Animal Encounter"[63] to differentiate itself from Disney. If Disney offered cartoons, movies, the castle, and a taste of America, Ocean Park showcased animals, natural surroundings, and a cable car ride with a fantastic view of Hong Kong.[64] Staying true to its mission, Ocean Park also decided to continue focusing on education and conservation in addition to providing entertainment. The Park envisioned its

---

[60] Ocean Park Corporation. (2003). "Annual Report."

[61] Gluckman, R. (September 2005). "Mickey Mouse Meets Mao," *http://www.gluckman.com/HKDisney.htm* (accessed July 25, 2006).

[62] Einhorn, B. (May 24, 2005). "Hong Kong's Theme Park Clash," *China Journal*.

[63] Ibid.

[64] Ocean Park Corporation. (2005). "The New Ocean Park" Press Kit.

future as a world-class marine-themed park.[65] "We are not trying to 'outdo Disney' but rather complement it," Zeman said. "With Disney, we have to go world-class, or we will fail."[66] The Park also believed that a focus on animals and marine life would offer something for everybody in the family from the oldest to the youngest.[67]

In contrast to the American brand, Ocean Park also positioned itself as Hong Kong's home-grown park. "Disney is a great brand, and one Hong Kong is lucky to get," Zeman said. "But a lot of people look at it as an American brand. Ocean Park is home grown, and Hong Kong people take a lot of pride in it. They have memories growing up around the park, and we want to build on that."[68]

Target Market

Ocean Park, similar to Disney, targeted the family market. The Park defined the family as everyone from children to grandparents. In order to attract repeat visits from local families, it ran special exhibitions that catered to everybody from kids to grandparents, such as the jellyfish aquarium. In addition, the Park ran programs to target secondary markets. The Ocean Park Academy catered to school children, and special yearly events, such as the Halloween bash, were geared toward teenagers. Ocean Park held its first Halloween bash in 2001, and its haunted houses and scary characters were such a success that the Park had to turn people away for the first time in its history.[69]

Attendance at Ocean Park could be categorised into locals; mainlanders, who visited mostly in group tours; and fully independent travelers (FIT) who do not travel as part of a tour group. Local visitors accounted for about 40% of the Park's attendance, mainland visitors 50%, and the rest were FITs. The three groups of visitors showed different patterns in park usage. Local visitors usually arrived at around 10 a.m. and stayed until 2 p.m.; FITs arrived at the same time and stayed until the park closed, while the group tours arrived

---

[65] Hong Kong Legislative Council. (December 2005). "Item for Finance Committee," FCR (2005-06)35.

[66] Chan, C. (March 19, 2005). "$5.5b Plan to Revamp Ocean Park Is Unveiled," *South China Morning Post*.

[67] Hong Kong General Chamber of Commerce. (March 24, 2003). "Ocean Park," *http://www.chamber.org.hk/info/member_a_week/member_profile.asp&id=36&P=3&KW=&search_p* (accessed October 8, 2006).

[68] Gluckman, R. (September 2005). "Mickey Mouse."

[69] Emmons, N. (November 18, 2002). "Hard Work Key to Success at Ocean Park Hong Kong," *Amusement Business*.

at around 2 p.m. and stayed for an average of 3.5 hours. Among the three groups, group tours, restricted by their itineraries and short stays, spent the least in the Park.

Pricing

The entrance to a Disney theme park in any market tended to allow local players to raise their price. Ocean Park's strategy was to "provide 80% of the bang at 60% of the buck."[70] It charged HK$185 for an adult day pass and HK$93 for children between the ages of 3 and 11. In comparison, Disneyland charged adults HK$295 on regular days and $350 on peak days, and children between the ages of 3 and 11 paid HK$210 on regular days and HK$250 on peak days [see **Exhibit 7**]. Zeman pledged that the price of Ocean Park would stay lower than Disneyland as long as he remained Ocean Park's chairman.

Exploring New Opportunities

When Mehrmann joined Ocean Park, the Park was drawing 85% of its revenues from its gates and 15% from in-park spending. Mehrmann saw the opportunity to boost the Park's revenues by increasing in-park spending.

Exhibit 7	Comparison of Admission Fee between Ocean Park and Hong Kong Disneyland	
	Ocean Park (HK$)	**HK Disneyland (HK$)**
Adult	$185	Regular: $295
		Peak: $350
Child	$93	Regular: $210
		Peak: $250
Senior (over 65)	Free	Regular: $170
		Peak: $200
SmartFun Annual Gold Pass (unlimited access)	Adult: $550	—
Adult	Child: $275	
Summer Pass (unlimited access for 3 months)	—	Adults: $450
		Children (3–11): $329
		Senior (over 65): $270

Sources: Ocean Park, *http://www.oceanpark.com.hk/eng/main/index.html;*Hong Kong Disneyland, *http://park.hongkongdisneyland.com/ hkdl/en_US/ticketsAndReservations/tickets?name=TicketsPage.*

---

[70] Whaley, F. (2001). "Move."

"It's what I refer to as the low-lying fruit," he said. The Park brought the retail operations in-house, ending third party relationships of its retail shops and food and beverage outlets to increase its income. It also began to explore the potential of adding three hotels both within the Park and in the neighbourhood of the Park, a move that would significantly boost in-park spending.

Service Excellence

Service was an integral part of the theme park experience, and Disney, which defined service excellence as exceeding customers' expectations, had made service excellence a cornerstone of all its theme parks. Following suit, Ocean Park also strived for service excellence. However, service-related complaints remained the most common complaints the Park received, even though it enjoyed more tolerance from visitors as a local park and the number two theme park in the market. "When you are in a service environment on a 38-degree day with 95% humidity, responding to the same questions and comments again and again, and employees need to treat each question or comment as the first time they've heard it, the repetitive nature of the business requires a great deal of patience and perseverance," Mehrmann said.[71]

Different types of visitors used Ocean Park in different ways, which made achieving service excellence more difficult. As a result of time constraint, group visitors tended to be more aggressive in using the Park compared with local visitors. They were also less protocol- conforming; for example, they were more likely to be found smoking in smoke-free areas or cutting through buildings. As a result, group visitors put a stronger demand on park management as the Park tried to ensure a satisfactory experience for both group and local visitors. The Park also had to keep its staff well trained in Mandarin in order to both serve and manage group visitors, who mainly comprised mainland visitors.

Ocean Park used no formal metrics for measuring service excellence, and the drive toward service excellence was achieved mainly through changing the management style. Mehrmann described the management team before he came on board as instigators of a "huge ivory tower situation" between management and employees. He adopted a different philosophy, walking the Park regularly, picking up rubbish along the way, and taking the time to get to know the employees personally. In addition to quarterly meetings with all the employees, he organised monthly exchange programs with the staff to solicit their input, and made sure that the management responded to that

---

[71] Interview with Thomas Mehrman on September 8, 2006.

input. "To the employees, it's a case of: 'If you take care of us, then we will take care of the guests,'" he said.

Whereas the old management focused on what the staff did wrong, the Park's new management focused on what they did right. The Park tracked visitors' experiences of the park by asking them to fill out a comment form. Helpful and outstanding employees mentioned by name in the comment form would be rewarded with trips abroad through a lucky draw. By giving employees recognition, Mehrmann hoped that they would have a stronger sense of belonging and would go that extra mile for guests, offering simple things such as returning a lost wallet or volunteering to take pictures for guests. "It's the little things that can make a difference," he said. Nonetheless, communication with staff was not always easy, as they did not immediately connect the message behind gestures to show appreciation for their work—such as free offers of ice cream and theatre tickets—and the Park's performance.

Master Plan

Ocean Park's vision of itself as a world-class marine park was translated into a HK$5.55 billion master plan to revamp the Park [see **Exhibit 8**]. Under the plan, the size of the Park would increase from 30 hectares to 43.8 hectares, the number of attractions would double to more than 70, the number of shows would triple to 12, and more than 30 new animal species would be introduced by 2010. The number of restaurants would increase from 7 to 27, and the retail area would more than double to 19,000 square feet. However, the construction of hotels was not included in the plan, as that involved amendments to the Ocean Park Ordinance, nor were they factored into the business models.

The revamping of the Park was planned to be carried out in eight phases over a six-year period. This would ensure that the Park would remain open during construction, until its completion in 2012. New attractions were to include an aquarium where guests could dine with fish swimming around them, an underground train, new thrill rides, and a rainforest, among others [see **Exhibit 9**]. The redevelopment would increase the daily attendance capacity of the park from 36,300 visitors to 53,600 visitors. Consultants estimated that, with the redevelopment, attendance at the Park would increase to 3.4 million in 2007–2008, more than 5 million by 2010–2011, and more than 7 million by 2021–2022 [see **Exhibit 4**]. Financial analyses projected the Park's revenue at HK$1.3 billion annually with the completion of the first phase, and HK$2.1 billion with the completion of the second phase.[72]

---

[72] Hong Kong Legislative Council. (December 2005). "Item for Finance Committee," FCR (2005-06)35.

Exhibit 8	Breakdown for $5.55 Million Ocean Park Redevelopment Project	
Item	**Cost Estimates (HK$ Million)**	**Remarks**
Capital Cost	4,525	Includes the following: ■ Demolition (HK$80 million) ■ Site formation (HK$328 million) ■ Access roads (HK$132 million) ■ Infrastructure (HK$304 million) ■ Facilities at the Summit (HK$1,705 million) ■ Facilities at the Waterfront HK$1,237million) ■ Funicular system and cable car upgrade (HK$464 million) ■ Area development (HK$230 million)
Contingencies (10% of capital cost)	453	
Animals	160	Includes relocation of animals, temporary facilities, and new animals.
Design and Project Management	362	
Interim Phasing Cost	50	Enabling works and interim facilities to keep the Park opening during redevelopment.
Total:	**5,550**	

Source: Hong Kong Legislative Council. (December 2005). "Item for Finance Committee," FCR(2005-06)35.

The revamping of the Park was expected to boost Hong Kong as a premiere destination for family visitors, to jumpstart the urban regeneration of the south side of Hong Kong Island and the development of Aberdeen as a tourism area. In terms of economic benefits to the territory, the Park was expected to contribute with 0.5% of Hong Kong's GDP by 2010.

CASH STRAPPED

Ocean Park launched a syndicated loan in April 2006 to raise funds for its redevelopment project. The master plan was estimated to cost HK$5.5 billion, and the Park did not have enough money to fund the project itself. As of June 2004, the Ocean Park Trust Fund had a balance of HK$288 million, and the Park had an operating cash reserve of HK$325 million. The operating cost of the Park for 2003–2004 was HK$338 million.

	Exhibit 9	Master Redevelopment Project Fact Sheet		

	Themed Zones or Facilities	**Attractions**	**Rides**	**Planned Completion**
		Dolphin show		
	Waterfront			
1.	Sky Fair	Helium balloons	Yes	Early 2007
2.	Temporary Entrance	Not applicable. Guest facility	N/A	Early 2007
3.	Astounding Asia	Asian animals	No	2008
		Exotic bird show		
		Nature trails		
4.	Funicular	Not applicable. Transportation facility	N/A	2008–2009
5.	Entry Plaza	Not applicable. Guest facility	N/A	2008–2009
6.	Lagoon	Nightly shows on the lagoon	N/A	2008–2009
7.	Aqua City I	Grand aquarium, including shark encounter	Yes	2009
		Underwater restaurant		
8.	Aqua City II	Shopping and dining with various attractions	Yes	2009–2010
9.	Whiskers Harbour	Many new themed venues for children: rides, animal interactions, birthday area, show venue, toy store	Yes	2010
	The Summit			
10.	Veterinary Centre	Not applicable. Back of house facility	N/A	2007
11.	Rainforest	Rainforest exhibits with adventure trails and discovery areas, along with dynamic and family-oriented ride attractions. Elevated aviary	Yes	2009
12.	Thrill Mountain	High-energy ride attractions for young adults, teenagers, and thrill seekers	Yes	2009–2010
13.	Polar Adventure	Polar animal experiences, shows, and attractions Ice palace	Yes	2010
14.	Ocean Dome Stadium	Stadium for marine mammal shows	No	2011
15.	Marine World I	Sea lion show	Yes	2011
16.	Marine World II	Renovation of Pacific pier, Ocean theatre	Yes	2012
17.	Cable Car	Renovation	N/A	2012

Source: Ocean Park Corporation.

In 2005, the government committed to revamping the park with a subordinated loan of HK$1,387.55 million at a fixed interest rate of 5% per annum and a loan term of 25 years [see **Exhibit 10**]. Ocean Park still had to raise the remaining 75% of the project costs through the commercial

Exhibit 10	Subordinated Loan from the Government
Amount	HK$1,387.5 Million
Lender	Hong Kong Government
Type	Term Loan
Purpose	To finance 25% of the Project Costs
Ranking	Subordinated
Loan Term/Final Maturity	25 years
Availability Period:	■ May be drawn at any time within 3 years after completion of loan documentation.
	■ To be drawn and used by Ocean Park Corporation before the commercial loan.
	■ At fixed interest rate of 5% per annum.
	■ To be capitalised at half-yearly intervals until the commercial loan is fully repaid. Thereafter, payable semiannually.
	■ Subject to agreement with lending banks, the intended commercial loan will be fully repaid after 15 years.
Other fees:	Nil
Repayment:	■ Repayment to commence 3 months after full repayment of the commercial loan.
	■ OPC should always "prepay" the commercial loans as far as possible (i.e., when there is idle cash after all the expenses are met).
	■ The total principal of the loan, together with capitalised interest, to be repaid by equal semiannual installments until final maturity.
Prepayment:	No prepayment until after full repayment of the commercial loan. Thereafter voluntary.
Security:	Nil.
Documentation:	■ Ocean Park to sign a loan agreement with government.
	■ Government to sign a subordination agreement with the commercial loan lenders.

Source: Hong Kong Legislative Council. (December 2005). "Item for Finance Committee," FCR(2005-06)35.

banking sector. Nonetheless, the government felt that it had to support at least half of Ocean Park's borrowing in order for the Park to secure enough loans for the project, so it offered additional support through a guarantee of repayment of one-third of the commercial loan (HK$1,387.55 million) plus the interest that arose from the loan, which was expected not to exceed HK$700 million. The government's support for Ocean Park's redevelopment entailed a total risk exposure of up to HK$3,475 million. The risk exposure of the loan was shared equally between the government and the commercial market.

The financial support given by the government was structured in a way that Ocean Park had to first draw the subordinated loan, followed

Exhibit 11	Hong Kong Government Guarantee for the Commercial Loan
Amount	Covering up to principal amount of HK$1,387.5 million of the commercial loan, plus interest accrued thereon
Guarantor	Hong Kong government
Terms of the commercial loan to be guaranteed	■ Major terms will be set out in Terms and Conditions of the commercial loan to be settled with relevant banks.
	■ Loan term will be 15 years
	■ The government-guaranteed commercial loan (Tranche A) will be drawn down by Ocean Park Corporation after the subordinated loan has been drawn, but before drawing on the remaining part of the commercial loan (Tranche B).
	■ The Tranche B commercial loan (which is not guaranteed by the government) will be repaid/prepaid first, before the Tranche A commercial loan.
Guarantee Fee	Nil
Documentation	A guarantee in form and substance acceptable to both the government and the banks.

Source: Hong Kong Legislative Council. (December 2005). "Item for Finance Committee," FCR(2005-06)35.

by the government-guaranteed commercial loan (Tranche A), and then the commercial loan (Tranche B) [see **Exhibit 11**]. At the same time, the Tranche B commercial loan would be repaid first, before the Tranche A government-guaranteed commercial loan. The financial package also stipulated that Ocean Park should always "prepay" the commercial loans as far as possible. The tenure of the commercial loans was 15 years.

The fact that Ocean Park was designated a public sector entity by the Hong Kong Monetary Authority favoured the Park when lenders assessed the risk in participating in the syndicated loan.[73] The government's guarantee also served as a strong token of confidence for the project. Nonetheless, its non-recourse nature meant that repayment would begin only when the redevelopment project was completed and the project began generating revenues, giving rise to the long tenure of the commercial loans. Although this structure allowed banks to earn higher margins,[74] it also increased their risk exposure.

[73] Ocean Park. (June 13, 2006). "It's Time. . . ." Press release, *http://www.oceanpark.com.hk/eng/main/index.html.*

[74] *Euroweek.* (May 19, 2006). "Ocean Park Loan Swamped after Blowout Syndication."

MASTER PLAN PUT TO TEST

Ocean Park's syndicated loan was launched with Bank of China (Hong Kong), DBS Bank, and HSBC as the mandated lead arrangers.[75] The launch of the syndicated loan essentially put the Park's master plan and major enhancement strategy to test in the financial market. Ocean Park's high attendance figure during the period of Disney's opening suggests the Park has adopted the right strategy, but competition from Disney remained intense. Theme parks were complex operations, and major glitches during their openings were not unprecedented in the industry. Universal Studio's theme park in Florida ran into major technical glitches when it opened, but it managed to rebound. How would the commercial banks respond to Ocean Park's strategic plan? Was the Park's positioning strategy strong enough to win their confidence in the face of competition from Disneyland?

---

[75] *Financial Times.* (June 14, 2006). "Hong Kong Ocean Park Gets HK$55.5B in Loans for New Project."

Six Flags: Is Recovery on the Horizon?[1]

Brian D. Avery and Fevzi Okumus

"We've been a company that's about hardware, but we need to be more than that. Theme parks take you away from the everyday, and they recreate a sense of wonder.... You're not checking your PDA. You're not checking your e-mail. You're walking around and you're escaping. That's the experience you're going to have at Six Flags."[2]

Mark Shapiro, CEO Six Flags, Inc.

INTRODUCTION

This case study first provides a brief history and development of the amusement park industry in the United States. It then looks at Six Flags' growth, the operational, HRM, financial and marketing strategies, and current challenges. Finally, the case study provides discussions about Six Flags' competitive advantage and its current strategies to turn around the company.

---

[1] This case study was written by Brian Avery and Fevzi Okumus. It is intended to reconstruct the challenges and issues facing theme parks operating in complex and dynamic business environments. It was written for the purpose of classroom discussion. It was not intended to convey any criticism of any individual or group of individuals.

[2] *Adweek.* Six Flags Expands Marketing. Retrieved August 1, 2006 from *http://www.adweek. com/aw/national/article_display.jsp?vnu_content_id=1001841971;* and Roch, J. (2006). "Six Flags Embarks on a New Adventure," *The Boston Globe*, May 21, 2006, retrieved on May 22, 2009 from *http://www.boston.com/business/articles/2006/05/21/six_flags_embarks_ on_a_new_adventure/.*

THE AMUSEMENT PARK INDUSTRY IN THE UNITED STATES

Some date the amusement park industry back to medieval Europe pleasure gardens. Many of these gardens were located on the outskirts of major European cities. The pleasure gardens featured live entertainment, fireworks, dancing, games, and even early forms of amusement rides and devices.[3] The amusement park industry has grown tremendously since its recognized inception, and yet it still maintains many of the characteristics of parks from yesteryear.

In the United States, Coney Island led the way in the amusement park industry. It was home to three of America's most elaborate amusement parks, along with dozens of smaller attractions. Coney Island of New York helped establish the future of the amusement park industry.[4] Since the early 1900s, new innovations in the amusement industry paved the way for an explosion of growth. Many of these innovations were realized at Coney Island. This explosion of growth and innovation led to the development and operation of over 1,500 amusement parks in the United States by 1919. The crowds were heavy and continued to multiply until the year 1929. The Great Depression of 1929 shut down many amusement parks, and by 1935 only 400 remained, leaving a lasting impression on the amusement industry.[5]

World War II continued to negatively impact the amusement park industry. Parks continued to close during this time, and others delayed or canceled the addition of attractions and venues. The impact of the Great Depression and the war was felt for approximately 26 years. It was not until 1955 that the amusement industry started making a comeback. This is the year Disneyland opened. The arrival of Disneyland was met with much skepticism. Disneyland was different and was void of many of the traditional attractions found at the existing parks. The removal of the traditional midway led to the development of five

---

[3] Goeldner, C.R. and Ritchie, J.B. (2006). Tourism: Principles, Practices, Philosophies. Hoboken, NJ: John Wiley & Sons, Inc., p. 235.

[4] Denson, C. (2002). *Coney Island: Lost and Found*. Berkeley, CA: Ten Speed Press.

[5] Potter, Laura. (2008) *U.S. Amusement Parks: An Industry That Entertains Million, Exciting rides, other attractions keep customers coming back.* Retrieved June 5, 2009, from *http://www.america.gov/st/peopleplace-english/2008/June/20080623135303LLrettoP0.3846552.html.*

distinct themed areas, providing "guests" with the fantasy of travel to different lands and times.[6]

Disneyland's success proved to be an amazing feat in the amusement industry. Disneyland had successfully differentiated itself from the traditional park model. It was not until 1961, after many futile attempts were made to capitalize on Disney's success, that a new amusement park, Six Flags Over Texas, was able to achieve success. Today, the landscape is filled with variations of the parks of yesteryear and the cousins of Disneyland. Amusement parks and theme parks currently make up the United States' 450 estimated parks. It is a far cry from the 1,500 amusement parks during its heyday in 1919, but the complexity and the size of today's parks make up for the decline in numbers.[7]

Catapulting forward to about 1990, we find a very different and much more complex industry. During the early 1990s, industry consolidation was all the rage. The larger, more established parks began to buy up the smaller and family-run operations. Amusement parks became hot commodities, and park acquisitions rose to record levels. The largest acquisition was the acquisition of the Six Flags park chain by Premier Parks. Premier paid a record U.S.$1.9 billion for the Six Flags parks.[8] Acquisitions went on at a feverish pace for about a decade.

Around the time the parks started looking for the rewards of their hard-fought acquisitions, the terrorist attacks on September 11, 2001, occurred. Park attendance was already on the slide, but the terrorist attacks closed the door on many travel plans.[9] In 2002, poor weather conditions across the country caused an additional drop in attendance, and in 2003 concerns about the U.S.-led war with Iraq and the potential for additional terrorist attacks led to a further decrease in park attendance. According to a 2002 *USA Today* poll, 10 percent of Americans rated amusement parks and sporting events as the most likely target for a terrorist attack, behind nuclear

---

[6] Potter, L. (2008). *U.S. Amusement Parks: An Industry That Entertains Million, Exciting rides, other attractions keep customers coming back.* Retrieved June 5, 2009, from *http://www. america.gov/st/peopleplace-english/2008/June/20080623135303LLrettoP0.3846552.html.*

[7] National Amusement Park Historical Association. *The Amusement Park Industry, a very brief history.* Retrieved April 17, 2001, from *http://www.napha.org.*

[8] Rankin, B. (April 4,2002). Former Six Flags management loses in court Ruling upheld again for Six Flags. *Atlanta Journal-Constitution.* Retrieved October 19, 2006, from *http://sfog. playride.com/lawsuit.html.*

[9] Thomson G. *Business & Company Resource Center Curriculum Support Demonstration.* Retrieved June 23, 2009, from *http://www.gale.com/BusinessRC/mgt525.pdf.*

plants and large city downtowns, yet ahead of airports, national monuments, military installations, and bridges/tunnels.[10]

Park consolidation and impacts from man-made and natural disasters had many negative consequences on the United States park industry. It had stifled growth and impacted the bottom line of most park chains and independent operators for many years. Park consolidation had an adverse affect that most park operators did not see coming. Park options had become limited, and operators needed to work harder to attract and retain guests by adding and developing new rides, shows, and experiences. Since around 2005, many theme parks generally stopped investing heavily in hard rides like roller coasters; instead, parks shifted focus to more family-oriented rides and amenities like convenience centers in restrooms, shows, and healthier and better food.

The amusement industry, as of the year 2005, had attendance figures of 335 million and revenues of 11.2 billion.[11] In 2007, attendance figures were 341 million and $12 billion in revenue.[12] The top 20 parks in North America accounted for 123 million visitors in 2008. There was an increase in attendance at the top 20 parks of 3.9 percent between 2005 and 2008.[13] While the economics of the amusement industry has changed over the years, the premise remains the same: it is all done in the name of fun. The amusement park was once considered the primary location for the escape of the urban working class. Over the last 50 years or so, it has transformed itself into an expensive and limited form of entertainment in the United States and the World.[14]

---

[10] Thomson G. *Business & Company Resource Center Curriculum Support Demonstration.* Retrieved July 27, 2006, from *http://www.gale.com/BusinessRC/mgt525.pdf.*

[11] International Association of Amusement Parks and Attractions. *Attendance Figures.* Retrieved May 22, 2009, from *http://www.iaapa.org/pressroom/Amusement_Park_Attendance_Revenue_History.asp.*

[12] International Association of Amusement Parks and Attractions. *Attendance Figures.* Retrieved May 22, 2009, from *http://www.iaapa.org/pressroom/Amusement_Park_Attendance_Revenue_History.asp.*

[13] International Association of Amusement Parks and Attractions. *Attendance Figures.* Retrieved May 22, 2009, from *http://www.iaapa.org/pressroom/Amusement_Park_Attendance_Revenue_History.asp.*

[14] Bennett, D. (1998). Roller Coaster, Wooden and Steel Coasters, Twisters and Corkscrews. Edison, NJ: Chartwell Books.

Table I	Park Attendance in the United States in 2008	
1	Magic Kingdom—Orlando, Florida	17m (Flat)
2	Disneyland—Anaheim, California	14.7m (–1%)
3	Epcot —Orlando, Florida	10.9m (Flat)
4	Disney-MGM Studios —Orlando, Florida	9.6m (+1%)
5	Disney's Animal Kingdom —Orlando, Florida	9.5m (+0.5%)
6	Universal Studios Florida —Orlando, Florida	6.2m (+0.5%)
7	SeaWorld Orlando —Orlando, Florida	5.9m (–2.9%)
8	Disney's California Adventure —Anaheim, California	5.5m (–2%)
9	Islands of Adventure —Orlando, Florida	5.3m (–2.4%)
10	Universal Studios Hollywood —Universal City, California	4.6m (–2.5%)

Source: http://www.themeit.com/TEAERA2008.pdf (accessed on May 22, 2009).
Theme park attendance figures are for the year 2008 and are represented in millions. Positive and negative numbers represent an increase or decrease in park attendance from the previous year.

There are five main players remaining in the amusement industry in the United States. Disney, Cedar Fair, Busch Entertainment, Universal, and Six Flags are considered the largest and most prominent park operators. Six Flags filed for chapter 11 reorganization bankruptcy on June 13, 2009. They remain an active company; however, they are in the process of reorganizing their debts.[15] In the United States, Disney operates the Walt Disney World Resort near Orlando, Florida, and Disneyland Resort in Anaheim, California. It has additional stakes outside of the United States. The Orlando resort is North America's most frequented tourist spot and has four theme parks (Magic Kingdom, Hollywood Studios, Epcot, and Animal Kingdom), hotels and resorts, water parks, and golf courses. In 2008, Disney's U.S. parks together drew more than 68 million visitors.[16] Disney's Magic Kingdom in Florida is the number one most visited park and the second most visited park is Disneyland California (see Table I).[17]

Cedar Fair owns and manages a diverse mix of amusement parks, water parks, and hotels. In total, they own and operate 22 properties. Those properties include ten amusement parks, six outdoor water parks, one indoor water

[15] Tirrell, M. (2009). Six Flags Bankruptcy May Take 4-6 Months, CFO Says. Retrieved June 24, 2009, from http://www.bloomberg.com/apps/news?pid=20601103&sid=atNAcbVRbTjE.

[16] Hoovers (2009). Walt Disney Parks and Resorts. Retrieved May 22, 2009, from http://www.hoovers.com/disney-parks-&-resorts/–ID__104368–/free-co-profile.xhtml.

[17] Themed Entertainment Association/Economics Research Associates. Attractions Attendance Report. Retrieved May 22, 2008, from http://www.themeit.com/TEAERA2008.pdf.

park, and five hotels. Some of their key properties are Knott's Berry Farm in California, Michigan's Adventure, and Cedar Point, located on Lake Erie in Sandusky, Ohio.[18] Knott's Berry Farm is one of their more unique locations and operates year-round, while other parks are open daily from Memorial Day through Labor Day, plus additional weekends in April, May, September, and October. Cedar Fair bought Paramount Parks from CBS Corp. in 2006. In 2008, Cedar Fair parks together drew more than 22 million visitors.[19]

Busch Entertainment Corporation (BEC), a subsidary of brewer Anheuser-Busch/In-Bev, is another large theme park operator in the United States. BEC has ten locations in five states. Their park collection includes a wide variety of educational experiences and entertainment. BEC parks have a total of three SeaWorld parks in California, Florida, and Texas. The Florida location also houses Discovery Cove, where visitors can swim with dolphins and other marine life. In addition, BEC has three water parks, two in Florida and one in Virginia.[20] In 2008, BEC's top three parks together drew more than 14 million visitors.[21]

NBC Universal is a multifaceted company that owns and operates a vast media entertainment operation. One of NBC Universal's core units is its theme park operations. NBC Universal operates many theme parks including Universal Studios Hollywood, Universal Orlando, and Universal Studios Japan in Osaka.[22] Their parks feature attractions based on movies from its movie studios such as Transformers, *Back to the Future*, *Jaws*, and *Jurassic Park*. Proprieties include hotels, IMAX theaters, and water parks. The Hollywood and Orlando parks also contain CityWalks, family-oriented entertainment centers that offer restaurants and shopping. In 2008, NBC Universal's U.S. parks together drew more than 15 million visitors.[23]

---

[18] Cedar Fair. *Cedar Fair Properties*. Retrieved June 22, 2009, from *http://www.cedarfair.com/ir/company/properties/*.

[19] Hoovers. *Cedar Fair, L.P.*. Retrieved May 22, 2009, from *http://www.hoovers.com/cedar-fair/–ID__10305–/free-co-profile.xhtml*.

[20] Anheuser-Busch Adventure Parks. *Park Information*. Retrieved June 22, 2009, from *http://www.becjobs.com/Scripts/ParkInfo.aspx*.

[21] Hoovers. *Busch Entertainment Corporation*. Retrieved May 22, 2009, from *http://www.hoovers.com/busch-entertainment/–ID__56327–/free-co-profile.xhtml*.

[22] NBC Universal. NBC Universal About the Company. Retrieved June 22, 2009, from *http://www.nbcuni.com/About_NBC_Universal/Company_Overview/*.

[23] Hoovers. *Universal Parks and Resorts*. Retrieved May 22, 2009, from *http://www.hoovers.com/universal-parks/–ID__106044–/free-co-profile.xhtml*.

SIX FLAGS, A PROUD PAST...

A generation ago, Six Flags operated a handful of parks around the country, including the flagship, Six Flags Over Texas. Most of the parks in the Six Flags chain were well respected, and, by some, even thought of as superior to Walt Disney World.[24] The founder of Six Flags, a Texas oil baron named Angus Wynne, would be proud of Six Flags' rise to preeminent standing in the family entertainment industry. Angus Wynne is considered the father of the modern-day theme park. Mr. Wynne broke new ground when he opened the first Six Flags park, Six Flags Over Texas, in 1961. Mr. Wynne studied other pioneers around him and applied his own vision and imagination to create a new form of family entertainment. He imagined regional parks large in scope but closer to where people lived, making them convenient and affordable.[25]

The first Six Flags park took its name from the six countries whose flags had flown over Texas throughout the state's extraordinary history. Six Flags Over Texas featured six sections reflecting the spirited cultures of those nations and offered guests a vibrant experience straight out of their dreams. Mr. Wynne envisioned theme parks of a grand scale, bigger than Disneyland. A broad entertainment product, featuring innovative rides complemented by brilliant theme presentations, became his formula for success, and his ingenious use of themes turned the centuries-old amusement park idea into the broader theme park concept. His vision was right on target, and the regional theme park industry was born.[26]

In 1982, the Tierco Group, Inc., originally an Oklahoma-based real estate company, purchased its first park: Frontier City theme park in Oklahoma City. It had plans to demolish the park and sell off the real estate. Tierco soon changed its tune and decided to invest in the dilapidated park and make a go at the amusement park industry. Over a period of time, Tierco developed a reputation for buying rundown parks and resurrecting them.[27] In 1994, Tierco changed its name to Premier Parks

---

[24] Niles, R. (June 30, 2002). Six Flags Looks to Scale Back Expansion. *Theme Park Insider.* Retrieved July 28, 2006, from *http://www.themeparkinsider.com/news/response.cfm?ID=573.*

[25] Six Flags Corp. *Investor History. Retrieved.* October 19, 2006, from *http://www.sixflags.com/investor_history.asp.*

[26] Six Flags Corp. *Media Information. Retrieved.* September 28, 2006, from *http://www.sixflags.com/media_info.asp.*

[27] O'Brien, T. (March 23, 1992). "Restructuring, Renaming, Renovations: Tierco Group Prepares Parks for '92," *Amusement Business,* pp. 17+.

and four years later upped the ante with the purchase of 24 Six Flags parks.[28]

In order for Tierco to fund its endeavor into the amusement industry, it needed large amounts of capital. Tierco decided to sell off most of its real estate holdings to bankroll new park purchases and make improvements at existing locations. During the late 1980s, it sunk nearly $39 million into Frontier City alone. During the early and mid-1990s, the newly formed Premier Parks went on a shopping spree, acquiring seven existing and struggling parks.[29]

For about a decade, from 1980 until 1990, Six Flags was experiencing growth of its own. It had acquired its seventh park: Six Flags Great America in Gurnee, Illinois. During this period, Six Flags experienced a "revolving-door" of sorts concerning owners and operators; they had three to be exact. The third owners, Cochran and Wesray Capital Corporation, managed to take Six Flags private with a leveraged buyout of $617 million. This proved to be costly for the company and shareholders, allowing the accumulation of large amounts of debt. In early 1990, cash-strapped Six Flags opened its doors to investors, allowing Time Warner to purchase a 19.5 percent stake in the company.[30]

In 1991, in an effort to gain financial stability, Six Flags was sold to Time Warner and two additional investors. The total deal was worth an estimated $710 million. This money was intended to further develop the brand and usher in the era of new, more thrilling coasters. In 1995, Time Warner sold 51 percent of its stake in the company for close to $1 billion to Boston Ventures. This capital allowed Six Flags to purchase additional properties over the next four years.[31]

In 1998, Premier Parks paid $1.86 billion for what was touted as the largest amusement park acquisition in history. A mixture of $965 million in cash and securities funded the purchase. However, Premier agreed to assume close to $900 million in debt. Many worried that Premier had grown too fast and wondered if they could ever overcome this debt load. It seemed like an

---

[28] O'Brien, T. (November 2, 1998). "Premier Converts More to Six Flags," *Amusement Business*, pp. 1, 44.

[29] O'Brien, T. (March 23, 1992). "Restructuring, Renaming, Renovations: Tierco Group Prepares Parks for '92," *Amusement Business*, pp. 17+.

[30] Goldman, K. (April 23, 1990). "Time Warner Buys 19.5% of Six Flags for $19.5 Million," *Wall Street Journal*, p. B6.

[31] O'Brien, T. (May 4, 1992). "Time Warner Changes Face of Six Flags Chain," *Amusement Business*, pp. 1+.

insurmountable task ahead of Premier Parks. Overnight, they had become the largest regional theme park operator in the world.[32]

It did not take long for rumblings to start regarding the cash flow problems Premier Parks was facing. In 1998, approximately three months after the acquisition, Premier Parks stock dropped 35 percent. They reacted by cutting close to 450 corporate jobs, leaving them with only 35 corporate staff. Additionally, they began an investment and improvement campaign allocating $200 million to 25 parks.[33] In recognition of its increasing brand importance, Premier Parks changed its company name to Six Flags in mid-2000.[34] During that same period, it spent $170 million on 4 parks, 13 roller coasters, and 60 rides. Six Flags continued purchasing parks during this period and even went international with parks in Canada and Holland.[35]

In 2004, Daniel M. Snyder began investing heavily in Six Flags. One of Mr. Snyder's objectives was to advise management on how they could improve the parks. It did not take long for the conversations to turn hostile. This resulted in Daniel M. Snyder starting a proxy contest for control of Six Flags. Mr. Snyder was under the impression that he could revitalize the ailing park chain with new and improved marketing. This endeavor resembled the efforts Mr. Snyder used to invigorate the Washington Redskins football franchise.[36] Daniel M. Snyder gained control of Six Flags in December of 2005.[37] After gaining control, he was determined to transform the Six Flags brand into a successful media and marketing company. He

---

[32] McDowell, E. (June 21, 1998). "The New Monster of the Midway," *New York Times*. Retrieved October 19, 2006, from *http://www.nytimes.com/1998/06/21/business/the-new-monster-of-the-midway-premier-parks-thrives-by-not-being-disney.html?pagewanted=1*.

[33] Garrity, B. (August 14, 2000). "Despite Recent Transactions, Six Flags Having a Rough Time on Wall Street," *Amusement Business*, p. 13.

[34] Ultimate Rollercoaster. *Premier Parks Officially Changes Name to Six Flags*. Retrieved May 22, 2009, from *http://www.ultimaterollercoaster.com/news/archives/july00/stories/070500_05.shtml*.

[35] O'Brien, T. (October 18, 1999). "Premier Purchases WB's European Parks Division," *Amusement Business*, pp. 1, 32.

[36] Gross, Daniel. (June 29, 2006). Six Flagging—Can Daniel Snyder Revolutionize the Amusement Park Business? *Slate*. Retrieved July 26, 2006, from *http://investors.sixflags.com/phoenix.zhtml?c=61629&p=irol-homeProfile*.

[37] Shin, A. (December 14, 2005). Snyder Partner Named Six Flags CEO. *Washington Post*. Retrieved October 19, 2006, from *http://www.washingtonpost.com/wp-dyn/content/article/2005/12/13/AR2005121301827.html*.

wanted to shed the modern-day carnival image and become a sophisticated player in the amusement industry.

Shortly after gaining control of the Six Flags chain, Daniel M. Snyder installed Mark Shapiro, a former ESPN programming executive, as chief executive officer (CEO). He also installed a new management team and added new board members. The new board included heavyweights such as Harvey Weinstein of Miramax fame. Mr. Snyder also created a new entertainment and marketing department and hired the direct-marketing agency OgilvyOne.[38]

RECOVERY ON THE HORIZON OR A STATE OF FLUX?

Six Flags' mission after the takeover by Daniel Snyder and the installation of Mark Shapiro was to surround the best rides in the world with entertainment from the fields of music, theater, sports, film, and television. Six Flags wanted to be about a wider, more fulfilling experience.[39] Six Flags hoped to energize the elements of the park so that Six Flags would become a destination for every member of the community.[40]

New York–based Six Flags owned and operated a combination of 28 parks in 2009. The collection included 14 theme parks, 12 water parks, and 2 animal parks, all in North America. There was a time when Six Flags owned and operated 15 of the United States' largest theme parks.[41] However, at the end of the fiscal year 2008, Six Flags had two theme parks in North America in the top 20: Six Flags Great Adventure and Six Flags Great America, listed 19 and 20, respectively. Six Flags North American water parks fared slightly better with two breaking the top 15.[42]

In 2005, the Six Flags parks in North America collectively saw its turnstiles turn approximately 33.7 million times. Since 2005, Six Flags has

---

[38] Gross, D. (June 29, 2006). Six Flagging—Can Daniel Snyder Revolutionize the Amusement Park Business? *Slate*. Retrieved July 26, 2006, from *http://investors.sixflags.com/phoenix.zhtml?c=61629&p=irol-homeProfile*.

[39] Adweek. *Six Flags Expands Marketing*. Retrieved August 1, 2006, from *http://www.adweek.com/aw/national/article_display.jsp?vnu_content_id=1001841971*.

[40] Six Flags Corp. *Shareholder Report. Retrieved*. July 28, 2006, from *http://library.corporate-ir.net/library/61/616/61629/items/196628/2005%20Annual%20Report%20 (2).pdf*.

[41] Dunn, J. and & Jackson, M. (August 7, 2006). Elitch's ticket: $170 million. *The Denver Post*. Retrieved October 19, 2006, from *http://www.cobizmag.com/articles.asp?id=1207*.

[42] Themed Entertainment Association/Economics Research Associates. Attractions Attendance Report. Retrieved May 22, 2008, from *http://www.themeit.com/TEAERA2008.pdf*.

reduced its number of parks to 28, and the attendance has dropped to approximately 25.3 million for 2008. Most of the revenue earned by Six Flags comes from its gate receipts. The additional income is generated from merchandise and food.[43]

Since Daniel M. Snyder gained control of Six Flags, the general strategy was to make the parks operate more like Disney. Prior to being selected as the Six Flags CEO, Mark Shapiro worked for ESPN, which was owned by Disney. Mark Shapiro has emulated some of the concepts and themes of the Disney brand—a potential coincidence because he might just be applying proven concepts within the amusement industry. However, it has been stated that Mark Shapiro has spoken in Disney-esque terms about rolling out character brunches and "focusing on an improved guest experience— from keeping our parks cleaner, to a more friendly and service-oriented staff."[44]

Mark Shapiro went right to work making several key changes that were considered critical to the short-term and long-term success of the organization. He immediately identified teenagers as a problem area. They were known for buying low-margin season passes and then hanging out around the parks, occasionally buying a soft drink. The parks had suffered greatly as a result of the loitering from teenagers. Six Flags wanted change the tune and wanted a more lucrative guest. Their objective was to target free-spending upscale families.[45]

The decision was made in spring of 2006 to shift focus and to target the newly identified upscale families. Six Flags implemented new park rules, forged new marketing ventures, and sought new capital to make improvements to the parks. One of the first actions taken was to make the parks smoke-free. On the marketing front it struck sponsorship and marketing deals with pizza chain Papa John's and Home Depot. Six Flags also struck deals with DC Comics and Warner Bros. These agreements allowed Six Flags the exclusive theme park rights to many of the world's greatest cartoon characters and superheroes, from Bugs Bunny and his Looney Tunes friends to DC Comics superheroes Batman, Robin, the Green Lantern, Wonder

---

[43] Six Flags Corp. *Shareholder Report. Retrieved.* July 28, 2006, from *http://library.corporate-ir. net/library/61/616/61629/items/196628/2005%20Annual%20Report%20 (2).pdf.*

[44] Gross, D. (June 29, 2006). Can Daniel Snyder Revolutionize the Amusement Park Business? *Slate.* Retrieved July 26, 2006, from *http://investors.sixflags.com/phoenix.zhtml? c=61629&p=irol-homeProfile.*

[45] Gross, D. (June 29, 2006). Can Daniel Snyder Revolutionize the Amusement Park Business? *Slate.* Retrieved July 26, 2006, from *http://investors.sixflags.com/phoenix.zhtml? c=61629&p=irol-homeProfile.*

Woman and the Flash.[46] As a result, Six Flags was able to offer its guests a full character program. Now, Six Flags could expand their experiences to include character meet and greets, themed meal opportunities, photograph and autograph encounters, and new retail options. Additionally, it sold off its Six Flags Astroworld property to raise $77 million in cash and put up other assets in order to raise much-needed cash.[47]

Some further actions that Six Flags took to improve service in 2006 included the launch of an online ticketing technology solution. Six Flags announced this at the same time that it relaunched its redesigned SixFlags. com website. This was all done in an effort to improve guest satisfaction and enable guests to more easily purchase daily tickets, season passes, and special event tickets for all 28 of its domestic parks.[48]

Since Daniel M. Snyder's takeover of Six Flags, his attempts to salvage the parks with marketing magic have fallen short. Six Flags high level of debt and other obligations have had extremely negative consequences on the parks and the investors. Six Flags has repeatedly stated since 2006 that they may not be able to satisfy obligations concerning outstanding debt. Additionally, they have addressed the concerns of obtaining essential financing in the future for working capital, capital expenditures, debt service requirements, Partnership Park obligations, refinancing, or other critical obligations. The economic situation of 2009 has not made satisfying park obligations any easier and has complicated matters further concerning the already negative circumstances surrounding Six Flags.[49]

As of December 31, 2007, Six Flags' total debt load was approximately $2.26 billion. It has grown slightly from the approximate $2.24 billion it owed in 2005. Six Flags has been strapped with debt of this magnitude for many years. Based on interest rates for debt and annual cash interest payments for nonrevolving credit debt, it is anticipated that Six Flags' debt level will continue to be a threat to the company's overall health. With the combination of the current debt level and the continuous increases in the

[46] Gross, Daniel. (June 29, 2006). Can Daniel Snyder Revolutionize the Amusement Park Business? *Slate.* Retrieved July 26, 2006, from *http://investors.sixflags.com/phoenix.zhtml? c=61629&p=irol-homeProfile.*

[47] Gross, D. (June 29, 2006). Can Daniel Snyder Revolutionize the Amusement Park Business? *Slate.* Retrieved July 26, 2006, from *http://investors.sixflags.com/phoenix.zhtml? c=61629&p=irol-homeProfile.*

[48] McMillan, I. (May 24, 2006). Technology. *Market Wire.* Retrieved August 1, 2006, from *http://biz.yahoo.com/iw/060524/0131193.html.*

[49] Six Flags Corp. *Shareholder Report. Retrieved.* May 22, 2008, from *http://library.corporate-ir.net/library/61/616/61629/items/287458/SIX_2007AnnualReport.pdf.*

cost of operation, it is hard to believe that Six Flags could make significant strides in the repayment of that debt. The current repayment levels of working capital borrowing for the year will aggregate approximately $170 million.[50] The one saving factor in all of this is that most of the debt does not mature until February 2010.[51]

Meanwhile, Six Flags has sold off several parks and real estate to trim debt. They have also reduced television advertising and marketing budgets, and increased parking fees.[52] They have publically stated that they may not be able to satisfy their financial obligations and might have difficulty obtaining necessary financing in the future for working capital.[53] International Theme Park Services, an industry consulting company, said previous management spent an "exorbitant" amount on testosterone-fueled rides, like the Kingda Ka, a $20 million, 460-foot-tall roller coaster at Great Adventure New Jersey, to draw teenagers at a time when consumer preferences were changing. Six Flags fostered a longer, higher, faster armaments war, and it didn't pay any dividends.[54]

SIX FLAGS—A THRILLING FUTURE?

Over the last several years, Six Flags and its management have made numerous changes to the park system. Some of the changes are obvious, while others are hardly noticeable. Some of the more stated changes include new child-care centers and cigarette bans. These changes were directly aimed to lure families back to the parks. They changed their advertising and did away with Mister Six, the Junior Soprano lookalike that did little to spur attendance. They replaced him with characters from the Marvel Comics Justice

---

[50] SEC Edgar Database. *Six Flags, Inc.* Retrieved October 19, 2006, from *http://www.secinfo. com/d11MXs.vgpz.htm.*

[51] Six Flags Corp. *Shareholder Report. Retrieved.* May 22, 2008, from *http://library.corporate-ir.net/library/61/616/61629/items/287458/SIX_2007AnnualReport.pdf.*

[52] Six Flags Corp. *Shareholder Report. Retrieved.* July 28, 2006, from *http://library.corporate-ir. net/library/61/616/61629/items/196628/2005%20Annual%20Report%20(2).pdf.*

[53] Six Flags Corp. *Shareholder Report. Retrieved.* May 22, 2008, from *http://library.corporate-ir.net/library/61/616/61629/items/287458/SIX_2007AnnualReport.pdf.*

[54] Roche, B.J. (May 21, 2006). Six Flags embarks on a new adventure—After years of steep financial losses, the amusement park chain is changing its strategy to focus less on thrill rides and more on families to boost its bottom line. *Globe.* Retrieved July 26, 2006, from *http://www.boston.com/business/articles/2006/05/21/six_flags_embarks_on_a_new_adventure/.*

League: Batman and Robin, the Flash, the Green Lantern, and Wonder Woman. Aside from the Marvel Comics characters, Six Flags has added Looney Tunes characters and will have them roaming Six Flags parks across America. These additions, plus the addition of a parade at each park, change the dynamics of the parks and focus more intently on the needs of families and not teenagers.[55]

Once Mark Shapiro was installed as the CEO of Six Flags, he quickly declared an end to the costly roller coaster "arms race," emphasizing instead what he calls the "DNA of the parks," entertainment, character interaction, maintenance, and customer service. "I don't want to lose the teenager," Shapiro said on a recent tour of the Agawam park. "But I don't think you ever make money on a $20 million roller coaster. We need to concentrate on families. I think we chased them away."[56] The amusement industry realizes that families are good business. It is estimated that families spend about 25 percent more on average at regional theme parks than teenagers. This averages to about $38 per day per person. There are various reasons given for this, but some of the more touted ones include longer stays, more game plays, they eat more food, and buy single-day passes as opposed to teenagers buying season passes and a couple of sodas.[57]

The family focus of the Six Flags chain warrants comparison to Disney. Interestingly enough, Mark Shapiro does not mind. He has stated that he loves Disney. He has also addressed the numerous differences between Disney and Six Flags. Mark believes these differences are the key to the success of Six Flags. Mr. Shapiro has identified the hardships on the American consumer as a competitive advantage. He stated that the American family goes to Disney an average of 1.2 times in their lives. He further stated that the additional costs of airfare, car rental, hotel stays, expensive food, and expensive merchandise can essentially prevent families from traveling to

[55] Roche, B.J. (May 21, 2006). Six Flags embarks on a new adventure—After years of steep financial losses, the amusement park chain is changing its strategy to focus less on thrill rides and more on families to boost its bottom line. *Globe*. Retrieved July 26, 2006, from *http://www.boston.com/business/articles/2006/05/21/six_flags_embarks_on_a_new_adventure/*.

[56] Six Flags Corp. *Shareholder Report*. Retrieved July 28, 2006, from *http://library.corporate-ir.net/library/61/616/61629/items/196628/2005%20Annual%20Report%20(2).pdf*.

[57] Roche, B.J. (May 21, 2006). Six Flags embarks on a new adventure – After years of steep financial losses, the amusement park chain is changing its strategy to focus less on thrill rides and more on families to boost its bottom line. *Globe*. Retrieved July 26, 2006, from *http://www.boston.com/business/articles/2006/05/21/six_flags_embarks_on_a_new_adventure/*.

destination parks like Disney. The objective of Six Flags is to capitalize on this and offer a similar experience for just a car ride away. Six Flags is being touted as more convenient and more affordable.[58]

During the 2006 season, Six Flags conducted surveys of guests at selected parks. This was done during the first full month of the operating season. The findings showed that guest approval ratings were on an upswing. The surveys were conducted by independent firm Delta Market Research of Hatboro, Pennsylvania, a nationally recognized company that has researched all aspects of the theme park industry for companies, including Disney. The survey asked guests to rate every aspect of their park experience. Some of the ratings included park atmosphere, food, rides, and cleanliness. Some broader questions such as "Will you recommend the parks to a friend?," "Will you visit again this year or next?," and "Was the experience worth the money?" were also asked.[59]

- 96 percent of Six Flags guests will or definitely will recommend the parks to a friend.

- 92 percent of Six Flags guests will or definitely will visit again this year or next.

- 93 percent of Six Flags guests agree or strongly agree that "my Six Flags experience was worth the money I spent."[60]

All in all, approximately 4,800 guests at 17 Six Flags parks were surveyed during the month of June 2006. The survey results returned some of the best responses since the inception of the study in 2002. For example, respondents visiting Six Flags Magic Mountain in Valencia, California, gave record ratings.[61]

---

[58] Roche, B.J. (May 21, 2006). Six Flags embarks on a new adventure—After years of steep financial losses, the amusement park chain is changing its strategy to focus less on thrill rides and more on families to boost its bottom line. *Globe*. Retrieved July 26, 2006, from *http://www.boston.com/business/articles/2006/05/21/six_flags_embarks_on_a_new_adventure/*.

[59] Coaster Grotto. Six Flags guest approval ratings at five-year high. Retrieved July 29, 2006, from *http://www.coastergrotto.com/news.jsp?argId=435*.

[60] Coaster Grotto. Six Flags guest approval ratings at five-year high. Retrieved July 29, 2006, from *http://www.coastergrotto.com/news.jsp?argId=435*.

[61] Coaster Grotto. Six Flags guest approval ratings at five-year high. Retrieved July 29, 2006, from *http://www.coastergrotto.com/news.jsp?argId=435*.

SUMMARY

As it moves into the future, Six Flags aims to provide families and guests of all ages with the best and most diverse entertainment experience they can find close to their home. A lot has changed since the opening of the first Six Flags park in Texas over 48 years ago. As of 2009, Six Flags is a company struggling to remain relevant, a company on the verge of collapse. Mark Shapiro, the former ESPN programming whiz, has been leading the charge to turn the company around since 2005. The strategy employed to turn the parks around might have fallen short—way short. The intention was right, but the action might not have been swift enough.

The operating seasons since 2006 have been unkind to Six Flags. It has been noted on several occasions that revenues have been down. Six Flags has stated that per capita guest spending rose over the last several years. That boils down to families spending more money while they are in the parks. The unfortunate part is that attendance fell over the same period. This has been attributed largely to the lower sales of season passes. Essentially, fewer teens are spending time in the parks. Mark Shapiro spun the numbers positively: "Make no mistake about it; families are coming back—as evidenced by our solid increase in per capita guest spending—but not as quickly as we had hoped. The markets are not buying it."[62]

Mark Shapiro understood that Six Flags had chased the families away, and clearly they needed them back. However, an equally destructive choice to chase the teenage market away ensued quickly after Mr. Shapiro was put in place. Families are obviously good business for the amusement industry, but the teenagers might have been discounted by Six Flags prematurely. Six Flags made a valiant effort to bring the families back but apparently misread the desire for families to come back. Six Flags had spent many years catering to the teenage market and ride enthusiast with the roller-coaster arms race. Poor guest service, management choices, and highly publicized ride accidents led many to choose alternative forms of entertainment.

In order for Six Flags to get families back they should have been more dramatic with their approach, even as dramatic as lifting single-ticket entry into the park. A throwback to the early Disneyland years or a carnival with pay-per-ride admissions, this would generate extreme buzz in this day and age and would allow for greater competition with other forms of entertainment. This is especially relevant due to the regional influence that Six Flags has on the theme park industry.

---

[62] Six Flags Corp. *Shareholder Report. Retrieved.* July 28, 2006, from *http://library.corporate-ir. net/library/61/616/61629/items/196628/2005%20Annual%20Report%20(2).pdf.*

Mark Shapiro needs to worry less about trying to become Disney and concentrate more on paring down his park system and finding a way to become more profitable. He should find a way to make his offerings more appealing to families and less expensive. The idea is to bring families to the Six Flags parks multiple times over a short period of time. Disney is a destination park and has little to no bearing on the plans of Six Flags. Six Flags' real competition are recreational facilities and other forms of entertainment within regional market areas, including movies, malls, and sports attractions.

In the second quarter of 2009, Six Flags was delisted from the New York Stock Exchange. They were placed on the OTC Bulletin board for trading.[63] The stock, as of May 22, 2009, was valued at .335 a share. The share price has fluctuated form 2005 significantly reaching $11.61 in February of 2006. As of April 16, 2009, Standard & Poor's had downgraded Six Flags from a "CCC" to a "D" credit rating.[64]

DISCUSSION QUESTIONS

1. Why has the amusement industry in the United States been facing challenges?

2. Are regional theme parks a thing of the past? Explain.

3. What is the current mission of Six Flags?

4. Why does Six Flags face current challenges? Explain

5. Is targeting families a sustainable business model? Explain.

6. Does Six Flags have any core competencies? If yes, what are they?

7. Does Six Flags have a sustainable competitive advantage?

8. What would you recommend that Six Flags do to revitalize the company?

---

[63] *Dallas Business Journal.* Six Flags delisted, announces OTC symbol. Retrieved May 22, 2009, from *http://dallas.bizjournals.com/dallas/stories/2009/04/27/daily40.html.*

[64] Standard & Poor's. Six Flags Inc. Ratings Lowered To "D" On Nonpayment Of Interest. Retrieved July 28, 2006, from *http://www.alacrastore.com/storecontent/spcred/716042.*

The Implementation Process of a Revenue Management Strategy in Britco Hotels[1]

INTRODUCTION

BritCo Hotels[2] was founded in the mid-1930s as a restaurant operator and moved into the hotel sector in the late 1960s. It was a publicly quoted company, and its head office was based in the United Kingdom. It operated at all levels of the hotel market. In the mid-1990s, a conglomerate (which will be called IBD for confidentiality purpose) acquired BritCo Hotels, and it became a subsidiary of this conglomerate. In January 1999, the company operated over 400 hotels in around 50 countries in Europe, the Americas, Asia and the Pacific, Africa, and the Middle East. A large proportion of these hotels were operated in the United Kingdom, the United States, and a number of European countries. The company operated four brands, and each targeted a specific market segments. After acquiring BritCo Hotels, IBD began a rationalisation process and subsequently disposed of all hotels in the early 2000s.

CONTENTS

---

[1] This case was written by Dr. Fevzi Okumus. The case study was derived from Okumus (2000). Some of the findings from this research were also published in Okumus (2001) and Okumus (2004). The author conducted over 30 in-depth interviews with company respondents across the different levels of the organisation from 1997 to 1999. He also spent a period of participant observation in the company and collected internal and external data about the company and the development and implementation process of the YMP. The case is intended to reconstruct the challenges and issues facing management in implementing strategic decisions. It is not intended to convey any criticism of any individual or group of individuals.

[2] For confidentiality purpose, the actual name of the case study company is disguised. Thereafter, it will be referred to as BritCo Hotels.

This case study looks at how BritCo Hotels developed and implemented their yield (revenue) management project (YMP). The research took place between 1997 and 1999. The strategic context of the hotel group and the implementation process of the yield management project (YMP) are summarised in a chronological order in Appendix 1, starting from the early 1990s to 1999. First, the strategic content of BritCo Hotels is discussed. Next, the external and organizational contexts of BritCo Hotels are evaluated. Then, the development and implementation process of the YMP is explained. The case study ends with a summary and discussion questions.

STRATEGIC CONTENT

The main goals of BritCo Hotels in 1997–1999 are outlined in Table 1. Many informants from the head office and the hotel units also referred to these goals, but certainly, increasing profit was the most important business goal. It is worth noting that during the takeover bid, IBD group strongly argued that BritCo Hotels had not been managed profitably, and they convinced the key stakeholders that they could manage the company better and more profitably.

Linking business goals to the YMP, informants, particularly from the head office, stated that this was a strategic initiative in order to improve the company's revenue and profitability. During a revenue management workshop, both the IT director and the Yield (Revenue) director told attendees that this project was one of the biggest underway in the company at that

Table 1	BritCo Hotels' Business Goals
1.	Operate profitable and sound businesses
2.	Provide high-quality services at an appropriate price
3.	Provide customer satisfaction
4.	Seek market leadership
5.	Pursue excellence in management
6.	Recruit, train, and develop talented people
7.	Give scope to our management and staff
8.	Recognise and reward success and achievement

Source: Adapted from the company reports and documents (1996; 1997).

time, and it would be the key driver to increase occupancy, revenue, profits, and, therefore, shareholder value. Most of the informants, both from the head office and hotels, stated that before the YMP there had not been a consistent and company-wide uniform approach to managing revenue. Hotels had used manual systems that were time consuming, inefficient, and often unreliable. During the interviews and also at the training workshops, it was emphasised by the senior executives that the project was essential for the company for the following reasons:

- To adopt technological developments to managing hotels

- To overcome unreliable forecasting

- To minimise hotels' vulnerability to staff turnover

- To give extra time for more accurate forecasting and other managerial duties

To achieve this, the company aimed at designing a computerised yield management system that could forecast and monitor the demand for each hotel and based on it, produce daily reports for the next several months. Informants mainly from the head office believed that by implementing the YMP, BritCo Hotels could overcome the limitations of previous approaches to managing revenue and occupancy.

One of the main aims of the project was to develop a new "revenue culture" across the company. This new strategy gave more emphasis to the whole hotel experience, and the "value" of the whole hotel experience became the central concept rather than just the room type or rate. Whereas in the past, reservation and sales employees had only been there to take bookings and respond to enquiries, they now needed to learn to negotiate and to say no when necessary. Even if there was a room available in a hotel on the desired date, the new strategy required hotels to be more selective and choose whether or not to take the booking.

While explaining the company's business goals, many informants referred to other projects and developments that were being designed and/or deployed in the company. In order to achieve the strategic goals listed in Table 1, several other projects were being developed and put into practice. Some of them were closely linked with the YMP, while some did not have any direct relationship. Table 2 lists these strategic projects that were identified during the research project. Strong links were recognised among these projects. For example, the YMP either complemented the previous or current related projects or the stability of the yield project relied on these projects,

Table 2 Other Projects		
Grouping	**Related Projects**	**Unrelated Projects**
Initiatives Implemented before the YMP	■ The Central Reservation System Project ■ Developing a data-base to store the necessary data	■ Restructuring process after acquiring a new hotel chain
Initiatives Being Considered and/or Implemented during the Life Cycle of the YMP	■ "Rate by length of stay" project ■ Implementing the YMP in international properties ■ Revenue Management 2001 [name disguised for confidentiality purpose]	■ A radical structural change at operational level (clustering strategy) ■ Overall structural change across the company and appointment of new senior executives. ■ Excellence in customer service project

particularly the Central Reservation System (CRS), database, and agent interface development (AI). Some of the future projects aimed to develop the yield project one step further. The unrelated projects, particularly "clustering" and overall structural change, had generally negative impacts on the implementation process of the YMP. Concerning developing and implementing multiple projects within the company, the Yield director complained that developing and implementing other projects often had negative impacts on the implementation process of the YMP and it made their task even more difficult.

Before going into an in-depth explanation of how the YMP was initiated and implemented in BritCo Hotels, the next section describes the environmental and organisational context in which the YMP was developed and implemented.

ENVIRONMENTAL CONTEXT

In relation to the YMP project, many informants indirectly or directly referred to the economic and technological environment. They often indicated that the project had been developed and implemented in a positive economic cycle. For example, the managing director of U.K. hotels stated, "The external environment is moderately positive, the economy is still reasonably strong, and unemployment is coming down a bit. GDP is continuing to rise." BritCo Hotels reported important increases in occupancy

Table 3	Performance of the Hotel Industry in the UK		
U.K. Hotels	1995	1996	1997
Average Hotel Occupancy in the United Kingdom (%)	67.60	70.9	71.90
Average Daily Room Rates in the United Kingdom (U.S.$)	81.88	79.7	91.90
London Hotels	1995	1996	1997
Average Hotel Occupancy in London (%)	83.87	84.6	85.00
Average Daily Room Rates in London (£)	80.49	90.47	98.97

Sources: Adapted from Bailey, M. (1998). *The International Hotel Industry: Corporate Strategies and Global Opportunities*, 2nd ed. Research Report, Travel & Tourism Intelligence; Todd, G. and Mather, S. (1995). *The International Hotel Industry: Corporate Strategies and Global Opportunities*. Research Report, Travel & Tourism Intelligence.

and revenue figures between 1995 and 1998 (Bailey, 1998, and company reports). For example, in 1996, the company was able to increase room rates by an average of 17 percent in London hotels and 6 percent in provincial hotels (Table 3).

On the other hand, there were sceptics about the yield system's capability of precisely predicting future demand. They argued that the hotel market, particularly in the United Kingdom, had been buoyant during the previous two years. Therefore, they had doubts that the YMP would be able to recognise any sharp decline in demand. Some informants also questioned whether the company would have invested in the project if there had been a recession in the United Kingdom.

The consolidation process in the hotel industry in the 1990s had both negative and positive impacts on the deployment of the yield management project. When BritCo Hotels acquired another hotel group in the mid-1990s, the yield project was suspended until the integration of this chain into the group was fully completed. However, the change of ownership of BritCo Hotels in 1996 had positive impacts on the deployment of this project as new owners (IBD) supported the YMP.

There were mixed responses concerning technological advances. Several informants perceived the project as a reaction to technological developments, while many others saw these technological developments as an opportunity to improve management practices in the company. Informants also stated that similar technological developments had been utilised successfully by airline companies, so hotel groups should also adopt these technological advances to keep up with their competitors.

INTERNAL CONTEXT

The company's overall <u>organisational structure</u> changed radically since it was acquired in 1996. However, during the development and implementation process of the YMP, numerous structural changes took place in the company. In 1997, the chief executive officer of the company left, and no replacement appointment was made for over seven months. Moreover, the Information Technology director, marketing director, and managing directors for London, U.K. and International Hotels were replaced, generally from outside organisations. In mid-1998, a new CEO was appointed from outside, and he recruited new executives from outside as well and changed the organizational structure to a brand-oriented structure (Figure 1). In this new structure, the Sales and Marketing departments were combined. Reporting to the Sales and Marketing department, a new Distribution and Revenue

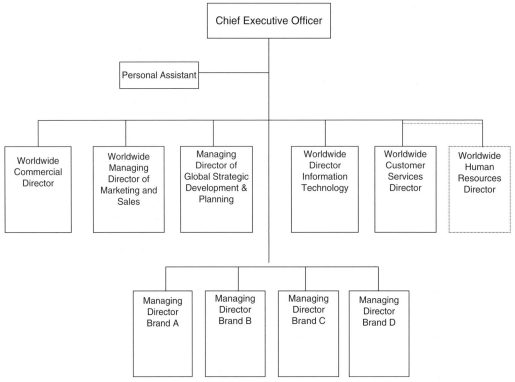

FIGURE 1 *BritCo Hotels' Organisational Structure after September 1997.*
Source: Company, May 1999.

department was formed, and an executive from outside the company was appointed as the managing director.

Radical structural changes also took place at regional and operational levels. After acquiring BritCo Hotels, the management team of IBD introduced the regional general manager concept, which was referred to as "clustering" project. The hotel general manager position was removed and the regional general manager position was created. Informants often claimed that this structural change not only caused a higher labour turnover across the company but also sent an important message to lower management levels about the company's new approach to managing hotels.

It was claimed that the organisational structure of the company had limitations, particularly when developing and implementing new initiatives. For example, the managing director of the U.K. hotels stated"

> *In terms of the implementation of plans and so on it [the company's structure] does make things slower. There are more people involved; there are multi-dimensional accountabilities. ... The structure does not facilitate strategy implementation.*

He further suggested that the company was too formal and bureaucratic, and people were often more interested in gaining and keeping new positions rather than delivering tasks and projects. Many informants stated that since 1996, BritCo Hotels had started using the project management structure to design and implement strategic initiatives. Unique project teams were set up for each project, and a *Project Management Handbook* was available that explained key issues and concepts in a step-by-step format. Informants from the head office often stressed the usefulness of using a project management structure for ensuring coordination and cooperation, and overcoming any potential cultural and political problems. However, a few informants further expressed their concern about the potential dangers and problems in utilising a project management structure in BritCo Hotels, claiming that some projects took too long and project teams often used projects to strengthen their own positions.

The overall communication style in BritCo Hotels was described as "top-down" and "formally documented." The communication mechanisms (technically and culturally) were not very effective at facilitating and maintaining collaboration among departments and getting the right messages across the company. For example, there were comments from senior executives like "Communication is poor and fragmented; that comes back to structure and culture. We are not good at making sure that people know what is going on in an adequate level of detail." It was stated that the communication and coordination between functional areas was problematic. To illustrate this, one middle manager gave the following example:

I found out recently that there is a person doing something in IT and that I should really be talking to this person about something that I am doing. If I had known that it was going on, I could help her, or she could help me. So that is the sort of communication we are lacking.

One of the regional general managers commented about why some communication efforts and activities are not always effective in big companies such as BritCo Hotels:

The worst type of strategy we have in a large organisation like this is one where you receive a memo that says "from Monday you do this." That puts people off. No explanation why we are doing it. That is very dictatorial. . . . If you do not sell it right, you face blockages. People will be determined to stop it.

Informants in hotel units further stated that they receive many letters and reports, but they are often not sure whether they are really important or not. For example, one manager stated, "I think some people justify their jobs by sending out all these memos."

It was further noted that prior to the change in ownership, BritCo Hotels was run as a family organisation, and the members of the previous owning family had been very influential in the company's culture. Prior to the change in ownership, the company was a very bureaucratic organisation, and there were conflicts within divisions and functional departments.

There were mixed responses as to how far the company changed since it had been taken over. A number of informants argued that the company had become less politically oriented and more open to change. On the other hand, more informants stated that although some positive changes had been made since the company's takeover, the company's culture had not changed much and there were still conflicts between departments and functional areas within the company. The managing director for the U.K. hotels stated:

Culture has not changed that much. Offices are still the same; the attitudes of many people are still the same. They have been here for 20 years; they are not going to change that quickly.

When introducing and implementing projects in BritCo Hotels, there were often conflicts and misunderstandings between head office and hotel units, and hotel units were often sceptical about the projects coming from the head office. Informants claimed that historically, hotels and their managers were powerful in the company and often paid little attention to the projects and instructions coming from the head office. Several informants claimed that by implementing the structural change (clustering), the company aimed to eliminate the hotel general managers' power in the company. In return, it was clear that this clustering project caused a certain amount of disruption and discomfort in hotels and made managers and employees even more sceptical about any new project.

Employees and managers from hotel units argued that in addition to requests from the head office, they had numerous other major duties, roles, and responsibilities. They claimed that new projects would often be introduced with great enthusiasm, but after a while this enthusiasm would diminish, and they were soon withdrawn and a new one would be introduced. One head office informant explained the situation between head office and hotel units: "There is always a 'them and us' situation between the hotels and the head office. . . . This is another project they are trying to give us—a waste of time."

It was apparent that despite all these structural changes introduced in hotels, the company's London hotels were still the most politically powerful and most influential in the company. For example, one yield analyst stated, "London hotels are very much separate from the remaining hotel. . . . They have so much power in the company that if the London hotels get together and decide not to do something, then it will have a great effect. It will not happen."

This section has so far described the environmental and organisational context in which the YMP was developed and implemented. The next section describes how the YMP was initiated and implemented in BritCo Hotels.

IMPLEMENTATION PROCESS OF THE YMP PROJECT

Appendix 1 explains the implementation activities, problems encountered, and how the project team responded to these issues. When explaining how the YMP emerged or was initiated, several informants referred back to the early 1990s and noted that a similar project with a different and less sophisticated format was first introduced, and this trial proved that a similar project could also be introduced in other brands. Further to this trial, a yield management project was introduced across the company in 1994, but due to other priorities at that time, such as implementing the company's central reservation system and integrating a recently acquired hotel chain into the company, the yield project implementation was suspended.

A number of senior managers who initially worked on the project left the organisation. At the time of the data collection process, several managers from hotels remembered this initiative. For example, one manager said, "The YMP has been going on for many years ... It must have been three years ago when we went to a meeting, of which we were told about." After the acquisition of BritCo Hotels by IBD, the implementation of the yield project was reconsidered in 1997. Many informants from the head office stated that after the change in ownership, IBD executives identified the yield management project as an important business initiative and therefore supported it.

At first, a Yield Department was created, and a Yield director was appointed. Several Yield analysts were recruited both from inside and outside the company to work with the Yield director. To design and implement the yield project alongside the Yield Department, a project team was formed that had several members from different areas. The Yield Department was also a part of the project team, working together on the implementation process. In order to gain the necessary financial resources, a formal project proposal was submitted to the Hotel Board and the parent company (IBD) board. Over $6 million was allocated to the development and deployment of the YMP. A significant proportion of this money was invested in software, and the rest was spent on training and other preparation activities.

At this early stage, a lot of discussions, presentations, and communication activities took place among the relevant parties, including the members of the BritCo board and the IBD board. These discussions were not primarily concerned with formulating the project, as it was believed that the concept already existed in the company. Their focus was more on how the project could be delivered successfully. However, it was clear that not all of the board members fully supported the project.

The Yield director stated that after the project proposal was approved, they went to all of the London hotels and talked to relevant managers about the benefits of the project and how they were going to design and implement it. They did this because London hotels were influential and politically strong in the company, and therefore their support and understanding was essential. However, it was apparent that managers from London and other hotels did not really get involved in the design of the project at this early stage.

After the takeover of the company, many IT activities were outsourced. Therefore, the company started to rely on the knowledge and skills of external companies, not only for adopting technological changes within the company but also for carrying out maintenance of existing software and systems. For developing the yield software, they had to work with two external companies. The first one was responsible for the development of the yield system as well as building the agent interface between the company's central reservation system and the property management systems in units. The second company was responsible for system maintenance. These two external companies played a key role in designing and implementing the YMP, as BritCo Hotels did not have sufficient knowledge and expertise in this area.

The members of the project team had numerous meetings, and eventually they developed an operational plan with clear objectives, action points, and deadlines. These preparation activities were time consuming for the company, but they were crucial in terms of building a sound infrastructure for the project. A specific step-by-step action plan was also developed for implementing the YMP in each hotel.

At the initial stage of the project, one of the project team's key preparation tasks was to collect information and data from hotel property management systems. Informants from both the head office and the hotels claimed that the content and reliability of the collected data was important for the YMP, as the software would provide recommendations based on this historical data and projected events. The informants further stated that finding and making sense of the collected information and data from hotels were difficult, as some of the previous data were missing or unreliable.

The real communication with managers and employees in hotels took place through training workshops. Hotel managers in London and regional general managers in provincial hotels were sent a formal letter inviting them and their key hotel staff to these workshops. Several informants from hotels indicated that this letter did not give much information about the project and that they did not know much about the actual implications of the project until they had attended the workshop.

The Yield Department initially worked with a specialised external training company when preparing these workshops. From May 1997 to September 1997, more than seven training workshops were organised for managers and employees from the head office and from 160 hotels. Each workshop lasted one day and was attended by between 60 to 75 people from 25 hotels. Overall, more than 450 people attended these training workshops. In explaining the importance of these training workshops, the Inventory director commented, "The idea was to give them some education and background to the changes and why we were doing them." Depending on the property management systems, hotels were grouped into different categories, and each group's training workshop was modified and adjusted accordingly.

A number of informants emphasised that in order to attend these workshops, people from hotels first had to attend training courses on property management systems, the company's central reservation system, and the agent interface. In other words, in order to be able to understand the Yield workshop, hotel staff had to first be competent in using the preceding systems. Managers and employees from hotel units were critical about the way the YMP was first communicated to them. When the YMP was first introduced, there were other changes taking place such as "clustering," and many employees were worried about their jobs. They seemed threatened by the way the YMP was introduced into the hotels. For example, according to one front office manager, people from the head office had indicated that:

The YMP was going to come and take over, and we would be replaced by all these machines. . . . It is going to be all done for you so it was like "we do not need you." That was how they put the message across.

Supporting this, the Inventory director claimed that:

We should have employed somebody specifically to spread the word constantly to keep talking about it. Telling people what is going on, describing the project, why we are doing it all the time, visiting the hotels. I think they would have got the message then and that would have taken us 50 percent of the way into the project and the actual "doing it" would be much easier for them.

The members of the Yield team and the project team stated that communicating and selling the project to so many people in these hotels was not an easy task. For example, one Yield analyst stated that:

It is difficult to get the message across to hotels. It is great at the managing director level, but we have been dealing with the reservation clerks in 160 hotels. Training people, getting information through, putting in a brand new communication network and a brand new technology at the same time is not so easy in many hotels.

When the project was first introduced, there were other changes happening in the company, and therefore people from hotels were worried about their future. One Yield analyst commented that:

The very first workshop we had was extremely negative. . . . People were very concerned about their job security. There were big changes being made, and they were called to come along to a Yield workshop. We were telling them about a new system where they initially perceived that we were just going to take all their responsibility away from them, which further led them to feeling even more insecure about their jobs. They were extremely negative.

Members of the Yield Department conversely thought that these workshops were effective and helpful in selling the project across the company, and in reality a very high majority of the informants from hotels who attended these workshops expressed their satisfaction with them. However, there were also a number of criticisms of the workshops' organisation and presentation. For example, some informants from hotels stated that there had been very limited opportunities for discussion and participation during the training day. Several informants also suggested that training workshops should have been arranged in their working environments. Many informants also complained about the timing of the Yield workshops. For example, a reservation manager stated, "I went to the workshop, and then several months later, I heard about the YMP again. ... There was a great gap."

Concerning this, the members of the project team and the Yield Department argued that this was almost beyond their control, as they had planned and arranged all these Yield training workshops in advance, assuming that the system would go live as planned. However, the Yield system unexpectedly started providing inconsistent and unreliable reports, and therefore the project team had to postpone its full deployment.

The YMP required a number of structural changes and adjustments at unit level. For example, each hotel was required to form a Yield Committee consisting of relevant managerial staff, including the hotel general manager, assistant general manager, front of house (or front office) manager, and reservations manager. In addition, every hotel had to appoint a new Yield manager internally. The project had implications for shift times, job roles, and job skills in hotels. For example, every hotel needed to look at the recommendation reports received each morning and confirm their content with the Yield Department at the head office before 10:00 a.m. More important, the project required reservation and front office employees and managers to be more revenue oriented. The Yield Committee members were also required to hold weekly meetings to examine the Yield recommendation reports and evaluate Yield and inventory issues.

There were differences among hotel units in terms of their capabilities and skills in yield management practices, and this had implications for the deployment of the YMP. For example, in large hotels, there were dedicated reservation managers and staff who could specifically focus on yield management practices. In smaller hotels, front office staff seemed to perform all these functions, which meant that they also needed to be trained and prepared for yield management practices. Some hotels were not connected to the company's central reservation system and were therefore excluded from the project. Across the different brands, there were several property management systems, and each required adjustments to implement the yield management system. Finally, hotels in some regions, such as London, attracted more employees, whereas some provincial hotels faced problems in recruiting qualified staff.

Overall, managers and employees seemed pleased to be associated with the YMP. However, it was often claimed that although the new project would provide new skills, it would not offer them any financial return in the short term. Senior managers also confirmed that employees would not receive any financial benefits from the implementation of the YMP. For example, the managing director of the U.K. hotels stated, "Employees will actually get nothing. ... It is just a tool to enable them to do their job properly."

The operational plans designed earlier were used for monitoring the progress of the YMP. Its progress and any problems encountered were reported to members of the project team and also to the hotel board. However, it was evident that the project team could not follow their initial plans precisely because there were unexpected problems and difficulties that resulted in delays when implementing the YMP. Several reasons were identified:

1. The database had to be moved to another country, thus delaying the project deployment as it took time to restart and restabilise the system.

2. The software was not reliable, and many hotel units received inconsistent yield reports. Informants argued that this was due to the fact that the wrong data had earlier been entered into the system, and to overcome this problem, the implementation team and many hotels had to reinput data.

3. The system was initially designed for airlines. The project group and the external companies were trying to adapt it to hotels.

4. The two external specialised companies responsible for developing and looking after the system were not particularly helpful in responding to the project team's demands and requirements in time, and this also delayed the implementation process.

5. Due to high labour turnover in hotel units, many hotels did not have trained staff to look at the yield reports, and therefore in some hotels, the implementation process of the project was delayed. This labour turnover

resulted in additional costs and also made it difficult for the project team to create a "yield culture" in hotels.

6. Managers and employees from hotel units directly or indirectly resisted the YMP, claiming that because of this project, they could upset and lose their loyal customers.

Additional resources were required to redesign some parts of the yield software and also to arrange more workshops. Members of the hotel board agreed to extend the extra capital and resources. The Yield Department continued working with the external partner firms to enhance the yield system and to overcome the existing challenges. However, the working relationship with one of the partners deteriorated, and the members of the Yield Department had to work with the other company to continue the implementation process.

Labour turnover created a major problem in implementing the YMP. Several reasons were given for the high labour turnover in BritCo Hotels, including low pay, unsociable working hours, the stressful nature of hotel work, and the structural changes across the company. The majority of informants stated that high labour turnover is a common problem in the hotel industry. This high labour turnover put extra pressure on members of the project team. For example, a yield analyst stated, "People have been on workshops, they have been trained, and they are leaving, leaving the hotels with nobody trained." The members of the Yield Department began arranging training workshops on a continuous basis in order to minimise the negative impacts of the labour turnover on the implementation process of the YMP.

A further issue was that these training programs were seen as vital in adapting a yield culture across the company. However, several informants referred to the cultural change involved as a slow process, and these informants claimed they had not perhaps given enough attention to this issue and that the company had not yet been successful in adopting the yield culture completely. For example, the managing director of the U.K. hotels stated, "I wish we could have thought more about the need to change attitude rather than just install the technology."

As mentioned earlier, after the appointment of the new CEO in September 1997, radical structural changes happened, and new senior managers were appointed from outside. Following these structural changes, the Yield and Inventory Departments were combined and became a Revenue Management Department. The existing Yield director was appointed as Revenue Director Worldwide, reporting to the director of the Distribution and Revenue Department, which was also a new department reporting to the managing director of Sales and Marketing Worldwide. The new Revenue director stated that they were going to continue recruiting more revenue managers/analysts for each brand to work with and to monitor revenue generation. These revenue analysts were required to report to the Revenue director, but they would also report to the managing directors of each brand. These new appointments meant changes in the project management group and required the Yield director and their teams to further communicate and sell the project to the new incoming executives, including the new CEO.

In later stages of the project, the members of the Yield team started carrying out a number of presentations to city analysts and potential investors about the YMP and its potential advantages for the company. About this, the Yield director stated, "Our shareholders and potential investors should know about this project and its advantages." However, perhaps the most important issue remaining to be addressed was the need to communicate with customers about the project. It was clear that relevant managers and employees in hotel units had not been clearly briefed about, and prepared for, explaining the implications of the new yield strategy to customers and handling customer complaints. Each person appeared to have a different interpretation. Therefore, further communication and training activities were needed to explain to relevant hotel people how they could talk to their customers about the new yield strategy and its implications.

Members of the Yield Department indicated that they aimed to design ongoing control and feedback mechanisms to closely monitor the progress and outcome of the project. For example, after every training workshop, attendees were given feedback forms and asked to contact the members of the Yield Department if they had any problems or suggestions about the project. The Yield director and a few informants from hotel units indicated that a yield users group was already formed, and informants from hotels and the head office were going to hold regular meetings to get feedback from hotels units and also to discuss the progress of the YMP. At the head office level, a further monitoring activity involved system checks by the Yield analysts on a continuous basis and making sure that it was consistent and working well. They also needed to monitor the daily and monthly revenue figures for each hotel and, when necessary, report these statistics to relevant departments or executives for further action.

At the operational level, relevant managers and employees were required to check yield recommendation reports every morning accompanied by regular weekly meetings. However, during the site visits to the hotels, the researcher observed that relevant people in the hotels did not check recommendation reports every morning, and some managers even claimed that they did not look at these reports daily. They argued that the system was still in its infancy and therefore they could not rely on these reports. Several informants from the hotels complained that reading long reports every morning was very time consuming and it was not a normal part of their daily working practices. It was recognised that unless relevant employees and managers believed in the system, it was almost impossible for the Yield Department to control whether the hotels were checking their reports regularly. In addition, informants from operations perceived the YMP as a new control mechanism over the hotels.

During the data collection process, several informants, including the two managing directors and the Yield director, noted that although they had already started implementing the project, by working on it and monitoring its progress and early results, they were making further changes and improvements and learning from the process. For example, the managing director of the U.K. hotels and the Yield director stated that initially they had failed to consider how they could use the information provided by the YMP in a broader way and maximise the management information. According to the managing director of the U.K. hotels:

> There was some failure to see the true strategic implications of what the system could do for us. It was seen as quite a narrow trace yield management setting system. There is a strategic opportunity that we were in danger of missing. ... We did not think about management information, but we thought about yield management in a very tactical way.

It was claimed that the project was new to them, and therefore its design and implementation process had been a learning process for them. Many informants believed that BritCo Hotels was perhaps the first hotel group in the United Kingdom to develop and implement a centralised yield project and that it was therefore ahead of the competition. However, they were equally aware of the need to update the yield software in order to maintain this competitive advantage.

OUTCOMES OF THE YMP

At the time of the research project, many informants, particularly from the hotels, believed that although the implementation process of the YMP was almost completed, the project itself was still new in the company and therefore it would take a few years to see its actual outcomes. However, a number of outcomes had already been achieved:

- An agent interface between the company's central reservation system and the property management systems was created, and they started communicating with each other.
- Despite minor problems with the system, the yield system started producing reports to over 160 hotels, and the majority of the hotels were regularly referring to them.
- The system started providing crucial information for marketing, sales, and HRM areas, and it was hoped that in the future the system would provide more reliable management information.
- Many employees and managers were trained at yield workshops.

In terms of future outcomes of the project, it was widely believed by the informants that the YMP would be an essential tool for the company in managing its revenues and occupancy in a more professional manner. The Yield director and the members of his team also argued that the yield system would help the company to minimise the negative effects of losing experienced hotel people. They claimed that the yield management system would be able to store historical data and consider planned events and, based on this, help the company to predict future trends. In this way the company would not solely rely on managers' experience and knowledge.

Concerning how customers reacted to, or would react to, the project, there were mixed feelings among the informants. Some clearly supported this initiative and claimed that as in the case of the airline industry, customers in the hotel industry would learn and adapt themselves to this new way of working. Other informants from the hotels were concerned about this new approach, and they argued that it could damage the relationship between the hotels and their customers. For example, according to one hotel manager:

> There is a culture beginning in BritCo Hotels whereby we do not actually sell a double or twin room to a customer; we just sell them a room. We are more interested in rate and revenue. I believe that it is wrong, and I think it is going too far. This new culture takes yield management a little too far.

SUMMARY

This case study has explained how BritCo Hotels developed and implemented their yield management strategy in their hotel units. In summary:

1. There were a number of other projects that were being developed and implemented at the same time, and the YMP was closely linked with some of these projects.

2. Increasing revenue and profit was the most important goal in BritCo Hotels, and the YMP was seen a strategic tool to assist the company to achieve this goal.

3. The YMP was introduced as a top-down initiative, and a project management structure was formed to actually initiate and implement the project.

4. The members of the project team, who were generally middle managers, developed plans, secured the necessary resources, arranged regular training workshops, and communicated to relevant parties.

5. After initiating the YMP, several unexpected challenges were faced that resulted in delays, and therefore the project team had to respond to those emerging problems and develop further contingency plans, ask for further resources, and carry out additional training and communication activities.

6. The main difficulties in implementing the YMP appeared to have emerged from the company's size, organisational structure, and culture.

7. At the time the YMP was being implemented, the participant company was going through a radical transitional period. There were structural changes going on that created an unpleasant working environment and made it difficult to introduce new initiatives.

8. The project was implemented across 160 hotels, and the project team faced further difficulties in deploying the project in multiple locations with differing resource and skills levels.

9. The project also required a radical shift in working practices, particularly in managing revenue in hotels.

DISCUSSION QUESTIONS

1. How was the YPM developed initially?

2. How did the implementation of multiple projects influence the YMP?

3. Is it common to implement multiple projects in an organization?

4. How did the external environment influence the deployment and the implementation process of the YMP?

5. How would you describe the organizational context of BritCo Hotels? How did this organizational context influence the implementation process of the YMP?

6. How was the YMP developed and implemented? How useful were their initial plans?

7. What were the challenges to the development and the implementation of the YMP?

8. The YMP was implemented only in the U.K. hotels. What other challenges would be faced if it was implemented in other countries and cultures?

9. Which school of thought would best explain the development process of the YMP?

10. What can we learn from this case study?

REFERENCES

Bailey, M. (1998). *The International Hotel Industry: Corporate Strategies and Global Opportunities*, 2nd ed., Research Report, Travel & Tourism Intelligence.

Okumus, F. (2000). Strategy Implementation: A Study of International Hotel Groups. Unpublished PhD thesis. Oxford Brookes University, Oxford.

Okumus, F. (2001). Towards a Strategy Implementation Framework, *International Journal of Contemporary Hospitality Management*, 13 (7), Special Issue, 327–338.

Okumus, F. (2004). Implementation of Yield Management Practices in Service Organizations: Empirical Findings from a Major Hotel Group, *The Service Industries Journal*, 24 (6), 65–89.

Todd, G. and Mather, S. (1995). *The International Hotel Industry: Corporate Strategies and Global Opportunities*. Research Report, Travel & Tourism Intelligence.

APPENDIX 1: STRATEGIC CONTEXT IN BRITCO HOTELS AND THE IMPLEMENTATION PROCESS OF THE YIELD MANAGEMENT PROJECT BETWEEN 1990 AND 1998

Date	Context	Process
1991	■ A family organisation. ■ Recession in the U.K.— lower revenue and occupancy figures. ■ Restructuring process was initiated and a brand-oriented structure was formed. ■ Bureaucratic and formal top-down management practices. ■ Problems with the coordination, cooperation, and communication practices between head office and hotels.	■ A centralised yield initiative was tested and eventually deployed at the budget brand of BritCo Hotels. Based on this experience, it was decided to utilise a more advanced project in other brands. ■ A centralised yield management project was initiated. However, due to other priorities in the company, such as the implementation process of the company's central reservation system and the integration of the recently acquired hotel chain, the yield project was suspended. ■ Informal and formal discussions started about the deployment of the yield management project.
1995	■ Difficult to implement strategic decisions because of the company's traditional culture and political conflicts between different functional departments and management levels. ■ A new hotel chain was acquired. ■ Signs of positive environment—positive revenue and occupancy figures. ■ Bid for the company by a conglomerate.	
1996	■ BritCo Hotels was taken over by IBD group. ■ Generally a positive economic cycle—seller's market. ■ Increased revenue and occupancy. ■ New owners initiated a restructuring process of hotel brands (hotels were grouped under three geographical areas: London, UK Provincial, and International). ■ New owners also started a disposing process (half of the hotels particularly outside the U.K. were disposed of). ■ New incoming executives into the company— generally from outside the hotel industry.	■ Discussions continued about the relaunching of the yield management project.

Date	Context	Process
1997	■ A positive economic cycle—seller's market. ■ Disposing process of hotels continued. ■ A radical structural change in operations. The hotel general manager position was removed, and the regional general manager position was introduced. This caused higher labour turnover than normal, and managers from hotels became more sceptical about the project coming from the head office. ■ The chief executive officer left the company, and no appointment was made for over six months. ■ A new chief executive officer was appointed in late 1997. ■ The new CEO made radical structural changes and reintroduced a brand-oriented organisational structure. ■ New incoming executives generally from IBD or outside the hotel industry. ■ Through these structural changes and new appointments, a more change-oriented culture aimed to be achieved. ■ Less politically oriented company culture.	■ The deployment of the yield management project was reconsidered. ■ A Yield Department was formed. A Yield director and several Yield analysts were recruited. (Recruitment for the Yield analyst's position became a continuous process.) ■ A project management structure was formed. ■ A project proposal was prepared, and a series of formal presentations were made to the members of the hotel board and IBD board. ■ The hotel board approved the project proposal and allocated £4 million for the project. ■ Hotels and other functional departments were formally informed about the project. ■ The Yield Department worked with two specialised external companies to design and implement the project. ■ A database was developed, and an agent interface between the central reservation system and property management system was designed. ■ Relevant documents, reports, and training materials were prepared. ■ Computers were installed in the hotels and connected to the main system. ■ A series of yield workshops were organised for relevant people from the hotels and the head office. ■ Data were put into the yield management system. ■ The system was tested in two properties. ■ The yield system was inconsistent and unreliable. Changes and improvements were needed. ■ Due to high labour turnover in the hotel units, more training programmes were needed. (Organising these training programmes became a continuing task for the Yield Department.) ■ Extra resources were required to be able to make these changes and arrange further training workshops. ■ Hotels started going live with the yield system and following the recommendations. ■ Problems with the yield system. The system provided inconsistent and unreliable recommendations for many hotels.

Date	Context	Process
		■ Problems were encountered with the external companies in getting sufficient support and knowhow.
		■ The yield management system and the data put into the system were checked and improvements were made.
1998–1999		■ Communication and presentations were made to new incoming executives about the project
		■ Rate by length of stay phase of the project was introduced.
		■ After the appointment of the new CEO, Inventory and Yield Departments were combined under a new department ,Revenue Management, and yield managers or analysts were appointed responsible for monitoring each brand's revenue and occupancy figures.
		■ New Yield analysts were recruited.
		■ Discussions about implementing the management project in international hotels.
		■ Working relationship with one external partner company deteriorated, and new working agreements were made with other external companies to work with to continue implementing the YMP and other forthcoming projects.
		■ Discussions about new complementary projects such as Revenue Management 2000.

Global Hotels and Resorts: Building Long-Term Customer Relationships[1]

THE EARLY YEARS OF GLOBAL HOTELS AND RESORTS[2]

For confidentiality purposes, the actual name of the case study company is disguised, and it will hereafter be referred to as Global Hotels and Resorts (GHR). GHR was founded as a subsidiary of an airline company in the mid-1940s and operated three distinct types of hotels: five star (up-market), four-star (midmarket), and global partner hotels. GHR was primarily a hotel management company, although it did own and lease hotels and undertake joint venture and franchise arrangements. As illustrated in Exhibit 1, the company had 178 hotels in over 70 countries, and a further 24 hotel units were under development in early 1999.

The hotel group owned 23 hotels from this total portfolio, the majority of the units being operated under a management contract. Throughout its history, several conglomerates had acquired the company, and these previous owners had tended to control the hotel group using a holding company structure. Until the late 1990s, a Japanese conglomerate had owned GHR, but in early 1998. a U.K.-based conglomerate acquired it. This new owner already operated a global hotel group, and this was a unique situation: For

---

[1] This case was written by Dr. Fevzi Okumus, University of Central Florida, and Dr. Angela Roper, University of Surrey, United Kingdom. The main author conducted nearly 60 interviews with company respondents across the different levels of the organisation. He also spent a period of participant observation in one regional sales office and collected internal and external data about the company and the implementation project. The case is intended to reconstruct the challenges and issues facing management in implementing strategic decisions. It is not intended to convey any criticism of any individual or group of individuals.

[2] For confidentiality purposes, the actual name of the case study company is disguised. Therefore, it will be referred to as Global Hotels and Resorts.

Exhibit 1	Portfolio of Global Hotels and Resorts	
Hotel Portfolio	**Number of Hotels**	**Number of Countries**
Management Contracts	62	36
Global Partners	41	14
Owned Hotels	23	11
Franchised Hotels	23	15
Joint Ventures	18	7
Leased	11	8
Hotels under Development	24	19
Total Number	202	75

Source: Company data (as of January 1999).

the first time in GHR's history, it was going to join an already established worldwide hotel portfolio that included hotels across the market segments.

GHRs stated strategy since its inception has been to provide "international" standards together with local flavour. It referred to itself as having the "unique ability to reflect the vibrance of the countries in which it operates." The main form of control in implementing this strategy has been through the agency of the General Hotel Managers and the senior executives who have been rigorously socialised into the company culture. People in the company argue that this culture is truly international, since it requires senior people to travel extensively with the company, cast off their own national roots, and "often marry outside their own nationality." National passports are seen to be insignificant due to the fact that the only passport that really matters is the "company passport."

DEVELOPING RELATIONSHIPS WITH BUSINESS TRAVELERS

Since its early days, the frequent international business traveler had been the target market of the company, accounting for more than 80 percent of the company's business worldwide. Moreover, a research project carried out by the company revealed that the typical GHR business traveler was from a large company originating in the United States, Europe, or Japan, and that this business traveler was male (over 85 percent), around 40 years of age, and occupied a senior management position. It was also identified that 80 percent of room revenue was generated by only 25 percent of total clients. In short, it was evident that the company had targeted a niche market segment for many years and that the success of the company was highly linked with working and satisfying business travelers. In order to maintain and strengthen this ongoing working relationship between the hotel group and the organisations originating frequent business travelers, in 1994 the company decided to introduce a Key Client Management Project (KCMP).

Company executives, mainly from the head office and regional sales offices, for a number of years had been of the opinion that finding new customers and building long-term reliable working relationships would become more difficult and expensive for the company. The KCMP was therefore seen as the best option for the company to strengthen its ongoing relationship with existing client companies. In addition, it was clear that the KCMP would play an important role in achieving the company's business objectives.

Key aspects of the company's business objectives were outlined by the chief operating officer in 1994 in a video presentation to managers and employees (Exhibit 2). Other managers referred to achieving high customer satisfaction and applying good management practices as other key aspects of the company's business strategy. Therefore, the key client management strategy was seen as the most efficient way to achieve the business objectives of the company, particularly financial ones. For example, in the project proposal it was stated that:

> In 1993, 66 percent of the business produced by our top 200 corporate customers came from just 20 accounts. It is probable that a small increase in a correctly qualified customer base would produce a large increase in room-nights. The same large accounts are also the major customers of our competition, so it follows that the single biggest opportunity we have to increase sales lies with our existing customers.

Prior to the KCMP, the company had mainly focused on local or regional markets. By introducing this new project, it aimed to look at the full needs of all the hotels and find a clear path to identify the key customers and markets on a global basis. Senior sales and marketing executives claimed that the KCMP was essential to fully utilise the full sales resources of the company in

---

Exhibit 2   Key Aspects of Global Hotels and Resorts Business Strategy

1. Increase revenues and profits of existing hotels
2. Renew 30 management contracts
3. Expand the company's portfolio to 200 hotels worldwide
4. Reduce corporate overheads
5. Create a sustainable competitive advantage with the customers, owners, and investors

meeting customers' needs and demands. Before the KCMP, there had been no reliable system for collecting, storing, and analysing information about the market and key client companies. Moreover, salespeople in regional sales offices and hotels had not had the knowledge or skills necessary to collect and analyse the information on a systematic and continuous basis. Therefore, through implementing this project, it was hoped that salespeople would improve their knowledge and skills and manage sales activities more professionally.

The KCMP was introduced as a more disciplined and focused sales approach, whereas prior to the project, there were variances in managing sales activities across the company. The key objectives for implementing the KCMP are illustrated in Exhibit 3. Company executives were particularly driven to achieve the objective of seven percent (7 percent) compound revenue growth from existing hotels. In the mid-1990s, the global economy was actually growing at a rate of around three to four percent (3–4 percent). Therefore, to reach this objective, the company wanted to develop and implement a strategy that would assist it in growing revenues at a rate faster than the economy was growing.

Sales executives in the company noted that due to the high globalisation of markets, many more client companies had started to operate worldwide, and therefore, in order to maximise the potential of these large corporations to the hotel group, these companies needed to be approached on a global basis. In addition, due to rapid technological advancements, more that 60 percent of the hotel group bookings were electronically generated, and over 65 percent of the clients never contacted the hotel unit until they actually arrived there.

Given this, having worldwide regional sales offices with the authority and skills was seen as essential to communicate and negotiate with key companies globally on behalf of the hotel units. The KCMP would require salespeople at

---

Exhibit 3   Key Objectives for Implementing the Key Client Management Project

- Increase the company's revenue through working with large global client companies
- Develop long-term revenue orientation rather than short-term yield orientation
- Develop a market-oriented sales approach rather than product orientation
- Have a global market focus in approaching large client firms
- Achieve a more strategic thinking and leadership position for the sales department
- Design a more focused and structured sales approach across the company, and aim to utilise fully the sales resources of the company

Source: Adapted from project proposal and interviews.

regional and hotel levels to work continuously with clients, monitor their activities, analyse their potential, and report all sales activities and progress for each client. The logic was that through understanding key clients' needs and expectations and offering them "a cannot be beaten deal," the company would increase its share and build a long-term working relationship with these clients. Salespeople from hotels and regional sales offices would have the authority to make commitments and solve problems. This would mean a leading role for the Sales and Marketing Department in the company.

In addition to the introduction of the KCMP, other projects and developments were also taking place in the company. For example, the KCMP was actually part of a reengineering process that consisted of several other projects:

- *Expansion Strategy*: Through joint ventures, franchising, and finding partnerships, the company aimed to expand its portfolio to 200 hotels by the year 2000 (a target that had already been exceeded by 1999). Executives indicated further expansion plans, particularly in South America and the Middle East.

- *Expansion of the Four-Star Hotel Brand*: This project had been under discussion for several years, and in 1997 a project proposal was awaiting authorisation by the board of the parent company. However, it was understood that due to financial difficulties faced by the owning company, no financial investment was to be made in this project.

- *A Revenue (or Yield) Management Project*: A project proposal had previously been developed and submitted to the previous owner. However, due to financial difficulties, the project had never been approved. The revenue management project would have been highly complementary to the KCMP.

THE GLOBAL HOTEL INDUSTRY IN THE 1990s

The global hotel industry had a difficult start in the 1990s, as the first four years of the decade were troublesome, with economic slowdowns in most parts of the world. In addition, the Gulf War in 1991 had forced many companies to cut their travel budgets (Todd and Mather, 1995). However, market conditions began to improve by 1994, and performance continued to improve from that point, although there were clearly some exceptions, such as Germany (Bailey, 1998). Between 1994 and 1997, the global environment was relatively positive, and there were increases in GDPs in many countries, which had a positive impact on the world's

| Exhibit 4 | The World Hotel Industry: Occupancy and Average Daily Room Rates 1994–1997 |

Occupancy (Percent)	1994	1995	1996	1997
Africa & Middle East	60.9	60.7	61.5	62.3
Asia	70.3	75.6	72.9	72.3
Australia	—	74.8	75.1	73.0
North America	70.5	69.2	69.2	70.3
Latin America	60.1	61.0	62.7	62.7
Europe	62.2	64.1	64.6	64.5
World	**66.5**	**67.2**	**67.7**	**67.6**
Average Daily Room Rate (US$)	**1994**	**1995**	**1996**	**1997**
Africa & Middle East	74.08	85.39	101.55	97.58
Asia	84.70	111.88	104.04	105.67
Australia	—	83.78	100.6	94.66
North America	80.84	95.44	90.65	93.93
Latin America	58.74	69.99	76.61	85.31
Europe	89.84	92.04	78.50	84.24
World	**81.02**	**88.57**	**87.02**	**88.83**

Source: Bailey, M. (1998). *The International Hotel Industry: Corporate Strategies and Global Opportunities*, 2nd ed. Research Report, Travel & Tourism Intelligence.

hotel industry performance. Exhibit 4 summarises the average occupancies and daily room rates for major regions of the world from 1994 to 1997.

People in the company remembered this period as being one where demand for the company's hotels had been buoyant, particularly in key cities. It was referred to it as a "seller's market." Bailey's (1998) report on the hotel industry also supports these views (Exhibit 5). This buoyant market for hotels meant that it was difficult to sell the idea of a KCMP in the company, particularly to hotel general managers.

The latter, of course, saw no immediate benefits from offering low rates to large key client companies. This created a major problem for the corporate executives responsible for implementing the KCMP because it was recognised that if the global economy had been less favourable, the project would have been received with "open arms." Having said this, managers in Asia Pacific, who were experiencing economic turmoil in their region, were not optimistic about the benefits of the project, arguing that client companies would always think about their budgets before their relationships. Internally, this different regional perspective was further emphasised by the fact that there were differences in working and developing relationships with key client companies across the globe. For example, client companies, mainly

Exhibit 5	Average Occupancy Rates in Major Cities Worldwide between 1995 and 1997		
City	1995	1996	1997
Amsterdam	74.9	79.0	83.3
Berlin	62.8	59.4	61.7
Brussels	65.9	69.7	71.4
Istanbul	70.2	72.9	75.9
London	83.7	84.6	85.0
Paris	68.2	71.0	74.5
Hong Kong (5 Star Hotels)	72.5	77.6	67.8
Singapore (5 Star hotels)	72.1	72.8	69.4
Tokyo (4 Star Hotels)	70.3	76.3	78.4
Cairo	—	74.0	76.8
New York	79.0	81.7	81.4

Source: Bailey, M. (1998). *The International Hotel Industry: Corporate Strategies and Global Opportunities*, 2nd ed. Research Report, Travel & Tourism Intelligence.

from the United States and the United Kingdom, had travel managers and worked in certain policies and procedures.

Meanwhile, companies in the Far and Middle East did not have travel managers or clear travel policies and therefore imposed no restrictions on their managers and executives when choosing airlines and hotels. Again in the Far East, Middle East, and Latin America, travel managers seemed to prefer more informal relationships rather than signing formal agreements or contracts. Conversely, managers at the corporate level argued against any major cultural differences in working practices. Instead, they argued that there was a growing global trend in the utilisation and popularity of the key client management concept, which had originated from the United States.

ORGANISATIONAL STRUCTURE FROM 1994 TO 1998

No structural changes took place as a result of the new ownership of the company until the beginning of 1999. Prior to this year, GHR was organised into three areas: operations, finance, and property management (Exhibit 6). The chief operating officer (COO) was responsible for managing all hotels globally. In operations, the scattered portfolio of the hotel group was managed by utilising an organisation structure based on geographic areas of the world.

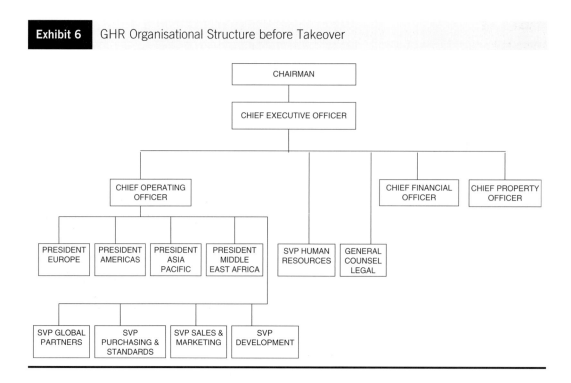

Exhibit 6 GHR Organisational Structure before Takeover

Four divisions therefore oversaw the operations of hotels in four continental regions—the Americas, Europe, the Middle East, and the Far East—and each area had a high level of decision-making power and freedom in running operations. In each region, hotels were further divided into separate territories, and local decision making finally rested at the hotel level.

MARKETING AND SALES ORGANISATION

As illustrated in Exhibit 7, the Sales and Marketing Department was divided into two subdepartments: the Marketing Department and the Sales Department. The role of the Marketing Department was to work on advertising and branding activities. This department was also responsible for having close relationships with customers who actually stayed in the hotels; these were referred to as "sleepers." In each region there was a regional vice president of Marketing, who mainly worked with, and reported directly to, the area vice president of Operations. The Sales Department's main task was to work with key client companies, particularly with their travel managers and other

Exhibit 7 Structure of the Marketing and Sales Organisation

relevant executives. There were three area vice presidents of Sales, and in total there were 15 regional sales offices worldwide. These offices were managed through a centralised organisational structure, and unlike the marketing function, corporate excutives in sales had substantial power to manage and control these offices. In South America the company did not have any regional offices, but instead independent sales agents were used.

At the operational level, each hotel had a Marketing and Sales Department and the director of this department reported directly to the hotel general manager. Although there was a dotted reporting line from this director to the regional vice president of Marketing, there was no direct reporting line between hotels and regional sales offices. There were also no formal procedures and guidelines for developing coordination and support between hotels and these latter offices.

At the head office level, there seemed to be no formal procedures and arrangements, such as a project management structure or project groups in developing and implementing strategic decisions. Each functional department appeared to develop its own proposals independently and then submit them to the hotel board. On the other hand, at the annual meeting where all hotel managers meet, overall problems and issues would be discussed, and, where appropriate, task groups would be formed to work on specific projects and initiatives to be implemented at the hotel level. Hotel managers tended to be critical about the relevance and the importance of the projects developed by the head office executives. For example, one stated that:

There should be programmes developed to support the hotels. ... I do feel that a lot of the programmes they [head office executives] develop are to make themselves feel better.

Hotel managers were also critical about what they saw as a lack of informal communication and coordination between themselves and the corporate office. For example, one hotel manager stated that:

If they expect that they gain trust and respect from the field by just sending out notes and memos and e-mails, and show up on general managers meetings for half a day of the meeting and then move off to somewhere else, they are very much mistaken. They need to make sure that they actually communicate. ... I have been seven years as a general manager, and there has not been one corporate guy who has come to my office, sat down with me, and discussed certain strategic issues, ideas, or plans. Or even asked, "How are you doing in the business? Where can I help?" You know, sure, if I call them, they talk to me. If they need something from me, they call me.

In fact, corporate opinion surveys carried out in 1996 and 1997 had indicated concerns about poor communication and coordination practices between the head office and the hotels. However, corporate executives and managers expressed the opinion that the overall coordination and communication practices in the company were satisfactory and that they used top-down, bottom-up, formal, and informal communication modes. They stated that the use of e-mails had been very practical and helpful. However, some corporate managers had contended that, as in any organisation, the communication and coordination between different management levels could be improved.

MANAGERS IN GHR

Area presidents and their teams were very influential in their areas; one was said to manage his region "as a personal and private kingdom." the senior vice president of Training Worldwide stated that:

Each area feels that they have ownership over their own decisions and the way they run things. So for the corporate office to dictate areas is not accepted very well, and there has not been a process to enable people to put in their own views and get sort of global initiatives. That has been one of the challenges to get some means to enable global initiatives to be owned by all areas and get a consensus.

Because the first hotels were not opened in the country of origin but in less-developed parts of the world, early managers had to have a pioneering spirit, and to an extent this culture continued to live on in the organisation:

The culture of this company is set up to reward maverick, independent people. Self-sufficient, resilient people . . . that culture of being able to survive and thrive by yourself. . . . The empowered, self-reliant culture of the company came from a really good roots, from a good source.

Hotel general managers also held very strong and powerful positions in the company. As mainly a contractor and franchiser, the company had little strategic power over much of its hotel portfolio. Having a relatively decentralised organisational structure with strong hotel general managers was seen as the most appropriate option in responding to complex issues in different countries. The latter could be responsible for revenue streams of over $100 million a year and could have a great impact on the unit's culture. For this reason the company was often called the "hotel general managers' company."

Having said this, the road to becoming a hotel manager was long—it was quoted at being at least ten years. Potential managers had to have worked in several hotel units in various countries, be fluent in at least two languages, and have spent a considerable length of time (8–15 years) working in the company. Hotel managers tended to be male and either trained predominantly in the front office or food and beverage operations. These "core" workers were carefully looked after. They received ex-patriate salaries paid in GHR's main operating currency, which was managed from another country, and they had their own pension scheme.

Many previous and current senior executives had actually started their careers working in the company's hotels and had made their way up to senior management positions. For example, the most senior operating officer had been with the group for over 20 years.

Hotel general managers talked to each other regularly, and without their understanding and support, implementing a strategy in hotels might well prove impossible. One executive officer stated that:

General managers have an immense amount of authority and power, and if they do not support what it is you are trying to roll out on a worldwide basis, they can make it very difficult.

One hotel manager also commented:

The biggest mistake in head office is that they think they are in charge of the business, but they are not. They should realise that they are the support for the individual units.

The company had many standards and traditions that employees and managers were said to work hard at to uphold. For example, one hotel manager stated that:

This company has a very, very strong culture. ... There are a lot of unwritten rules, and, you know, instinctively I will do exactly the same thing as my colleagues in New York or London. That is because the culture in the field is very tight.

However, some executives were beginning to question the company's traditions because of their belief that they made managing change and implementing strategic decisions difficult.

As the company operated in over 70 countries, many national cultures had influenced the company's corporate culture, and there appeared to be no single dominant national culture in the company. For example, the area vice president of Operations, Latin America, stated:

The company does not have a national culture. Our company does not have a flag that reflects nationalities or languages. Our company is an international [company] that cannot be described as a single culture.

Having said this, North American and British national cultures had perhaps been most influential in shaping the company's corporate culture and working practices.

THE INITIAL IMPLEMENTATION OF THE KCMP: 1994–1997

Exhibit 8 outlines the main implementation activities, problems encountered, and how the project team responded to these issues. There was little participation and consultation in the development of the KCMP. Head office executives had little time to consult all 200 hotels, and they were certain anyway about how the project needed to be designed. The project was essential for the whole company to achieve the company's business objectives, and therefore implementation had to start in 1994. Interestingly, many hotel managers expressed the view that the key client management

Exhibit 8 The Key Implementation Activities for the KCMP

Date	Implementation Activities and Some other key events
1994 Spring	A Sales Executive was recruited from another international hotel group. This incoming executive developed a project proposal. There was limited participation when designing the project (−). The proposal reviewed by the Senior Vice President of Sales and Marketing and the Chief Operating Officer.
	↓
Mid 1994	The Hotel Board approved the proposal.
	↓
Late 1994	Relevant Parties were informed about the KCMP. Planning and preparation activities took place at the Head Office Level. Specific documents and manuals were prepared.
	↓
Early 1995	Preparation activities began in Regional Sales Offices and Hotels. The project was piloted and started at the RSO and Hotels in London. An external consultancy company was hired to carry out training activities (+). Training programmes were piloted and then fully introduced (+). Structural changes could not be introduced (−).
	↓
Mid 1995	Project was piloted and started at RSO and Hotels Worldwide. Client companies were informed about the project. There was resistance to the project from hotels and RSOs (−). Monitoring and controlling process of the project began (+). Training Programmes were piloted and introduced worldwide (+). Basic software was developed to be used at the RSOs and in hotels (+). A proposal for the installation of advanced software was not approved (−).
	↓
1996	Change occurred in Senior Management Positions (−). The project had to be communicated to new executives (+). New Area Vice President of Sales, the Americas appointed (+). Training programmes and communication activities continued (+). More emphasis given to implementing the KCMP at the RSOs and hotels in the Americas and Middle East regions. Lack of understanding and support from HGMs (−). A one-day training programme was designed for HGMs. Each hotel's and RSO's results in revenue and room-nights started to be monitored. A list of key client companies and their performance was distributed to RSOs and hotels.
	↓
1997	Training programmes and communication activities continued (+). Lack of support from HGMs as the project continued (−). Revenue Plan and Year Budget were combined in hotel units (+). The training department started delivering some of the programmes independently. Monitoring of each hotel's and RSO's results in revenue and room-nights continued. The list of key client companies and their performance was Distributed to RSOs and hotels.
	↓
Early 1998	Training programmes and communication activities continued (+). GHR was acquired by a British conglomerate company. The project and its results were communicated to new owning company key executives.

Key: − activity or change that had a negative impact on the implementation process.
+ activity or change that had a positive impact on the implementation process.

concept was not a new idea in the company because they had always had key clients and regional sales programmes. Meanwhile, executives argued that the main difference between this initiative and the previous sales approaches was that for the first time the company had begun to approach key client companies globally, with a uniform sales approach.

Following the approval of the project by the hotel board members, the aims and details of the KCMP were communicated via a formal memorandum to area vice presidents worldwide. The KCMP was also discussed and explained to hotel managers at an annual meeting. As the area vice presidents of Marketing directly supervised individual hotel sales activities, they also communicated the implications of the project to sales people at the hotel level.

Sales employees and managers from regional sales offices and hotels learned more about the project through the sales training workshops. There were also other types of communication activities, such as video presentations by the COO, the area presidents of Operations, and the vice presidents of Sales. In his visual presentation in 1994, the COO of the company emphasised the importance of the KCMP to the company as follows:

> The KCMP project is a critical element in our revenue generation strategy, and, hence, it is also critical to the success of our business strategy. . . . I want you to understand that the entire senior management team is fully committed to do whatever it takes to help you to achieve our strategic revenue objectives.

Managers from regional sales offices and hotels stated that when the project was first introduced, there was confusion, a lack of information, and little support. Many felt they still did not know why the project was needed.

PROJECT ROLLOUT

The project was first piloted at the London regional sales office and some hotels in London (as the head office of the company was based in this city). These pilots helped the company executives to have close supervision of the sales team. Further to these pilots, the project was then piloted and finally introduced in the regional offices and hotels in Europe, America, and the Far East. The time scale of this planning and piloting stage was over a year, starting in late 1994 and finishing in late 1995. In order to initiate the project, both regional sales offices and hotels were required to carry out a number of preparation activities (Exhibit 9).

Exhibit 9 Planning and Preparation Activities required in Both Regional Sales Offices and Hotels

1. Checking all client companies' past performance, room nights, and revenue.
2. Identification of the top client companies.
3. Based on the past performance and potential of these companies, grouping them into "key clients," "niche clients," "prospect clients," or "suspect clients."
4. Devoting company resources and sales personnel to the first 20–30 percent of clients.
5. Carrying out a potential analysis of each client company to identify its potential in terms of room nights and room revenue. This analysis was carried out in several stages: information gathering, analysis, and action.
6. Signing contracts with client companies: Salespeople were required to contact key decision makers in client companies and build reliable long-term working relationships with them and sign yearly contracts.
7. Putting all the sales activities and relevant information about the client company into the database.
8. Reporting sales activities and generated revenue and room nights to the relevant executives on a monthly and yearly basis.

The KCMP required each salesperson in hotels and regional sales offices to evaluate and monitor every client's potential on a regular basis and, based on this, develop the Strategic Sales Path document (SSPD). Each hotel and sales office was required to produce the revenue plan for the next year, clearly stating each month's revenue and room nights targets. This revenue plan included each hotel's market position, information about competitors, and, most important, data on key clients on whom resources and efforts should be concentrated. The potential analysis, strategic sales path, and revenue plan were seen as working documents, as salespeople and executives were required to review and update them regularly. These activities carried out in each hotel and sales offices were the key components of the implementation process of the KCMP, and the preparation activities listed in Exhibit 9 were expected to become routine working practices.

TRAINING

The major financial resource allocation for the KCMP was to fund the training programmes, which were designed and run by an external company. Hotels and regional sales offices paid for the cost of these training programmes. Franchised and partner hotels, in particular, were not very keen on devoting resources to these training courses. Some financial resources were also devoted to designing and improving information systems, such as the Sales Software and Fidelio. In addition, in order to support and fully utilise the KCMP, a proposal for advanced software was developed and submitted to the hotel board. However, due to financial constraints and lack of consensus, the hotel board did not approve this proposal.

Exhibit 10	Initial Training Programmes			
Level	Target Participants	Focus and Concepts Covered	Duration	Began
Level 1:[1] A Basic Training Programme	Employees with limited knowledge and experience in sales and, particularly, the key client management concept	The concept of "key client management" was briefly introduced and explained.	3–4 days	Late 1994
Level 2: An Advanced Sales Training Programme	Employees and managers with substantial experience in sales	Concepts related to "key client management" were explained in some depth.	2–3 days	1995

Initially, two specific training programmes were designed to prepare relevant employees and managers from hotels and regional sales offices in utilising the KCMP. These training programmes began after the KCMP had been introduced. Concerning this, the senior vice president of Training stated that:

> As a training community we arrived a bit too late to make everything happen in the right order. They had already done half the launch before they did some of those things [i.e., training], so we had to do a kind of backward action trying to fill in the gaps, which is not the best way to carry out a change.

As shown in Exhibit 10, each workshop was aimed at different employees and managers.

The Sales and Training Departments worked with an international training consultancy company to design and operate these training programmes. This external company had regional offices worldwide and could deliver similar training programmes in different countries. A trainer in GHR said:

> They were free of political and emotional value. They were able to give us examples and share how this particular strategy had been implemented successfully in other companies and had achieved the results we were looking for.

---

[1] This was delivered in English in the United Kingdom, United States, and other English-speaking countries. In Germany, Spain, Latin America, and other locations, it was run in the local language, and manuals were translated.

IMPLEMENTATION CHALLENGES

The process of implementation was controlled and monitored as it was introduced. Employees and regional sales managers felt a certain amount of discomfort and dissatisfaction, and this was demonstrated in resistance to the project. Several other problems with the initial deployment of the project could be identified:

- The first challenge was for salespeople to adapt themselves to follow a specific pattern in carrying out their sales activities. They were not used to spending time in their offices in order to analyse data, prepare action plans, and undertake the potential analysis, strategic sales part document, and revenue plans. They found all these activities very time consuming.

- The second issue was that salespeople faced difficulties in finding and obtaining relevant and reliable information about the client companies. This was due to the fact that they did not always disclose information about their travel budgets.

- The third problem was that salespeople needed to carry out all these required planning and preparation activities manually, as there was no software available at that time. In later stages of the project, basic software was made available for salespeople, and it did make their jobs much easier. A further problem was that each hotel management team was required to produce an annual revenue plan. However, in addition to the revenue plan, each hotel had to prepare an annual budget. Both of these tasks were very similar, time consuming, and were viewed as a duplication of efforts. As a result, the hotel management teams did not show any interest in producing the annual revenue plan document.

- The fourth issue was that there was not substantial support for, and understanding of, the KCMP by hotel managers. The latter were operationally focused and often did not support or believe in structured, planned, and globally focused sales activities. A more substantial problem was the fact that according to the company's policies, each hotel manager performance was measured and monitored on the basis of the hotel's revenue and occupancy figures. However, the KCMP often required hotels to offer lower rates to key client companies. This could mean less revenue for hotels in key cities where the demand was high. In other words, the hotels in these cities could earn more by selling their rooms to higher-rate customers, who did not need to be from the key client companies.

- Finally, salespeople and managers from different countries, to an initial extent, found the KCMP difficult to understand and apply in their own cultural marketing settings. For example, salespeople in Germany stated that managers and executives from client companies preferred formal relationships and therefore do not always accept any incentives or free nights from hotels. In Japan, client companies were very bureaucratic, and it was very seldom that there would be a travel manager who had authority to make travel budgets or impose rules and regulations across the company. In every region or country, personal relationships between client companies and managers from hotels were found to be particularly important. However, a corporate executive stated that "strategic intent needs to remain untouched; the way it is implemented has to be adapted into the cultures."

Although initially there were difficulties and misunderstandings about the KCMP, after salespeople had attended the training sessions and had participated in formal and informal discussions with their colleagues, they gradually learned to adopt the requirements of the project into their own cultures, with their own specific interpretations. In short, although there were initial misunderstandings and problems adapting the KCMP in various cultures, this did not create a major barrier to implementing the KCMP across the company.

THE IMPLEMENTATION PROCESS BETWEEN 1995 AND 1997

Major changes occurred in senior management positions in 1995. In the initial stage of the project, the COO had been a key actor in designing and advocating the initiative. However, further to some structural changes in 1995, this executive moved to a senior position in the parent company, and a new COO was appointed internally. Other new appointments were made, which meant that the project needed to be recommunicated. Senior executives in sales and marketing claimed that the new COO did not openly support the KCMP (he had previously been an area president). They felt they were left alone in advocating the project in the company, and as a result, those in operations saw no immediate reason to enforce the implementation process in their particular regions and hotels.

After the first introduction, the need for continuous communication and selling the project was recognised in order to emphasize the importance and

Exhibit 11	Training Programmes Introduced after 1995		
Level	**Target Participants**	**Focus and Concepts Covered**	**Duration**
Level 3: An Advanced Sales Management Training Programme	Sales managers and executives	This workshop focused on how the key client management concept could be applied and managed strategically.	2–3 days
General Sales Training Programme	Hotel general managers and their deputies	The logic behind the key client management concept was explained.	1 day

implications of the KCMP across the company. A further reason for such assiduous communication and training activities was that the company had new hotel openings or new franchise and management contract agreements that required that the management team, and particularly the sales force, in each new hotel were informed and fully trained. One of the purposes of the KCMP was to build a continuous communication channel and good working relationship between GHR and travel managers and senior executives in key client companies. Regional salespeople, in particular, worked very hard at achieving this.

Exhibit 11 illustrates two further training programmes introduced after 1995. The second of these was aimed at hotel managers. Executives had realised that at the start of the project no specific training session had been designed to sell the project to this important group and that this may have been a reason why they had initially resisted the project. Trainers still continued to learn and respond to cultural differences. Training programmes were delivered continuously across the regions because the expansion of the company meant that employees and managers from new hotels needed to be trained and prepared to utilise the requirements of the KCMP.

However, resistance from hotel managers to the KCMP continued throughout the rollout process, and this problem appeared still to be unresolved. This almost ceaseless resistance was put down to the fact that the project still provided them with no incentives, the incentive system not having been adjusted. One hotel manager stated that:

If my results are poor in the end, they will fire me, and I will accept that. … They can give me any programme they want as long as they give me written confirmation that as long as I implement everything, I will not get fired and I will keep my job until I am 65.

The key actor in designing and implementing the KCMP was the vice president of Sales. He was often described as the "father" of the project. He was not very keen on providing any specific incentives to hotel managers for the implementation process of the KCMP. He perceived them as recipients of change and implementers of strategy. In fact, his view was that the company's organisational structure should be changed and that contrary to the company's administrative heritage, the area presidents of operations and hotel managers should be seen as managers rather than leaders or heroes in the company.

There was an ongoing monitoring and feedback process of the KCMP, and from 1997 onward, the company executives decided that while auditing each hotel, one of the areas to be checked was whether the hotel sales department was following the requirements of the KCMP.

IMPLEMENTATION UNDER NEW OWNERSHIP

Further to the change in ownership of GHR in early 1998, the integration process between the two companies began. It was known that the new owning company had a centralised organisational structure and that the area presidents of Operations and the hotel general managers did not have substantial power and influence over company policies. In order to inform relevant executives about how GHR managed their sales activities globally, key members of the implementation team prepared a number of reports and undertook formal presentations. It was apparent that these presentations were mainly about the KCMP explaining how successful it had been and how it had helped the company in increasing revenue. In these presentations and reports, the existing problems and issues and also future plans were also stated. For example, in one particular presentation to the CEO of Bass plc, the vice president of Sales clearly emphasised two key issues:

1. The need to have a "command global sales structure" across the company, including the sales departments in hotels.

2. The need to have the necessary funds in order to install the electronic solution software in both regional sales offices and hotels globally.

This executive argued that these two issues needed to be tackled if the company was to continue to successfully increase its revenues in coming years.

OUTCOMES OF THE KEY CLIENT MANAGEMENT PROJECT

It was widely believed by the sales managers and executives that the KCMP had helped GHR to increase its revenues by over 7 percent consecutively since 1994. Supporting this, the Revenue Plan documents for 1997 and 1998 also showed revenue increases of at least 7 percent every year since 1994. However, some hotel managers did stress that the individual efforts of hotels and the positive economic cycle worldwide should have also been considered when looking at these increases in revenue. The tension and competition between the head office (the sales department) and the hotel units therefore seemingly continued.

A more focused and structured sales approach was adopted at the regional offices and partly adopted at hotel level. The difference in outcomes was put down largely to the lack of the specific sales software at the hotel level. One of the important outcomes often stated by people in sales departments was that across the company they were now better trained, prepared, and equipped to manage their sales activities. For example, one Marketing Information manager stated that:

> Everyone feels proud of what they have achieved in the last four years with the same or less resource. They have achieved a significant increase in room nights and room revenue from the point of view of pure targeting. I think they have been able to prioritise and control their time better. They do not feel that they are out of control.

By implementing the KCMP, a new standardised mechanism was created to monitor all sales management activities across the company.

DISCUSSION QUESTIONS

1. How did the external environment influence the deployment and the implementation process of the KCMP?
2. How would you describe the organizational context of Global Hotels and Resorts?
3. How did this organizational context influence the implementation process of the KCMP?
4. How was the KCMP developed and implemented?
5. How useful were their initial plans?

6. What were the challenges to the development and the implementation of the KCMP?

7. Which school of thought would best explain the development and implementation process of the KCMP?

8. What were the main barriers and challenges when implementing the KCMP?

9. What can we learn from this case study?

REFERENCES

Bailey, M. (1998). *The International Hotel Industry: Corporate Strategies and Global Opportunities*, 2nd ed. Research Report, Travel & Tourism Intelligence.

Todd, G. and Mather, S. (1995). *The International Hotel Industry: Corporate Strategies and Global Opportunities*. Research Report, Travel & Tourism Intelligence.

Entrepreneurship and Leadership in Hospitality: Insights and Implications for Hospitality and Tourism Education[1]

Mr. Harris Rosen, in Conversation with Drs. Sandra Naipaul and Youcheng Wang

Rosen College of Hospitality Management, University of Central Florida, 9907 Universal Boulevard, Orlando, FL 32819

INTRODUCTION

The twenty-first century has ushered in changes that have been both unprecedented and unpredictable in many sectors of the business world, including the hospitality and tourism industry. Globalization, technological advances, and worldwide economic crises, among others, have put the hospitality and tourism industry in an environment of uncertainty and unpredictability that calls for different management and educational mindsets in order to achieve success. Gone are the days when textbooks and conventional wisdom are consulted and referred to when prescribed solutions are needed (Russell and Purphy, 2004), particularly in an environment in which the only condition we can be certain of, is uncertainty.

The nature of the business environment we are now confronting calls for a different set of management qualities, of which entrepreneurship, leadership, adaptability, risk taking, and creativity (thinking out of the box) must be the vital components. Indeed, such entrepreneurial-type people will be highly sought after because they are likely best suited for the turbulent economic conditions of today and tomorrow (Maccoby, M. 2001; Russell, R. and

CONTENTS

[1] Original version of this article is published in *International Journal of Contemporary Hospitality Management*, 21 (6), 2009.

CONTENTS

Murphy, P. 2004). To survive, the new global economy must be an entrepreneurial economy where entrepreneurial leadership will take center stage (Zahra, 1999). In order to be an effective and successful leader in such an ever-changing business environment, hospitality managers must demonstrate these management qualities in their work environment.

One challenge confronting hospitality researchers and educators is to make certain that their efforts in research and teaching address these changing needs (Russell and Murphy, 2004). Examples of leaders in the history of hospitality and tourism industry, such as Conrad Hilton, Walt Disney, Kemmons Wilson, and J. Willard Marriott, have provided us with valuable lessons we can learn from. In addition to these leaders with global significance, there are also regional leaders who are lesser known but whose leadership skills and entrepreneurial spirit are equal to or perhaps even more exceptional.

Mr. Harris Rosen, president and CEO of Rosen Hotels and Resorts in Orlando, Florida, embodies such an example (Please see Appendix A for his background information.) He has demonstrated entrepreneurial and leadership qualities, such as seeing opportunities in times of economic downturn, creativity, and risk-taking, that have made his business successful over the past several decades, a benchmark for success in an ever-changing and competitive business environment. He has also earned tremendous respect in central Florida for his passionate support and dedication to education, as well as his philosophy of giving back to his community. Learning from his example can provide insights and challenges for hospitality education which should be brought to the forefront of research and ultimately what and how we teach in our classrooms.

PROCESS AND PROCEDURE

With this premise in mind, an interview was arranged with Mr. Rosen in April of 2008. The interview approach was structured to provide Mr. Rosen with an opportunity to share his perspective on a number of issues. The interview took place in his office and lasted about an hour. For data analysis purposes, the interview was recorded using a digital recorder and was then transcribed verbatim. An interview protocol was prepared to facilitate the interview process. The interview protocol included several open-ended questions in order to solicit Mr. Rosen's views on key issues the researchers were interested in. Such topics as entrepreneurship, leadership, education, management philosophy, and philanthropy were discussed at some length.

INTERVIEW FINDINGS

Mr. Rosen provided his perspective on several key issues as well as his life's experiences as a hotelier in central Florida. Key findings from the interview revealed Mr. Rosen's strong beliefs regarding entrepreneurship, leadership, and philanthropy. For example, according to Mr. Rosen, it is his belief that entrepreneurship is in the DNA (he believes a "defective" gene) of an individual, which drives one's desire to expand and grow one's business seldom ceases. As a successful entrepreneur, he believes that he has been blessed beyond anything he ever imagined in his lifetime and has thus decided at this time and place in his life to contemplate a multitude of ways in which he can give back to society. In order to retain the originality and totality of his insights regarding these issues, the researchers reported the majority of the transcribed interview and organized the interview transcripts, following the order of the questions in the protocol.

MR. ROSEN ON ENTREPRENEURSHIP

Some people possess what I refer to as the entrepreneurial gene (most likely a defective gene) which I believe you are born with. I am not sure if it is a blessing or a curse, but it is something you discover you have at an early age. Even though you possess this gene, it is nonetheless a necessity, if you wish to be successful, to keep an open mind, and to read as much as you can in an attempt to keep expanding your knowledge. The desire to achieve never ceases.

Being an entrepreneur is not an easy voyage, particularly when you start from a poor neighborhood (as many successful entrepreneurs have). I was born and lived until age 16 in New York City's Lower East Side in a community referred to as "Hell's Kitchen." Early hardships teach you to never give up and to always persevere. In addition, you learn to work hard—harder than anyone else. Along the way, you will learn that there really is no substitute for hard work. To succeed you must above all love what you do and you must be passionate (an overused word) about your work. If you are passionate about your work, the likelihood to succeed increases, exponentially.

I truly enjoy what I do. Is it on occasion aggravating? Yes, of course, and, yes, there are days when I scratch my head and wonder why am I doing this? But I have been doing this work for 34 years, and I love it. To me, it is really not work at all. Although on occasion I still do some of the same stupid things I did 34 years ago, I have learned not to get crazy about these miscues and to just keep pressing forward. In a nutshell, my philosophy is to first discover what you really love to do, then work hard at it; if you are fortunate enough to succeed, then I believe that you have an obligation to demonstrate your gratitude by giving back to those who need a helping hand.

I do not believe you can teach someone to be an entrepreneur. It's a bit like trying to teach someone to be 6' 8" tall. You cannot, for instance, teach someone to be a risk taker, because you cannot change an individual's personality. You would have to change their heart and mindset and infuse their being with courage, which I believe is impossible to do. You see, entrepreneurship is a rather unique phenomenon, and when I contemplate what I've been through and what other successful entrepreneurs have been through, I often wonder, how did we ever do it? What gave us the courage to carry on? You simply cannot teach that. I believe it is inborn.

I have been entrepreneurially inclined throughout my life; even when I was in the Army serving in Frankfurt, Germany, I engaged in a business venture. I enjoyed traveling to Holland on the weekends because it was so beautiful there. Just by chance one day I found myself in the tulip business. I had a conversation with an owner of one of the big tulip growers (De Groot). I mentioned to him that I was in the Army, and I had never seen a tulip bulb in a PX. I told him that I believed we can sell them there. My new friend said, well, why don't you take some bulbs with you and see if you can sell them, then perhaps we can do some business together? So I took several dozen boxes of tulip bulbs (he packed them, three bulbs in a little container), and he sold them to me for 25 cents for the three bulbs. I took them to the PX in Frankfurt, and I put together a little display and I sold them for 3 bulbs for $1.50. Well, we sold out in just a few hours, and I was now in the tulip business. Each weekend I went back and forth to the little town of Hellicom where my "partner's" tulip farm was.

We were doing this for several months, and I was making about $300 or $400 a week profit, which was HUGE back then. (You see, as a first lieutenant I was only earning about $400/month.) We were thinking about expanding and going into PX's all over Germany (perhaps Europe), and I was already dreaming that I would remain in Germany and become very wealthy selling tulip bulbs and perhaps other things. Well, one day I got a call from the post commander, and I had no idea why he wanted to see me. When I stepped into his office, he asked me if I knew that as an officer in the U.S. Army, I was not permitted to work in the private sector while still on active duty. I said, no, sir, I didn't know that. He said you have 24 hours to get out of the tulip business before you get court-marshaled. I said, sir, I'm out right now, ... and so I was out of the tulip business, but I realized that for me there would be many more opportunities ahead.

Here is another interesting story which speaks for the difference between an entrepreneurial mindset and that of a top Fortune 500 company executive. Bill Marriott called my office about four months before we completed construction at Shingle Creek. (Shingle Creek is our newest hotel in our company (no. 7).) Mr. Marriott said that he was going to be in Orlando attending a time-share symposium at the Peabody Hotel and wondered if I could meet with him and tour Shingle Creek. I said I would be honored. He came with some of his associates but promptly asked if he could be alone with me. We shared a golf cart and toured the entire resort. While walking through one of the ballrooms, he asked me if the rumor he heard was true, that I was building Shingle Creek for $300 million including the golf course and with no borrowed funds. He said he did not believe it. I asked him why he didn't believe we could build Shingle Creek for $300 million, and he responded by stating that his company built the J.W. Marriott and the Ritz Carlton just down the street from Shingle Creek (which combined has approximately the same square footage (± 2 mil sq. ft.) as Shingle Creek) for about $640 million.

I responded by neither confirming nor denying his statement but instead by indicating that our development of Shingle Creek was an example of how a small company can on occasion actually have an advantage over a much larger organization. I stated that because Marriott had so many projects (all over the world) going on simultaneously it would be impossible for any one individual to devote the time, effort, and energy that I was able to devote having just one project to focus on. It was easy for me to concentrate all of my energy and time on Shingle Creek, whereas, you, Mr. Marriot, have too much on your plate to do that. I informed Mr. Marriott that I was on site every day, walking the site, talking to everyone I came in contact with, seven days a week, 15 hours a day, or more. I also informed Mr. Marriott that our company was intimately involved in the construction as well. I shared with him that we had done all of the framing, drywall, finish, trim, painting, carpet installation, furniture installation, and all of the ceiling beams. I also shared with him that I met with the construction crew every day and that we had done a little buffet picnic outside once a week to keep everyone happy and motivated.

I also stated that I personally negotiated every contract for the Shingle Creek project. I recall that Mr. Marriott just shook his head in disbelief. When we drove back to the parking lot, he got into his van, thanked me, and left. He was extremely cordial but clearly incredulous. A funny thing happened just before we opened Shingle Creek: The Marriott Corporation sold their interest in the Ritz and Marriott for approximately $750 million (about $100 million profit). I wondered if this was just a coincidence or perhaps if he was not very excited about competing with Shingle Creek when it was clear that we had a significant advantage in the marketplace (no debt).

MR. ROSEN ON HIS HOTEL BUSINESS

It was 1973, and the oil embargo was in full swing. Orlando was in terrible shape; virtually every hotel in the area was in serious financial condition. Very few tourists were coming to Orlando, people weren't driving here because they couldn't buy gas, and just about every hotel in Orlando was for sale. I was not working at the time, having been recently fired from Disney, and I had started looking for a hotel to buy. One day in the spring of 1974, I drove by this little hotel, the Quality Inn, and I just liked the way it looked. I also liked the fact that you could see it from I-4 and that it also had International Drive exposure.

I went in and asked the front desk clerk if the owner was available. She said, yes, Mr. Morgan is here, and what is it that you would like to talk to him about? I said that I was looking for a hotel to buy. Within minutes, a short, stocky fellow came out and shook my hand and took me into his office (his name was Jim Morgan). He said that he was the owner and that he was losing his mind because business was so terrible and that his wife and three daughters were anxious about his health and were encouraging him to sell the hotel. He said to me, "God must have sent you to save me." I asked him how much he was asking. He said I had to discuss the price with his lender who would be in Orlando tomorrow and that he was certain that something could be worked out. He said once again, thank God you are here.

The next day the lender arrived, and he asked for my resume. He read it and said, you certainly have a great resume, and no doubt can operate this hotel successfully. He then asked me how much money I had in the bank. I asked, why? He said it would help him determine if we could do business together. He repeated the question. I believed that this might be some sort of test, and I was determined to be honest. I really thought that there might be some way he could find out how much I actually had, so I told him the truth. I said that I had a little more than $20,000 in the bank. The lender (he was from the Travelers Insurance Company) looked at me and said, you are a very lucky man. I asked why, and he said, because that is exactly what the down payment is going to be. I said OK, let's do the deal, and we shook hands, ... but I knew I had made a big mistake, revealing my bank balance.

At closing several days later, my two partners, Kelly Smith and Alan Dayton, and I assumed the mortgage (approximately $2.5 million), and I handed the lender my $20,000 (which meant that I was now penniless).

On June 24, 1974, I stepped into the hotel I had just purchased, believing that I was the dumbest person God had ever created. I sat at the desk, became depressed, and soon convinced myself that I probably would not last for very long. However, I had done some prior planning and knew that there was still one viable market out there: the motor coach market. I just knew that if I could talk to the owners of the motor coach companies, I would be able to convince them to stay at my little Quality Inn. I was also convinced that tourists who couldn't drive because of gas shortages would come to Orlando by bus. In fact, for the time being, this was perhaps the only way tourists could come to Orlando. An immediate problem, however, was that I didn't have any money to travel to New England where many of the motor coach companies were located. So I called a friend and asked if she could sit at my desk in the hotel and look important while I was away. (We didn't have that much business anyway.) So I hitchhiked to New Bedford, Massachusetts, and I got a hotel room for around $12. Maybe I had a total of $30 or $40 with me, so I could stay for a couple of nights if I had to.

The next day I went to my first meeting with a big motor coach company. I believe it was Paragon Tours. I told them my story, and I handed out some business cards and some brochures. I stated that my Quality Inn was a beautiful little hotel and that I lived on the property, enabling me to take excellent care of their guests. (I stated that I am there 24/7.) I asked the owner of Paragon, Mr. Jim Penler, and Mr. Ed Camara, the operations manager, to take one of my business cards and to write down a room rate on the card (any rate that they were willing to pay) and that I would honor it. They were incredulous. No matter what rate and I said yes. Mr. Penler conferred with Mr. Camara and then wrote a rate of $8.50 on the card and handed it back to me. I looked at the rate and quickly shook his hand and said, Mr. Penler, we have a deal. I said, from now on, all of your buses will come to Rosen's Quality Inn, and you will pay only $8.50/room, and I promised that we will take excellent care of your clients. So I signed the card and handed it back to Mr. Penler, indicating that I would send a formal contract once I returned to Orlando. I then stated that I didn't have a car or much money with me and really wanted to see some of the other motor coach operators. Did they have any suggestions? Surprise! Mr. Camara said he would drive me in his bus to my next contact, which he did. Now that's really quite amazing, isn't it? This is exactly how I got to make all of my other sales calls.

While in New England, I visited about eight motor coach companies in two days and signed them all up using my little business cards as a contract. The rates ranged from $8.00/room to $9.50. When I came back to Orlando, I was so happy because I now had all of this new motor coach business on the books, but then another miracle occurred. Approximately a week or so after I returned from my trip to New England, the oil embargo was lifted, and thankfully people started traveling again—with a vengeance. We actually made a profit our first year and have made a profit every year since, and I am proud to report that more than a few of the original bus companies still stay with us. During our first six months in business, our success in the local market became very well known, primarily because we always had so many buses parked at our hotel. Everyone was jealous of us, and many hotels were still having severe financial difficulties.

One day a Philadelphia, Pennsylvania, bank (Continental Bank of Philadelphia) came to Orlando to foreclose on a hotel on north I-Drive that was called the Solage. Because they heard of our success, they came over to visit with me, suggesting that it was well known that for some reason we were doing better than most of the other hotels in the area. They asked me some general questions and then asked if I had an interest in purchasing the Solage. I said, oh, my God, I don't think so. My hands are full, and I cannot afford to purchase another property. They said they would make it very attractive for me and asked me to think it over. So against my better judgment, I did think about it over the weekend and asked them to return to discuss my offer.

Before I met with them again, I went down to take a look at the Solage and liked what I saw. I then met with them and put forth a rather novel purchase plan. My idea was that I would assume the mortgage (approximately $2.5 million) with no down payment and that I would operate the hotel for five years with no management fee or salary for myself and that I would give every penny we earned to the bank. They in turn would match whatever I gave them, dollar for dollar in the first year. (For instance, if I gave them $1, they would give me credit for $2.) In the second year the match dropped to $1.75, then $1.50, then $1.25, and in the final year to $1.10, and then at the end of the five years whatever balance remained on the mortgage, I would have the option to pay and would then own the hotel free and clear. At the end of the five years (I believe it was actually four years and 9 months), I paid off the entire $2.5 million mortgage, and I now owned the hotel free and clear.

The bankers were happy because they were essentially out of what they considered to be a poor investment, and I was happy because I now owned a new hotel, my second one (debt free). I renamed the hotel the International Inn, and I was now the proud owner of two hotels. Interestingly, I signed the contract with Continental Bank on June 24, 1975—exactly one year to the day that I purchased the Quality Inn. So from $20,000 in a savings account and no job, in exactly two years I now had a 256-room motel and a 250-room hotel. Not bad, and off to a nice start, if I say so. Well, that was our beginning. As soon as I paid off the (Solage) International Inn mortgage, I purchased some additional property on International Drive and built the Quality Inn Plaza, the largest Quality Inn in the chain with 1,020 rooms.

Several years later we purchased property in Lake Buena Vista and built the Comfort Inn in two phases: 320 rooms followed a year later with an additional 320 rooms, making it the largest Comfort Inn in the chain. Amazingly, the Comfort Inn did not carry a vacant room for five years, even as it grew from 320 rooms to 640 rooms. Of course, no one believed us, but we really did run at a 100 percent occupancy rate every day for 365 days for five straight years. How did we do it? Well, we were the only economy hotel in the Lake Buena Vista area for some time. We were selling rooms for $29.95/night, while everyone else was in the $75 to $200 range. We had a big reader board on I-4, and walk-in traffic (guests without reservations) was just unbelievable. We would easily do 100 to 200 walk-ins a day. That, of course, was before travel websites and the Internet, and many tourists would arrive in Orlando without reservations, knowing that there was an abundance of good, inexpensive hotel rooms available on a daily basis. Tourists would see our sign from the highway, and the cars would literally line up outside the hotel lobby, waiting for rooms. I recall that our public relations company did call Great Britain to speak with the *Guinness Book of Records* people, requesting that they authenticate our record of operating at 100 percent occupancy for five years. We stated that we were convinced it had never been done before and most likely would never be done again. For whatever reason, they said they just weren't interested but would consider presenting us with a certificate recognizing our claim, although it would not be authenticated as a *Guinness* record. We accepted the "nonauthorized" certificate from *Guinness Book of Records*, stating that we "claimed" not to have carried a vacant room for five years. Big deal!

Shortly after we completed the 640-room Comfort Inn at Lake Buena Vista, we noticed that the tourist sector seemed to be slowing down ever so slightly as thousands of new hotel rooms, time-shares, and condos were added to the central Florida inventory. I became concerned and had a gut feeling that Orlando might be ready for yet another market. I believed that Orlando just might become an attractive convention destination, if, of course, we had a large convention center. I must confess that practically everyone thought I was crazy. To test my idea, I called Bob Tish, president of Loews Corporation, and I asked him if I could run an idea by him. He said yes. I asked him if he believed Orlando could become a convention destination if we had a convention center. I shared with him that we would soon have a public referendum on whether or not to establish a tourist tax on all hotel rooms to generate funds to build a convention center. I told him that I was certain it would pass, and when it did, the convention center would most likely be built on International Drive, where I was thinking about taking an option on a 10-acre parcel contiguous to the parcel we believed the convention center would be built on. I asked Mr. Tish if he would like to be my partner. He just laughed and said Orlando will never be the likes of New York, Chicago, Atlanta, or Las Vegas. He said, Harris, you are just wasting your time. Boy was he wrong!

The referendum passed, and the convention center was indeed built on the site I had hoped it would be built on. So in I went to visit with Martin Marietta, the company that owned the parcel I wanted to build my hotel on and asked Jim Brown, president of Orlando Central Park (a subsidiary of Martin Marietta) if I could purchase the parcel. He disappointed me by saying no. He indicated that they were in active negotiations with Hilton, Marriott, Hyatt, and Westin and were looking for a big name, not a Rosen to be the two anchor hotels to the convention center. Jim said that although he appreciated my interest, there were too many hotel companies expressing a keen interest in the site.

Well, in due course, it became clear that they were not successful in selling the particular parcel I was interested in; however, for some reason, they did sell a parcel directly across from the convention center. It was purchased by the Belz family from Memphis, owners of the Peabody hotel chain. For some reason the major hotel companies just did not have any confidence that Orlando would one day become a powerful convention destination, and they failed to purchase the contiguous parcels. How wrong they were! And so I was pleasantly surprised when in late November, Jim Brown called and said, "Harris, do you still want to buy that parcel?" And I said, "Yes, sir!" He asked me if I would be able to close quickly, and I asked how quickly? And he responded, "before the end of the year," and I said, "Yes, I can." "Well, bring us the check." I asked him how much, and he said "8 million dollars." I said OK. So I wrote the check. (I had the money in the bank. I had by now been in business for about 15 years and had been saving money like crazy, just waiting for an opportunity like this.) I will never forget when in early December I brought the check (made out to Martin Marietta) for $8 million to Mr. Brown's office in Orlando Central Park. Jim never received me or met with me. He merely requested that I leave the check with the receptionist, which I did. Prior to the end of the year, we closed on the property, and within two years, we built the Clarion Plaza Hotel. Jim and his company, Martin Marietta, were very pleased with the Clarion because after a brief period of time, it was doing exceptionally well, and Martin Marietta was selling property all around us like crazy. Back then, our four tourist hotels ran occupancies in the upper 90 percent range, and that's what drove our little company. We were never concerned about ADR (average daily rate), only about occupancy. Our motto: You can't generate revenue from an unoccupied room.

After the Clarion Plaza was up and operating for several years, I received a phone call from Martin Marietta headquarters in Bethesda, Maryland, asking if I would visit them. They said they just wanted to chat with me. I decided to take my attorney along just in case. Kelly Smith, my attorney, and I went to Maryland, and we had a meeting scheduled for 9 o'clock the next morning. We walked into what was the largest board room I had ever seen in my life, with a table that comfortably sat 40 to 50 people. I sat all the way down at the end with Kelly next to me, and I was scared to death. Why did they ask me to come? Mr. Bennett, Martin Marietta's chief financial officer, introduced me as his very special guest, Harris Rosen from Orlando, the gentleman who built the beautiful Clarion Plaza Hotel, which is doing very well. He shared with the group that he gave us a month to come up with the $8 million to buy the property, and we did it. He then stated that Harris showed us his plans for his hotel, and he built exactly what he said he would. He also assured us that the hotel would be successful, and it has been even more successful than we ever imagined. So now, Harris, we want you to continue to work with us.

You see, we've been asked by the government to get out of the real estate business and to focus on defense. So we have an interest in selling about 250 acres, all on International Drive, and we would like you to buy it all from us. I was shocked, and I said that I had never done anything like this before and I would need some time to think about it. Mr. Bennett said that I didn't have to pay a dime for another year, and in the meantime I would be able to sell as much property as I wanted for whatever price I could negotiate as long as I met their purchase price, and … you can keep anything you sell above whatever we want. I turned to Kelly and asked his opinion. He said, let's do it. I said to Mr. Bennett, it's a deal.

It was two hundred plus acres of prime property on International Drive, which Martin Marietta wanted approximately $60 million for. We sold it for about $80 million, so we made a $20 million profit. We traded our profit for approximately 23 acres next to the convention center we wished to own. Indeed, it is 20 acres the Rosen Centre is built on contiguous to the convention center on the south. In addition, we purchased the helicopter site contiguous to the Quality Inn Plaza, which is approximately three acres. So I wound up with two prime parcels (essentially for free). We decided to build a sister convention hotel, now the Rosen Centre, on the 20-acre site, and because we did not have any immediate plans for the smaller site, we decided to lease it to a helicopter ride operator on a long-term lease (with options to cancel). Our initial faith that Orlando would one day become a great convention destination has been proven correct. And just imagine that it is *our* little company that has a hotel on either side of the Orange County Convention Center—what a blessing!

Before long, we had two convention hotels: the Clarion Plaza, our first, and the Omni Rosen, our second. Soon after we opened the Omni, I began to dream that one day I would own a large resort with a golf course. This was the same dream I had as a child growing up in New York City. I had this dream for several years and then decided to get serious about it. We soon started searching for a large parcel for my dream resort. The first parcel we looked at was a property at Disney's Celebration. I must confess that it was 750 of the most beautiful acres I had ever seen in my life. It was just so beautiful. … I immediately began thinking of building two golf courses, a very large (2,000 rooms) beautiful resort attached to (a 500,000 to 1 million sq. ft.) convention center. Within weeks of walking the property, we made Disney an offer, which they seemed pleased with, and they said they would take it directly to Michael Eisner in California for his approval. They felt confident that everything would be fine.

In several weeks I called my Disney contact to see if everything was moving along, and he informed me that things did not go well at all with Mr. Eisner. I asked what happened. … He told me that when he presented Michael with our proposal, Michael asked, "Who is this guy Rosen?" I've never heard of him." We explained to him who you were and the fact that you have been a successful hotel owner/operator in town for more than 20 years. Michael responded that he never heard of the name Rosen and said that he doesn't do business with people he doesn't know. I, of course, was taken aback and asked if anyone else had expressed an interest in the parcel, and the answer was (surprise) yes. I was informed that Disney may have a deal with the Four Seasons Company (a company Michael was very familiar with) and were at this point working very closely with them. I said, okay, it is too bad it didn't work out.

This rejection, however, turned out to be a huge blessing because when we continued our search for land for our resort, we found a lovely 270-acre site very close to the new convention center on a beautiful 1,200-acre site originally owned by Martin Marietta, which they later sold to Universal Studios. I fell in love again, and we negotiated a price and closed on the site on October 6, 2000. We designed a magnificent 1,500-room resort with about 500,000 square feet of meeting space and decided to name it after the creek that flows on the eastern boundary of the property (Shingle Creek), which also happened to be the headwaters to Florida's Everglades. After we designed the resort and Dave Harmon designed the golf course, we decided to gift 20 acres to UCF to build the Rosen College of Hospitality Management contiguous to our resort. We completed construction of the golf course first, and then approximately two years later, four and a half months ahead of schedule and on budget, we opened Shingle Creek in 2006 on my birthday, September 9. Shingle Creek recently celebrated its first anniversary and has achieved much greater success than we ever imagined.

In summary, we started our little company in 1974 with a 256-room Quality Inn, which we paid $20,000 for, and today, 34 years later, we have approximately 6,500 rooms and we are planning to add more meeting space to the Rosen Centre and the Rosen Plaza. In addition, we shall add a retail component as part of our plan to physically connect both the Centre and the Plaza to the convention center. We have grown from one small motel to a medium-size company with seven hotels and approximately 6,500 rooms, and we enjoy a very significant advantage in the marketplace because we are essentially a debt-free company (Please see Appendix B for a more detailed Rosen Hotel & Resort portfolio.)

MR. ROSEN ON MANAGEMENT PHILOSOPHY AND STYLE

We are not a stereotypical company. For example, we have never had an organization chart. I don't like them. I don't believe they serve any real purpose, and instead they can inhibit a free flow of ideas and suggestions crucial to the success of any company. In addition, we are not a public company. We don't have shareholders and don't issue stock. We therefore have no shareholder meetings and no public disclosure. Thankfully, we are a private company, a very private company.

I do believe that people who work for us will tell you that they enjoy working here because we're not a "typical" company and that we never pretend to be something we are not. My office is really kind of indicative of who we are and what we are all about. It is located on the second floor of the Quality Inn hotel, the first hotel I acquired back in 1974. To get to it, you must walk up a couple of flights of stairs. The office is no big deal, and I actually lived in it for 16 years. I once had a small kitchen, and you can still see the stove vent in the ceiling. I keep it there as a constant reminder of how we started. My current office is in what once used to be my living room, and the adjacent room where my assistant works was my bedroom. Yes, it is true that I lived in this hotel room for 16 years with my dog Rin Tin Tin, who died at the age of 13 and who is buried in the courtyard near my office.

My management philosophy is a simple one: You must first of all love what you do and work hard at it. It is also important to set aside some time to dream. And, of course, always be honest and unselfish, and always treat others with respect. Our company does not tolerate dishonesty, and we do shop our various departments continuously. We shop our bartenders, our restaurant servers, our front desk agents, and so forth on a regular basis to make sure we stay on track. In addition, I read every single guest comment card that is turned in. There is a new book out, *Winners Never Cheat* by John M. Huntsman, which states that you must always play the game fairly. He also admonishes us not to get carried away with whatever success we may achieve and always remember that there is much in life that you simply cannot control. So if you catch a good wave, ride it for all it's worth and have as much fun as you can. As I have said, always treat everyone with honesty and respect, and love what you do. If you do that, I believe you will really live a great life.

I firmly believe that our 4,000 associates appreciate the fact that we really do care a great deal about them. The benefits package (featuring our own on-site medical clinic) is probably amongst the best in the industry. Interestingly, we now hear that Disney is replicating our wellness clinic for their employees finally, after they shopped us for 15 years. We have also learned that the city of Ocoee has replicated our health care program, as has the Harris Corporation in Melbourne. We've had our clinic 18 years, and we now have two full-time docs and a total of 28 people on staff. I have to believe that our health care benefits are amongst the very best in the nation. In addition, our scholastic scholarships program is also excellent. If you work for us, you can study any subject in college, and we will pay for it. Also, dependent children can also attend college on Rosen scholarships. I think that our people really do appreciate the connection we have with them. (Please see Appendix C for examples of Rosen Hotel & Resorts Employee Programs.)

MR. ROSEN ON LEADERSHIP

I do not believe that you can teach someone to be an entrepreneur. However, I do believe that it is absolutely possible to teach someone to be a good leader. The military does it all the time. The three years I spent as an officer in the Army certainly helped me tremendously. The question is, are there natural-born leaders? Perhaps there are individuals who carry themselves a certain way and who speak with a certain authority. However, I believe that you can also train someone who wishes to be a leader or someone who has the passion to learn and who also possesses the necessary skills to do so. No doubt you can teach someone to be a good leader if they have the desire to do so.

To be a leader, you must always set the example. This is really the key. Please remember never to ask someone to do something that you, yourself, would not do, and always be fair to everyone, treat all equally, and don't play favorites. Never treat some individuals differently than others. Treat everybody the same. It is also important to praise whenever appropriate and to offer constructive criticism when necessary. Criticism may be directed at an individual quietly or perhaps not so quietly; however, to be effective, it must be unequivocal. People must understand when they have done something inappropriate or incorrectly; however, you must explain why it was inappropriate and then make sure to correct the situation for the future. Simply speaking, it is a balancing act where fairness and respect must always be emphasized.

It is also important to let your staff know that you are always anxious to hear what they are thinking. Remember, the best ideas often come from those who are working within the company, usually in the middle and lower levels of the organization, not the top. I've certainly had my share of ideas, . . . and our company has certainly grown based on my intuitiveness and my gut feelings (it is the entrepreneurial gene that often gets my attention). I have often gotten wonderful ideas from those associates within the organization, such as housekeeping, the front desk, the culinary departments, engineering, sales, food & beverage operations, and so on. Great ideas come from all corners of the organization, and it is vital to develop a culture that encourages the sharing of ideas and suggestions. Everyone should be comfortable when offering a suggestion. And, of course, never ridicule anyone for a silly idea. I never have, and I never will. No matter how silly the idea might be, never make someone feel uncomfortable about sharing an idea with you. It is also important to realize that on occasion the craziest (out of the box) ideas can turn out to be exciting and productive.

Sadly, however, I have discovered that in academe, in the public sector, and sometimes within large private organizations (GM, Ford, AIG, Citicorp, etc.), there seems to be a disinclination, almost a fear, for those who work within these organizations to think out of the box. Perhaps it is akin to a fraternity, where like-minded people are comfortable with each other and don't ever wish to be considered as outcasts or mavericks by thinking differently.

Indeed, it is often the private sector where the outcasts and mavericks excel. Neither Donald Dell nor Bill Gates graduated from college. They both decided to first develop their ideas in the private sector before completing college. It is most often those who have different ideas and who also have the courage to act upon them that succeed, and I suspect it is why the United States has been such a fertile ground for the entrepreneur, the thinker, the maverick, and why it is such a great place to live, especially if you posses the troublesome "defective" entrepreneurial gene.

I tell youngsters all the time that it is not a gene I wish upon those I really care for because it can drive you mad. I am often asked, how do you feel when you walk into one of your hotels? I respond that I don't really feel anything because I am usually too busy looking for cigarette butts, litter, or checking if someone's nametag is on straight or perhaps if paintings are hanging correctly, or if the carpet has been recently vacuumed. I wish that just one day I could crawl into Donald Trump's shoes and see how it must feel to be an "important" person, being driven around in a stretch limousine, flying in private jets, and wearing very expensive suits. How must that feel? I suspect I will never know!

MR. ROSEN ON EDUCATION

It is important for parents to encourage their youngsters to do well in school and to make sure whom they select as their friends and to be aware of whom they are associating with. Parents must observe if their children's friends are ambitious and eager to achieve something in life or if they are just comfortable hanging out. School is important because it is really the first opportunity for youngsters to learn and to socialize. Youngsters must be encouraged early on to dream—to dream about anything, perhaps of being a leader, a manager, a business owner, a teacher, a scientist, and so on. I absolutely believe that dreaming is necessary if one is to achieve success in life.

School is also a great period to learn about oneself. What are your likes and dislikes? What excites you? What do you love to do? You must learn all about yourself; you have to be confident with yourself, who you are, what you are, and you must learn to be tolerant and kind to others and to be sensitive regarding their thoughts. Yes, I think teachers plant the seed, but eventually youngsters have to do it by themselves. An education can help you learn what you must know to be successful, but the rest is really up to you.

Of course, the beauty of our hospitality college (the Rosen College) is that you are in a classroom learning the basics, the essentials, creating a foundation you can build upon. And then it's off to the real world, where you can put your education to good use. It is really nothing more than on-the-job learning, which may be the perfect combination of classroom learning, and then putting what you have learned to good use on the job. I suspect that there are some who might frown upon this "learn and work" concept because it may be perceived as a form of vocational training. Well, perhaps this is the new education paradigm, which I suspect can accelerate one's ability to succeed. I believe this new paradigm can be effective no matter what you are studying: engineering, hospitality, business, fine art, medicine, and so forth. I have no doubt that higher education must absolutely include real-life experiences as part of the education experience. If you don't have real life, hands-on experiences, you will most assuredly struggle after graduation. Just think of all of the training our astronauts go through . . . my dear God! You just can't sit behind a desk in a classroom and learn everything you may need at work. You have to learn to be successful. You absolutely need real-time, real-life work experience along with your classroom learning. I believe that academe is beginning to understand and appreciate this approach because it is gradually becoming the standard teaching methodology, one which I believe is a more legitimate approach for our higher education system to utilize.

MR. ROSEN ON INDUSTRY-ORIENTED SKILLS

It once was believed that it was enough to just roll into a classroom, submit your homework on time, do well on tests, and boom! Off to graduate school . . . and then in no time out in the real world. My firm belief is that if you can't function confidently in the workplace, you will likely not achieve your life's goals. I don't care how smart you are. Indeed, I believe that there may be little relationship between one's ability to excel in the class room and one's ability to achieve success. Many people who are not successful in school are extremely successful in business, and many people who are brilliant in school are not at all successful in the real world. Nonetheless, you must be able to make the transition from the classroom to the real world; some people succeed, some are moderately successful, and some fail. Not everyone is ambitious; not everyone wishes to be a supervisor, a manager, or an owner; and not everyone is a leader or a risk taker. And this is the way it should be because there is a great need for good, honest, hard workers who aspire to do their job to the best of their ability without complaint and who are quite content doing what they are doing.

MR. ROSEN ON PHILANTHROPY ("RESPONSIBLE CAPITALISM")

I do believe that those of us who achieve a modicum of success in our careers must (at the end of the day) say thanks to God for his blessings, and once you reach that point in your life, I firmly believe that you have an obligation to give others a helping hand. As you traverse your 70, 80, or 90 years on earth and you are fortunate enough to have achieved success in your chosen field, at some point in time you must realize that this wonderful nation has provided you with extraordinary opportunities to succeed, please remember then to always be thankful for your successes and to demonstrate your appreciation by helping others. (See Appendix D for a list of Mr. Rosen's philanthropic activities.)

I realize that some people are a bit leery when I talk to them about my concept of "responsible capitalism," but I absolutely believe that we do have an obligation to give back. For me, someone who has been blessed beyond anything I ever imagined, it is important that I demonstrate my gratitude. And so, as I move into the twilight of my career, I contemplate ways in which I can give back to this incredibly generous nation. It has not been an easy voyage from the Lower East Side of Manhattan to International Drive in Orlando, but it has taught me perseverance, to never to give up, and most importantly, that there is absolutely no substitute for hard work. But please never forget that we all have a responsibility (when you succeed) to demonstrate your gratitude by helping others

CONCLUSIONS AND IMPLICATIONS

The insights highlighted in the interview with Mr. Rosen in this study provide important implications to hospitality education in many aspects, such as the importance and the quality of entrepreneurship, the significance of leadership, the philosophy of giving back to the community, the balance between academic functional knowledge and industry experience, which are all of vital importance if one is to succeed in the hospitality industry. The interview findings imply that to be a successful entrepreneur, one has to possess some inherent gene to pursue this course of life. While it is difficult to prove or even debate as to whether entrepreneurs and/or leaders are born or made, the common denominator shaping and defining them, according to Mr. Rosen, is certain restlessness, a capacity to dream and to inspire, business intelligence, confidence, diligence, and high personal values. They are the people who have the ability to challenge established procedures and assumptions, and a continuous pursuit of one's dreams. These results and associated implications are by and large consistent with previous studies in the area of entrepreneurship and leadership (e.g., Morrison and Johnson, 2003; Morrison, Rimmington, and Williams, 1999).

Regarding the essence of philanthropy, the implication from this research is that giving back after you have achieved a modicum of success in your own career is an obligation to be taken quite seriously. Many entrepreneurs find it important to share their wealth with many causes within their community as well as nationally and globally—for example, Bill Gates, John Huntsman, Chuck Feeny, Don Della, and Warren Buffet. Mr. Rosen's philanthropic activities demonstrate his commitment to giving back. It might be argued that money and profit are motivating factors driving entrepreneurships, but there are numerous examples in which enjoyment of the game and the thrill of the chase become the main incentives for entrepreneurs, especially when they have created wealth far in excess of their own or their families' needs. Mr. Rosen is a fine example of sharing his success with the community via numerous philanthropic activities he has been involved with and continues to be involved with. It is because of his contribution to the community through his innovative entrepreneurial spirit and philanthropic activities that he has garnered respect and recognition nationally and internationally. (Please see a list of Mr. Rosen's Awards and Recognition in Appendix E.)

In regard to hospitality students' success in their careers, the insight Mr. Rosen has shared seems to suggest that there is a need for students to find a balance between classroom education and industry skills. This raises a question as to vision and mission of hospitality education, which in turn guides hospitality curriculum development. Obviously, hospitality education is multifaceted as well as a very applied discipline, and there is always the need for a curriculum to integrate functional knowledge in the classroom with practical skills needed in the industry, recognizing the interdependence of many parts that make up a business so students cannot only think but must also act strategically. This may require an attempt to link theory and practice; encourage imaginative, creative, and innovative interpretation of conventional business practices; and understand the specific interface between entrepreneurship and hospitality operations, leadership, and management strategy (Hinkin and Tracey, 1994; Jayawardena, 2001; Russell and Murphy, 2004).

For hospitality educators, there is a need to contextualize our teaching philosophy and the design of hospitality programs in a transitioning economy, always making certain that the programs delivered meet the requirements of this new economic paradigm. In order to prepare the future managers for our industry, there is a call for an integration of entrepreneurship and leadership into the curriculum and the need to nurture our students through appropriate teaching and learning strategies with an emphasis on reflection and critical thinking in order to adequately prepare nascent entrepreneurs and leaders so they cannot only think big but are also able to execute these big ideas. This implies that creativity and critical thinking should be the constant focus of hospitality educational thinking. This may also mean that for many hospitality programs, there is a need to distance themselves from the traditional preoccupation with a vocational orientation (Morrison et al., 1999). As a result, the curriculum content should have more emphasis on self-discovery and critical and creative thinking in order to produce future entrepreneurs, managers, and leaders who are intellectually able to think outside of existing business practices and paradigms and compete in a more challenging work environment. Last, but not at all least, we must inculcate within the minds of our future leaders to always be respectful of others, to listen to what others have to say, to be ready to give back and serve others, to always be honest and forthright, and to remember "to always do the right thing."

REFERENCES

Hinkin, T.R. and Tracey, J.B. (1994). Transformational leadership in the hospitality industry, *Journal of Hospitality and Tourism Research*, 18(1), 49–63.

Jayawardena, C. (2001). Challenges in International Hospitality Management Education, *International Journal of Contemporary Hospitality Management*, 13(6), 310–315.

Maccoby, M. (2001). Successful leaders employ strategic intelligence, *Research-Technology Management*, 44(3), 58–60.

Morrison, A. and Johnson, B. (2003). Personal creativity for entrepreneurship: teaching and learning strategies, *Active Learning in Higher Education*, 4, 145–158.

Morrison, A., Rimmington, M., and Williams, C. (1999). *Entrepreneurship in the Hospitality, Tourism and Leisure Industries*. London: Butterworth Heinemann.

Pittaway, L., Carmouche, R., and Chell, E. (1998). Clevedon: Channel View Publications. pp. 44–65. The way forward: Leadership research in the hospitality industry, *International Journal of Hospitality Management*, 17, 408–426.

Russell, R. and Murphy, P. (2004). Entrepreneurial leadership in times of uncertainty: Implications for tourism research and education. In J. Aramberri and R. Butler (Eds.), *Tourism Development Issues for a Vulnerable Industry*. Clevedon: Channel View Publications. 44–65.

Zahra, S.A. (1999). The changing rules of global competitiveness in the twenty-first century, *The Academy of Management Executive*, 13(1), 36–42.

APPENDIX A: BACKGROUND OF MR. HARRIS ROSEN, PRESIDENT AND CEO OF ROSEN HOTELS AND RESORTS

Mr. Harris Rosen grew up in a poor neighborhood in New York City's Lower East Side. His hospitality career began by helping his father stack his beautifully hand-written banquet place cards in his small office at the Waldorf Astoria Hotel in New York City. This experience gave Mr. Rosen much more than the penny he earned per card alphabetized. He enjoyed seeing the lavish ballrooms and meeting people like Douglas MacArthur, the famous general from the World War II; Marilyn Monroe; Pope John Paul II; Ty Cobb, one of the greatest baseball players ever; and Jackie Robinson, his hero and the first African American in the major leagues. This experience led him to believe that the hotel business was fun. Upon graduation from high school in New York City, he pursued a degree in hotel administration at Cornell University, Ithaca, New York. During Mr. Rosen's college years, he held jobs such as a pot washer and bartender for a sports fraternity. He also sold programs at football and basketball games. During his time at Cornell, Mr. Rosen took four years of Army Reserve Officers' Training (ROTC). ROTC is a college-based, officer commissioning program in the United States Army. This commissioning program is designed as a college elective that focuses on leadership development, problem solving, strategic planning, and professional ethics. Mr. Rosen's strong beliefs and success can be attributed in no small part to his participation in the ROTC program and to his military service.

After graduation, Mr. Rosen was commissioned as second lieutenant, and his first assignment was in Korea, where in addition to his military assignments, he taught English in a Korean high school and studied judo, earning a black belt. From Korea, he went on to Frankfurt, Germany, where he spent two years. It was during his service in Germany that Mr. Rosen began his entrepreneurial career. After his tour in Germany, Mr. Rosen returned to New York, seeking a job at the Waldorf Astoria. He always dreamed of one day working there as his father had.

As a Cornell graduate with three years in the Army, sadly there were no jobs at the time at the Waldorf to fit his education and experience, so he accepted a job in the personnel office as a file clerk. His job turned out to be quite fortuitous because he was able to learn very early on all the new jobs that were available. This allowed him to quickly interview for the jobs he really wanted. Finally, he interviewed for and was offered a job as a convention coordinator. This job proved to be the stepping stone to convention sales, which was what he really was interested in. After several months as a convention coordinator, he was offered a sales position. Within a year he became one of the top convention salespersons in the office.

While working at the Waldorf Astoria, Mr. Rosen was sought out by Mr. Bob Tish, owner of Loews Hotels, to be the assistant director of sales at the Americana Hotel, not far from the Waldorf. After the interview with Mr. Tish, an offer was made at quite a substantial increase in pay, an impressive title, and an office. He sought out the opinion of Mr. Frank Wangeman, senior vice president of Hilton Corporation, who recommended to Mr. Rosen that he stay with Hilton, offering him an opportunity to attend the University of Virginia to pursue an advanced management degree.

Three months after being at the University of Virginia, Mr. Rosen's career took off. His first position was resident manager at the Cape Kennedy Hilton, then as the director of Food and Beverage Operations at the Pittsburgh Hilton, then back to New York City as the resident manager of the New Yorker, and from there to the Dallas Statler as resident manager. He then left Hilton to become the general manager of a luxury resort in Acapulco, Mexico (Tres Vidas), a wonderful job in a spectacular setting. However, this position was short lived due to a political change in Mexico. The company Mr. Rosen was working for had to be dissolved, leaving him without a job. He left Acapulco and went to California. It was in California that Mr. Rosen read about Disneyland in CA. He then went to Burbank (Disney headquarters) and was hired as the hotel planning administrator and coordinator for the hotel division. There he spent his time working with the architects designing the Contemporary and Polynesian resorts, the golf resort, and Fort Wilderness before heading to Orlando in 1969 to help with the construction and the opening of Disney World in October 1971.

Disney opened in 1971, and in addition to his job as planning coordinator for the hotels, he was also the character Winnie the Pooh. In 1973, Mr. Rosen was let go by Disney because his supervisor felt that he would never become a "real Disney person." This was the second job he had been fired from in four years, so he vowed never to work for anyone ever again. He purchased his first hotel for $20,000, the Quality Inn on International Drive in Orlando, Florida, on June 24, 1974, at the peak of the oil embargo. As of 2009, Rosen Hotels & Resorts is the largest private hotel company in the southeast, owning and operating seven hotels in the Orlando area with a combined total of nearly 6,500 rooms.

APPENDIX B: ROSEN HOTELS AND RESORTS PORTFOLIO

Hotels	Amenities
Quality Inn International, June 24, 1974	Quality Inn International includes 728 spacious semisuite guest rooms, 2 large pools, a children's wading pool, and spacious courtyards.
Rodeway Inn, June 24, 1975	The Rodeway Inn is the largest in the United States. It includes 315 semisuite guest rooms, the Palms dining room, and Shogun Japanese Steak House.
Quality Inn Plaza, February 26, 1984	Quality Inn Plaza includes 1,020 guest rooms, 3 attractive pool areas, and beautifully landscaped gardens.
Comfort Inn Lake Buena Vista, May 17, 1987	The Comfort Inn includes 640 semisuite guest rooms and 2 swimming pools. This property occupies 23 acres.
Rosen Plaza, September 13, 1991	Rosen Plaza includes 800 deluxe guest rooms, 32 suites (executive, king, presidential, hospitality, and parlor suites), over 60,000 square feet of modern meeting and exhibit space, a 26,000-square-foot grand ballroom, 22 meeting rooms, and a business center; adjacent to the Orange County Convention Center.
Rosen Centre, October 31, 1994	Rosen Centre includes 1,334 hotel rooms and suites, over 100,000 square feet of meeting and conference facilities, 3 large restaurants, a beautiful swimming grotto, and tennis courts; adjacent to the Orange County Convention Center.
Shingle Creek Resort, September 9, 2006	Shingle Creek includes 1,500 guest rooms, 445,000 square feet of meeting space, a 13,000-square-foot spa with 9 treatment rooms, on-site fitness center, tennis courts, and a golf course spread across 230 acres.

APPENDIX C: ROSEN HOTELS & RESORTS EMPLOYEE PROGRAMS: WORK/LIFE BALANCE WEEK

The Annual Work/Life Balance Week (formerly known as Celebrating Family Week) includes free seminars with translations available on topics that impact our daily lives. In 2008, they included Debt Management seminars, Preventing Foreclosure seminars, and Personal Solutions for Today's Financial Problems. In the past we have also included topics such as Identity Theft and Energy Conservation in the Home. During the week, human resource members visit all of the hotels and distribute free books to the children of associates to encourage literacy and reading between parents and children. Finally, we offered free golf clinics in our golf course for children of associates. Work/Life Balance is extremely important to have a happy, healthy, and productive workforce, so we do everything we can to maintain a good morale among our family of associates.

Educational Programs

Rosen Hotels & Resorts provides a wide variety of seminars, workshops, and classes to assist associates in becoming the best associate they can be. These include certification courses, language classes, and computer workshops. They are dedicated to the professional growth of our associates. The Rosen Hotels & Resorts Management Training Program is a series of workshops covering topics such as Personality Styles, Effective Teams, Communication Skills, Presentation Skills, and Motivation. The series lasts ten eeks and runs twice a year. Our Certified Leader Program consists of courses like Maximizing Personal Potential, Selecting the Right people, and Fundamentals of Employment Law. This course, presented by the Leadership Difference, has proven to be a major success for our managerial associates who have learned to apply the most recent industry techniques in their teams.

For the past 12 years, Rosen Hotels & Resorts has provided English classes for associates who are non-English-speakers. Since the program's inception, over 1,500 associates have participated. This program provides basic conversational English, with the idea that associates will be able to understand and learn everyday vocabulary. The classes are offered at each hotel property for an hour a week during company-paid time.

Health and Fitness Programs

Aside from the company's own medical center, which offers medical care and a dietician, Rosen Hotels & Resorts offers an on-site Weight Watcher's program in which the company pays for associate's memberships based on annual salary. The company initiated its Weight Watcher's at Work Program on June 10, 1997, with 33 members and one meeting. Today the program has grown to close to 100 members for each 12-week session throughout four different locations in the company. The company is very proud of its associates who have lost thousands of pounds on the program and the members who have reached their weight-loss goals.

The newest wellness initiative at Rosen Hotels & Resorts is the Wow Factor Program. Wow stands for Workout for Wellness and includes a monthly wellness newsletter, daily walking clubs, and weekly high-intensity aerobic classes and Tai Chi exercises to help improve balance and flexibility.

Family-Friendly Benefits

Rosen Hotels & Resorts has a Family Outreach Center that employs a full-time social worker. The center's mission is to help associates and their families with child care subsidies, educational reimbursement, foreclosure prevention, credit counseling, debt management, company loans, immigration assistance, citizenship review courses, a food pantry for times of need, furniture and clothing donations, and any other issue that could crop up. The Family Outreach Center also works with our Finance department and human resources in offering free tax preparation for associates during tax season. Additionally, Outreach Center staff are available to accompany associates on appointments to serve as translators if language is a barrier (Spanish, French, or Haitian Creole).

Employee Events

The company enhances morale by providing fun events for associates throughout the year. Such events include National Housekeeping Week, Administrative Professionals Day, and the company's Anniversary Celebration, among others. Guests at the Anniversary include associates who have been with the company ten years and above. This event celebrates the accomplishments of all associates who are turning 10, 15, 20, 25, 30, and 35 years with the company that year by recognizing all of them on stage, giving them a "years of service" pin, and providing them with a special anniversary bonus. We also have an annual health, benefits and safety fair where associates can receive free health screenings, information, flu shots, and massages. Every holiday season the company hosts a tree-decorating contest that each hotel competes in. This is a great team-building event because it encourages associates to work together and have pride for their property. One winner is selected, and every holiday tree is donated to a charity of the hotel's choice. This event also includes a talent show for associates.

Many internal employee events are open to family members, including all community/volunteer events. The largest annual family event is our company carnival, which is usually held on a Sunday and invites associates to bring their families for a day full of carnival games, dancing, prizes, and food—all at no cost to the associate.

APPENDIX D: MR. ROSEN'S PHILANTHROPIC ACTIVITIES

Hospitality Education Development

- Benefactor of the Rosen College of Hospitality Management, University of Central Florida. Mr. Rosen donated money and land to build the Rosen College of Hospitality Management in the sum of $20 million.

- Mr. Rosen's scholarship endowment provides $120,000 in yearly scholarship funds to the Rosen College of Hospitality Management Students.

Tangelo Park Community Program

Tangelo Park is a predominately African American neighborhood in South Orange County. The neighborhood is made up of 900 homes. Mr. Rosen has made a continuing multimillion-dollar ($8 million) donation to the Tangelo Park neighborhood that supports two major educational programs.

- *Tangelo Park Free Preschool Education*

One to three years of free preschool education is provided for the Tangelo Park preschoolers. The Tangelo Park elementary school was only one of very few urban elementary schools in Florida to receive an "A" (FCAT score) in three of the last four years. Due to this program, there has been a dramatic increase in PTA and SAC participation, meaning that parents also want to be more involved in their children's education.

- *Tangelo Park High Education Scholarship Program*

An all-expense-paid education is provided for graduating high school students who reside in the Tangelo Park community and are accepted to a vocational school, a community college, a junior college, or a four-year public college or university in the state of Florida.

Since its inception, approximately 350 high school graduates from the Tangelo Park community have been provided with full college scholarships. Prior to the program, the vast majority of high school students from Tangelo Park did not go on to college, and the dropout rate was close to 25 percent. In 2007, 100 percent of the students graduated from high school, and 75 percent of the students graduate from college.

Since the inception of Mr. Rosen's Tangelo Park program, the average home in Tangelo Park has increased in value from an average of $45,000 to an average of $150,000. Mr. Rosen's program has made the neighborhood desirable to parents who want the educational benefits for their children.

- *Tangelo Park Reading Program*

The Rosen Hotels & Resorts has supported the Tangelo Park elementary school with various programs, including an associate reading program. Rosen associates are divided into teams and assigned to classrooms. Teams work with students once a week throughout the school year. This program is geared toward helping the students learn to read and improve their literacy skills.

Southwest Jewish Community Center

- Mr. Rosen donated $3.5 million to the Southwest Jewish Community Center. The new center, when completed, will be named the Jack & Lee Rosen Jewish Community Center (after Mr. Rosen's mother & father).

- The 33,000-square-foot center, which opened in June 2009, has classrooms, a fitness center, a swimming pool, and a gymnasium and will serve the southwest community of Orange County.

APPENDIX E: MR. ROSEN'S AWARDS AND RECOGNITION

Mr. Rosen as an entrepreneur and philanthropist has been honored and recognized for his outstanding contribution to his community. He has received the following awards and recognition:

- 2007 Black MBA Award—National Black MBA Association
- May 2005 President's Award—Mr. Rosen was honored by the U.S. Dream Academy at the "Power of a Dream Gala" in Washington, D.C. Mr. Rosen was presented with this prestigious President's Award by Oprah Winfrey in recognition of his work on the Tangelo Park educational pilot program.
- Florida Reading Association Literacy Award
- 2007 Most Influential Executive—*Orlando Magazine*
- 2006 Best Corporate Citizen—*Orlando Magazine*
- Onyx Award
- Junior Achievement Hall of Fame

Index

329